AIR AMERICA THE PLAYBOOK
★ ★ ★ ★ ★ ★ ★ ★ ★ ★ ★ ★ ★

DISCLAIMER

Dear Reality-Based Readers,
Air America Radio wants you to know that no politicians, lobbyists, or their lackeys were harmed during the making of this book. However, many were subjected to mockery and ridicule. The majority of the book is made up of actual transcripts and original essays filled with 100 percent factual information (suggesting the mockery is, perhaps, well deserved). In fact, many improbable-sounding statements in this book concerning the actions and beliefs of politicians, lobbyists, and their lackeys are verifiably true. However, please be aware that the editors have included certain "false" items—depictions of conversations and events that could in theory have occurred but in fact might not have (yet). These falsehoods might be called satire or just speculation. We invite you to make the final judgment.

★ ★ ★ ★ ★ ★ ★ ★ ★ ★ ★ ★

AIR AMERICA
THE PLAYBOOK

★ ★ ★ ★ ★ ★ ★ ★ ★ ★ ★ ★

What a Bunch of Left-Wing Media Types Have to Say about a World Gone Right

David Bender
Chuck D
Rev. Dr. C. Welton Gaddy
Thom Hartmann
Robert F. Kennedy Jr.
Rachel Maddow
Mike Malloy
Mike Papantonio
Randi Rhodes
Mark Riley
Sam Seder
Introduction by Al Franken

With text by Jon Hotchkiss
Information graphics by Don Asmussen
Original illustrations by Dustin Amery Hostetler

  MELCHER MEDIA

RODALE

Rodale books may be purchased for business or promotional use or for special sales. For information, please write to:

Special Markets Department, Rodale Inc., 733 Third Avenue, New York, NY 10017

Printed in the United States of America

Rodale Inc. makes every effort to use acid-free ∞, recycled paper ♻.

Library of Congress Cataloging-in-Publication Data

Air America : the playbook / Air America Radio.
       p.   cm.
    Includes transcripts of radio broadcasts from 2004 through 2006.
    ISBN-13 978–1–59486–514–5   hardcover
    ISBN-10 1–59486–514–0   hardcover
    1. United States—Politics and government—2001– 2. United States—Politics and government—2001–
—Humor. 3. Liberalism—United States. 4. Right and left (Political science)—United States. 5. Air America
Radio. 6. Interviews—United States. I. Air America Radio. II. Title.
    E902.A428 2006
    973.931—dc22   2006024721

Distributed to the book trade by Holtzbrinck Publishers

2 4 6 8 10 9 7 5 3 1   hardcover

RODALE
LIVE YOUR WHOLE LIFE™

We inspire and enable people to improve their lives and the world around them
For more of our products visit **rodalestore.com** or call 800-848-4735

Our enemies are innovative and resourceful, and so are we. They never stop thinking about new ways to harm our country and our people, and neither do we.

—PRESIDENT GEORGE W. BUSH

Contents

Introduction

Al Franken

In February of 2003, while George W. Bush was checking with God one last time on whether to invade Iraq and then choosing to ignore him when, in response, God asked him to give the weapons inspectors more time to complete their work, I was working on a book that was in large part about the myth of a liberal bias in the Mainstream Media.

In that book, *Lies and the Lying Liars Who Tell Them: A Fair and Balanced Look at the Right*, I argued that the Mainstream Media has plenty of biases—get it fast; get it cheap; stoke controversy; politics as horserace; pack mentality; keeping access to administration sources; laziness, etc., but there is no "liberal media," I argued, notwithstanding that the right has been trying—and largely succeeding—to make a case to the contrary. In fact, at that very point in time, Judy Miller of the *New York Times* was making my case for me.

There is no liberal media, but there is a right-wing media. It's Fox, the *Washington Times*, the *Wall Street Journal*'s editorial page, and, of course, talk radio in general.

Researching the book, I ran across a Gallup poll showing that 21 percent of Americans said they got most of their news from talk radio.

That's when I decided to take seriously an offer to do a daily three-hour radio show from some folks who were putting together what would become Air America Radio.

Lies would become my first number-one *New York Times* bestseller in which I didn't call Rush Limbaugh a big fat idiot.[1]

I wrote my first *New York Times* bestseller, *Rush Limbaugh Is a Big Fat Idiot and Other Observations*, immediately after leaving *Saturday Night Live*. During my fifteen seasons on SNL (1975 to 1980, 1985 to 1995), I had written, with other writers, a lot of the show's political sketches. For a number of reasons, though, we felt at the time that the show's political satire should not reflect a particular political point of view.

First and foremost, the other writers and I felt it would be inappropriate. We were a late-night comedy variety show, the collective work of scores of creative people who hadn't signed on to do a show with a liberal (or conservative) axe to grind. It's not like we were doing *Murphy Brown* or something. Secondly, we writers had differing political philosophies ourselves. Jim Downey, a brilliant writer with whom I have collaborated on a great number of political pieces, is conservative, though admittedly, a thinking conservative who could

---

[1] On the cover.

often see the foibles of Republicans more clearly, I'll admit, than I could see those of Democrats. At any rate, Jim and I kept each other honest, and I look back with pride at that body of work.

But when I left the show in 1995 with a book contract in hand, I felt it was time to write about what I believed politically. And, frankly, I was a little angry. The Gingrich Revolution was ascendant, and Rush was its big, fat mouthpiece. They wanted to gut the EPA, get rid of the Department of Education, dismantle the social safety net, and they were hypocritical and uncivil to boot.

That's why I wrote *Rush Limbaugh Is a Big Fat Idiot*. The title was meant as an ironic comment on the decline of civility in our discourse. I'll give you two examples. When the Clintons moved into the White House in 1993, Rush called twelve-year-old Chelsea Clinton "the White House dog." Newt had compiled a list of words for Republican candidates and officeholders to use against Democrats. Words like "treason-ous," "corrupt," and "depraved." I especially like depraved.

Irony as a satiric device is sometimes lost on certain people. Especially when those people are *determined* not to get it. Since I wrote *Rush Limbaugh Is a Big Fat Idiot*, I've been depicted by some on the right as a "smear merchant," as a "far-left hatemonger," and, of course, as "depraved."

Those Americans who are able and willing to get irony seemed to take to the book. I received a reaction unlike any I had received in my years of comedy. Don't get me wrong. There is nothing better than making people laugh. But folks all over the country were thanking me for standing up to these guys. *Rush Limbaugh Is a Big Fat Idiot* was on the *New York Times* bestseller list for eight months. Somehow I managed to write a bestseller without accusing any widows of enjoying their husbands' deaths.

With the book's success, a number of Democratic leaders asked me to do a syndicated radio show to counter Rush and the impressive number of Rush wannabes on the right. But it seemed like too big a com-mitment. I liked the freedom afforded me by show business. Besides, Clinton had won in '96 and things weren't going so badly. The economy was expanding. Poverty and crime were down. And we were at peace. Also, the Gingrich Revolution had collapsed. I wasn't angry anymore.

By late 2002, I was pissed off again. Bush had had the gall to claim he had won political capital from his 2000 victory margin of a negative 540,000 votes. Even though he ran claiming that "by far, the vast majority of my tax cuts go to those at the bottom," he passed a tax cut for which the vast majority went to those at the top. By far.

It took the man who had said we should have a "humble" foreign policy about a week to alienate the entire world by withdrawing from a long list of international agreements, including the Kyoto Protocol. He appointed lobbyists from Big Oil, Big Coal, and Big Timber to regulate Big Oil, Big Coal, and Big Timber. He reversed himself on his promise to regulate CO_2 emissions—the kind of thing that would later be characterized as a "flip-flop"—but only when a Democrat does it.

But worst of all was how Bush had squandered the unique opportunity handed him after 9/11. When people ask me today why our political discourse is so venomous, I remind them that it wasn't so long ago that that wasn't the case. I ask them to remember how they felt on 9/12. We were all united. What's more, the world was behind us.

George W. Bush had the opportunity to lead this country and the entire world in a spirit of mutual purpose and mutual sacrifice. And he blew it. He blew it by hijacking 9/11 for his own petty political purposes.

By January 2002, Karl Rove was telling the Republican National Committee that national defense would be a great issue to exploit in the 2002 midterm elections. It wasn't long before the president was accusing Democrats of not caring about our nation's security and Republicans were running ads against Max Cleland, who'd lost two legs and an arm fighting in Vietnam, and stooping so low as to juxtapose his face with Osama bin Laden's and Saddam Hussein's.

What seemed most disturbing to me, though, was that an acquiescent mainstream media was letting the Bushies get away with it, as the right-wing media did the administration's dirty work, blaming Clinton for 9/11 and calling anyone who urged caution on Iraq a traitor.

I researched _Lies_ during the 2003 winter-spring semester with fourteen students at Harvard where I was a fellow at the Kennedy School of Government. As we watched the inexorable lead-up to war, I had a sickening feeling. But we gave the president the benefit of the doubt when he told Congress that a vote for the authorization to use force against Iraq was a vote for peace because it would allow him to go to the United Nations. When Colin Powell laid out the case before the UN, I believed him.

As we now know, the Bushies were misleading us about the intelligence on WMD and Saddam's links to al Qaeda and lying to us about Bush's intention to go to war only "as a last resort."

By the fall of 2003, it was becoming apparent that there were no WMD in Iraq. A growing insurgency was killing our troops. With 21 percent of Americans getting their news from talk radio and no liberal voice responding, I decided I had to get on the air.

Air America didn't exist in 2003. It was a glimmer in the eye of a couple from Chicago, Sheldon and Anita Drobny, who couldn't get the thing off the ground—i.e., financed. I had been casually mulling the idea since they first approached me at the end of 2002. The idea of doing three hours a day, five days a week, week in and week out, was daunting. Franni and I were just becoming empty nesters, and I had visions of us traveling together between ridiculously lucrative speaking gigs and book deals.

But then I read that Gallup poll. And there was this little thing called the Bush administration. And this other little thing called the Republican Congress. And, of course, the war. And this other thing called patriotism.

I decided to do Air America for the same reason that everyone at Air America chose to do Air America. We all wanted to make our country a better, fairer place. Yes, we all brought our egos and ambitions and neuroses to Air America. But everyone joined in because we love our country.

Everyone, except maybe for Evan Cohen.

Who is Evan Cohen? That's a good question. And one I probably should have asked myself a little sooner than I finally did. First, let me say that we never would have gotten on the air without Evan Cohen. For that, I will be eternally grateful to the man.

Cohen, we were told by Cohen, was a multimillionaire from Guam who had made his money managing businesses in the Pacific Rim. According to Cohen, he had survived a brain tumor and was now going to use his life, and his money, to do good. During the early months of Air America, we heard a lot about the brain tumor. If some needed phone lines weren't in place, Evan would remind us of his brain tumor. If a copying machine hadn't been ordered, Evan would remind us of the brain tumor.

Cohen had picked up the ball from the Drobnys and managed to convince enough people, including some other investors, that he had put together enough financing to keep Air America on the air for three years before it started turning a profit.

As it turned out, Cohen only had enough money to keep us going for three *weeks*. We launched on March 31, 2003, with five stations—New York, Los Angeles, Chicago, Portland (Oregon), and the Twin Cities. On April 13 and 14, we lost Chicago and LA.

The right gloated. And who can blame them, really. Chicago and Los Angeles are two of America's best-known cities. Bill O'Reilly predicted we'd be out of business within two months and that this proved there was no audience for liberal radio. What it proved was that Air America was undercapitalized. Capital is important when starting up a major media network.

Take, for example, the Fox News Channel, on which O'Reilly frequently appears. Just to get on the air, Rupert Murdoch had to pay cable carriers $11 per viewer. In other words, $5.50 per eyeball—roughly.

That cost approximately $187 million. Add to that the $130-million operating deficit in the first two years, and you're looking at more than a $300-million loss.

As anyone who watched the HBO documentary about Air America knows, the months following the loss of the LA and Chicago stations were traumatic. I became what I called "an involuntary investor," meaning I continued doing the show without being paid. That was not a hardship for me or my family financially. But more than anyone else, I was publicly associated with the network, and it was clear I had a lot to lose if the network failed.

And obviously I was concerned about everyone else working on my show. Katherine Lanpher, my cohost, was wondering whatever had possessed her to uproot herself from a successful career and a comfortable home in St. Paul. The day we lost LA and Chicago, Katherine got the word from Minnesota Public Radio that it had found a replacement to host her popular midmorning show.

As new investors moved to save the network and ease Evan Cohen back to Guam or wherever he had come from, they made sure that Katherine and the staff were paid and got their health insurance. But we were all operating in a thick cloud of uncertainty. Would they have jobs tomorrow? Would I be the poster boy for a giant failure that would forever kill the idea of liberal radio? Had Evan Cohen really had a brain tumor?

And, if so, could we please see it?

Frankly, if this had happened when I was twenty years younger, I might have freaked out. But I've absorbed a few lessons in my life. My dad told me not to regret any decision you made for the right reason. And I knew that the only thing I could do under the circumstances was to try and do three great hours of radio a day.

With the very survival of Air America in question, you can imagine how hard it was to get new affiliates to sign on. Our only hope was to prove that there was an audience for what we were doing.

Fortunately, our first quarter ratings were surprisingly high, especially in New York and Portland. In New York, my show clobbered O'Reilly's in the hour that we went head-to-head, and I beat Limbaugh in the coveted twenty-five to fifty-four demographic. Air America had captured and continues to capture a younger, better-educated audience than right-wing talk. For example, the average age of my listeners is about forty-seven. Doesn't sound that young until you understand that O'Reilly's listeners average around sixty-seven years of age. That means for every twenty-year-old listening to O'Reilly, there's a 114-year-old listening. In other words, his audience is dying off as you read this.

Our biggest success was the Portland station, KPOJ, owned by Clear Channel, the evil megacorporation that would soon become Air America's best friend. In its first quarter with Air America, KPOJ more than quadrupled its ratings from its previous format. Clear Channel owns more than 1,100 stations nationwide, almost four times that of its nearest competitor. Aside from the scary concentration of media implications, this means that Clear Channel owns stations in a number of cities that are in the toilet with their current format. Since Air America turned around one of its stations in liberal Portland, Clear Channel decided to give us a try in conservative San Diego.

It worked, and now we're carried on twenty-six Clear Channel stations around the country, including Los Angeles, San Francisco, Denver, and Miami. Some of our stations don't have the strongest signals. And our marketing budget is slightly less than that for the *Sporting News*. But as I write, more than 6 million distinct individuals listen to Air America every week in our eighty markets, covering about 63 percent of the country. We're also extremely popular on the Web and on XM satellite radio.

That hasn't stopped O'Reilly from predicting our demise some forty-two times over the past two and a half years. On his TV show alone. He's done it when we had four stations, eight stations, twenty stations, forty stations, seventy stations, and he continues to do so to this day. Every time he does it, he says no one is listening to Air America and predicts we'll be off within two months. So far, anyway, he's been wrong.

But in one sense, we have failed. Because we haven't made everyone like us. Still, unlike the other guys, we acknowledge our faults and are open to criticism. That's why on *The Al Franken Show* we started the popular hate e-mail segment.

We got the following from a guy who appears to be an O'Reilly fan:

> **JON K. (9/27/05)**
> **SUBJECT: WEBSITE FEEDBACK: YOU STILL AROUND**
>
> Al, you f**king loser. I haden't heard from you loud whiney mouth in a long time. I thought maybe Bin laden had captured you and was doing America a favor and keeping your soory ass in the dessert...I hear your show ratings are even worse then before...Hope your Birthday went like crap and you SUCK. If you have kids I do feel sorry for them...Have you given up on trying to be like your idol Bill O'Reilly? You don't even come close to accomplishing all that Bill has done good for the U.S. If you do leave the country, let me know. I want to punch you in the mouth first!

Jon's is an especially good one because it includes so many of the elements common to our favorites: obscenity, a threat of violence, the ubiquitous assertion that I "SUCK," and typo after typo after typo.

To really appreciate our hate mail, you'd have to read a good eighty or ninety of them. If we wanted to, we could fill this book with them. But I just thought I'd cover the basic types of hate e-mails as a jumping-off point to discuss the reasons I'm so proud of our show.

First, there is the basic "you suck" e-mail exemplified by these from Steve L. and a guy named Bob.

> **STEVE L. (8/18/05)**
>
> you suck you stupid piece of crap. i think your radio show sucks just like you. you are a cry baby liberal who lies all the time,so you should write about your own lies you lying liar. i think you suck so much. please e mail me back if your not a loser liberal[2]

> **BOB (9/6/05)**
>
> Al you no talent muthaf**ka....you sucked on SNL and you continue to suck. You are a bitter, jaded scumbag with no talent and little reason to get up in the morning. F**k you asshole.

---

[2] I didn't e-mail Steve back, even though that might confirm in Steve's mind that I am a loser liberal.

By the way, kudos to Bob for his mostly accurate spelling and punctuation. Now what is it about these e-mails that could possibly make me proud of my show? Well, nothing. Except that I know for a fact that these idiots represent only a small percentage of the conservatives in this country and of those who listen to our show.

See, I get stopped all the time by Republicans who actually listen to the show and thank me for presenting a smart, fair (but not necessarily balanced) program. Even on the floor of the Republican National Convention in Madison Square Garden, a number of delegates told me that, while they didn't necessarily agree with me, they enjoy listening. And more than occasionally I meet a former Republican who's come over to our side because he listens to me or to the other hosts on Air America. Of course, you've got to give Bush some of the credit.

Anyone in our business gets these stupid letters. David Brock, a weekly guest on my show, is the founder and head of Media Matters for America, a liberal media watchdog group that monitors the right-wing and mainstream media. When Media Matters finds an egregious error or lie, they put it up on their fabulous Web site MediaMatters.org and post the e-mail of the offender. I'd venture a guess that the Michael Medveds and the O'Reillys and the Hannitys receive a higher-quality hate mail than I get. But that doesn't stop them from claiming that these letters are further proof that all liberals are just irrational Bush-haters filled with pathological rage.

Of course, they're smart enough to know that isn't true, just like I know that Jon, Steve, and Bob represent only a small segment of the right. But it's just another part of their campaign to marginalize anyone who has the temerity to be critical of them or the administration or the commander in chief. In a time of war, yet.

One common theme in our hate mail that is an especial delight is the vicious antisemitism. Here's a representative sample:

SCOTT (9/13/05)

That Al Franken is a mench, its too bad the US troops got invovled in WWII or that Jew might not be here... And you wonder why Hitler hated them so much, you weirdos don't know how to shut up, even for your own good. Heil George Bush...LOLOLOL You dumb stupid bitch bastard (Andrew Dice Clay, another Jew). Go take a hike kike.

JIM C. (9/14/05)

You are a dumb jew f**k. Jesus Christ is going to come down and f**k
You in your stupid Jew rectum with his fat Republican c**k. I hope you get cancer in your ballsack.
Yhank You for your time. F**ker.

GENE K (1/11/06)

Let he preface this first by saying yes, I am an anti-semite. I Believe the Jews are ruining the world by using their money to unduely influenceUS elections and trying to funnel military and policy support to Israel. jack abramoff is a jew. al franken is a jew. need i say more? somepeople in our history had the right idea—now that is not a knock against you, mr. franken, but that is a knock against you believing in your jewish practices. good day.

TOM J (2/13/06)

Mr. Franken,
With all due respect, I cannot stand to see your snob-nosed, ugly-f**kface on TV criticizing. You are like many of your NY-Jew friends who think their money and private school upbringing qualifies them to critize and mock the rest of the country. To that I say shame—and shut up. Please, for your family's sake and our stomachs.

RUSS (11/22/05)

Subject: Website Feedback: Suck ON It

Dear Al,
Went to a BBQ over the weekend. I was cooking up a whole slew of great things that you liberals wouldn't enjoy—pork, beef, chicken. Yeah, a whole lot of things people like you never get to enjoy. Youknow pork? Yeah, bet you don't. That's the problem with people like you—you wish to take away our freedoms. Our right to say what we want, do what we want, and eat what we want. That's why voters have been eating your sorry ass for the last ten years. HA! Suck on that, Russ—The Truth (you're a joke).

I found this last one a little odd because I love to barbecue and talk about it a lot on the show. (As I've said, talk radio is a cult of personality.) In fact, one of our regular features is called "Good Ribbin'" during which I talk to folks at a barbecue joint (usually in the South) who hate me and my politics but love good barbecue. We talk about what they're eating and politics. It's almost always a fun time, and we discover that we have at least something in common.

It almost makes me think sometimes that some of the hate e-mailers don't really listen to the show. That they just find our Web site and have a lot of free time, but not *so* much free time that they can use spell-check, and a desperate need to vent.

Take, for example, this one from someone who indicated for some reason that his/her name was "not applicable":

NAME N/A (8/26/05)

Al, you need a wife and children and grand children.. This would more than likely give you something worthwhile to do in life, other than making such a fool of yourself on national TV and radio. You continually deny common sense thinking to rant about how much you hate George Bush.You on the other hand are just like many of your "hollywood" buddies. You have been greatly overpaid for being a F**king Clown and you think that makes you an average American. NO, I dont think there is anything average about you. You are simply one of those people that has a silver spoon in your mouth (or up your nose) and you think that that gives you credibility. It DOESNT. You are a worthless hollywood "nouveau riche" idiot that thinks that you have earned the right to tell the people of this country what they should think and what they should say...I hope terrorists will come visit you soon.

See, what makes me suspicious here is that anyone who listens to *The Al Franken Show* for any time at all has heard me brag about my kids and complain about my wife. And talk about all my Hollywood friends.

Now what really bothers me is when someone listens to the show, as this next fellow obviously did, and instead of it helping our cause, I somehow turn someone off our message:

MIKE B. (6/16/06)

Subject: SHOCKED!

I AM A DEMOCRAT AND HAVE BEEN EVER SINCE I STARTED VOTING.I LISTENED TO YOUR PROGRAM FOR THE FIRST TIME TODAY.I AM VERY ASHAMED OF YOUR STUPIDITY, ON YOUR RADIO PROGRAM. DON'T YOU PEOPLE UNDERSTAND WHAT OUR PRESIDENT IS TRYING TO DO. HE IS TRYING TO PROTECT YOU. YOU PLAY INTO THE HANDS OF PEOPLE LIKE OSAMA. SHAWN HENNITY IS RIGHT. YOU ARE GOING TO DESTROY THIS COUNTRY WITH YOUR BELIEFS. I AM DEATHLY AFRAID IF PEOPLE WITH YOUR BELIEFS TAKING CONTROL OF THIS COUNTRY.YOUR SHOW IS A JOKE.BECAUSE OF LISTENING TO YOUR SHOW TODAY, I WILL CHANGE MY VOTING AFILIATION TO REPUBLICAN.

GOD BLESS AMERICA!

I gotta tell you. That was probably the most disturbing hate e-mail we've received in the two and half years we've been on. I mean here Mike was a lifelong Democrat and one sampling of my show turned him into a Republican! That's exactly the *opposite* of what I'm trying to do!!! I have to tell you I lost a lot of sleep after receiving that one. Mike, I hope you give us another chance.

I guess the most common hate e-mail we receive accuses me of hating America. No doubt those people are probably reacting to my weekly "Why I Hate America" segment, in which I espouse Marxist economic theories and make excuses for al Qaeda and Osama bin Laden.

DIANE M. (8/25/05)

We are aware of your Communist beliefs. Won't work in America. Sorry. Try another country. Go away, you evil bastards. You don't have a chance in America.

CHRIS N. (11/29/05)

Subject: Website Feedback: you

Hope the terrorists kill you and your family first.....

I think what Tony and the others don't understand is that the "Why I Hate America" segment is actually an imaginary segment that exists only in their minds.

Regular guests on *The Al Franken Show* include communists like Norm Ornstein of the American Enterprise Institute, former *Boston Globe* columnist Tom Oliphant, Jonathan Alter and Howard Fineman of *Newsweek*, Paul Krugman of the *New York Times*, and Joe Conason of the *New York Observer*.

As far as I know, we were the first in the media to champion Operation Helmet. Its founder, Dr. Bob Meaders, is a retired Navy medic and a Republican redneck from Texas. We've put him on our air a number of times to enlist our audience to contribute in order to provide helmet liners for our Marines. Two-thirds of those wounded in Iraq now have brain injuries because so many of the injuries are concussive rather than ballistic. The liners, which the Marine Corps should be providing (but are not), absorb the shock and save lives and brains.

I'm proud of what I do on Air America. Every one of my shows has its own mix of substance, heart, outrage, humor, and, sometimes, tears. Since our very first show, we have discussed Iraq in depth with journalists like George Packer of the *New Yorker* and James Fallows of the *Atlantic Monthly,* with Ambassador Peter Galbraith, and with counterterrorism expert, Marine Colonel T. X. Hammes (retired), who served in Iraq.

In his book, *The Sling and the Stone*, Hammes decried our military's failure to use established counterinsurgency doctrine in Iraq. One of the main problems: Rumsfeld's stubborn refusal to admit the existence of an insurgency. At one point in our interview, Hammes complained about not having access to a single interpreter when he was serving in Basra. I asked him how he felt about the military discharging six gay Arab-speaking interpreters before the war.

"That's all you guys care about," Hammes said, with some disgust.

"What's that?" I asked.

"Gays."

"And who are *we*?" I wondered.

"Liberals," Hammes shot back. "That was six guys. What we need are hundreds of interpreters."

"Yeah, but wouldn't it have been nice to have *one* in Basra?" I countered.

Hammes admitted that one interpreter would have been helpful, and Katherine and I continued our conversation with Hammes. As we went to commercial, I said, "We'll be right back with Air America Radio and our gay agenda."

Hammes laughed. Later, he e-mailed our producer that he had been on a lot of radio shows, most of them right-wing talk, and that Katherine and I had understood his book better than any of the other hosts and asked the most pertinent questions.

Yes, we catch the administration and the Congress and the right-wing press in their lies and subject them to scorn and ridicule. That *is* my job.

We discuss the cronyism and corruption of the Republicans in Congress and in the White House. And the outing of Valerie Plame. We fought the attempt to partially privatize Social Security. I railed against the bankruptcy bill written by the credit-card industry and learned from Elizabeth Warren of Harvard Law School that more than 90 percent of bankruptcies are caused by a health problem, a job loss, a divorce, or a death in the family.

We discuss policy. In depth. And we advocate. For universal health care, and an Apollo program for renewable energy, and public financing of elections.

And I've gone after Bush, et al., endlessly for lying us into a war and then bungling virtually every aspect of it. I've lambasted the Republican Congress for failing to do oversight on war contracting and virtually everything else.

But we've done our share of segments on Saddam's atrocities. I'll never forget my interview with Zainab Salbi about her memoir *Between Two Worlds*: *Escape from Tyranny: Growing Up in the Shadow of Saddam*. I asked Zainab to read something from the book, and she chose a passage from the introduction, which pretty much told the reader what the book was about.

Zainab was eleven years old when her father was chosen to be Saddam's personal pilot. Saddam brought the family into his world, inviting them to his country estate for creepy weekends. As she witnessed Saddam's cruelty and his willingness to kill and rape those around him, Zainab watched her parents become complicit in their own oppression. As Zainab grew into a beautiful young woman, it became clear that Saddam, who insisted she call him "Amo" (uncle), had developed an unhealthy interest in her.

Zainab's mother managed to get her to the United States by arranging a marriage to an abusive husband. Zainab escaped that relationship and founded Women for Women, an organization that helps women survivors of war.

I had read the book the night before and found it harrowing. I was especially taken by Zainab's growing understanding of what the terror of living in Saddam's shadow had done to her and was moved to tears as I read a passage about a confrontation with her mother, who, after several years, had come to visit her in America.

On the air with Zainab, I asked her if she would read the passage, which I had highlighted. She looked down at the page and hesitated, then nodded, and read:

> We went to the Kennedy Center to see *Phantom of the Opera,* the story of a young opera singer held captive by a hideously deformed phantom in a mask. "Those who have seen your face draw back in fear," the young singer told her tormentor. "I am the mask you wear." There it is Mother, look! I wanted to say. That's the nightmare of my life you created for me. Can't you see it? I was the mask Amo wore. I still have this nightmare that my face will disintegrate and people will see his face underneath mine. Can't you *feel* it Mama? But all she said was how much she enjoyed the show.

As Zainab read, her eyes welled and her voice choked. But she was happy that she had read that on the air because it gave our audience, an American audience, a real glimpse of Saddam's grip on one human being.

As I write this, I've been at it for about two and a half years. When I started out, I said to myself that if I'm going to be on the air three hours a day, I might as well learn something. And I have. We've taken the show on the road to more than thirty affiliates in cities—from Miami to Seattle; from Portland, Maine, to Portland, Oregon; from blue markets like Madison to red markets like Reno and Fresno. I've seen what mayors and state legislators and governors are achieving while Washington has been in the grip of a Republican White House and Congress. More than 200 mayors have agreed to abide by the Kyoto Protocol. They're saving money on energy and creating new high-tech jobs in conservation technology and renewable energy.

We've visited cities and states that have passed living wage laws, which have led to a greater increase in jobs than in the cities and states around them. We've seen Illinois provide universal health care for kids. In Asheville, North Carolina, we talked to a state legislator who had led the fight in a very red state for a clean smokestack law, which reversed Bush's rollbacks in the Clean Air Act.

And we've seen that Americans are catching on. And I like to think that we've had at least some small part in that.

As I said before, I'm proud of my show. I'm proud of everyone on our staff. And I'm proud of my association with Air America.

And most of all, I am proud of this book. Though I haven't read it.

Ramon developed a way to hack into EVERYONE'S Palm Pilot in the administration. Here is Vice President Dick Cheney's schedule from one day shortly after the '04 election.

OIL LOVER41
TODAY'S SCHEDULE:

7 am Wake up. Ask Lynn whether I died over the weekend and if this is Hell. Also have inquiries made: If I did die and this is Hell, would Lynn tell me?

7:30 am Breakfast. Oatmeal with extra oat bran. Wheatgrass juice. Bowl of pills. No butter, no salt, no bacon. This _is_ Hell, and Lynn didn't tell me.

10 am Get on remote controls during president's meeting with veterans' group. Now that election is over and it won't make any difference, make Prez look like Rip Taylor and have his arms flail around like Kermit on the Muppet Show.

3 pm Meet with ambassador from Zoltan Nebula 4 and allow him to harvest the population of Maine for his nutrition and obscene pleasures. In exchange, receive more vast amounts of wealth, with which I can continue to pay my way out of death.

7 pm Watch the news. Using only brain waves and angry thoughts, see if I can make the anchorman's face melt again.

10 pm Bedtime. Get back in bed with Halliburton.

"Broadcasting Live from a Bunker 30,000 Feet Beneath Dick Cheney's Bunker . . . "

Air America Radio went live on March 31, 2004, at noon with *The O'Franken Factor,* hosted by Al Franken. Al's guests that day included several lions of liberal politics: Bob Kerrey, Al Gore, and Michael Moore. While there was near chaos in the halls and the executive suites, the show went off with barely a hitch—sure, there were some technical issues, but one thing was certain: Based on the tenor and wit of the conversation, this was not your father's liberal radio station.

Al Franken was followed by Randi Rhodes. Randi was, at the time, largely unknown outside of Florida, where she had hosted a daily radio show that regularly beat her time-slot competitor, Rush Limbaugh, in many key demographics. For her Air America debut, her producers arranged a call with a progressive icon: Ralph Nader. For more than forty years, Nader had successfully kept liberal issues at the forefront of the American consciousness; he'd championed monumental changes in auto safety, worker's rights, and environmental protections. But this was 2004, the White House was up for grabs, and Nader was feared, not revered, in many liberal circles. After running for president in 2000 on the Green Party ticket and siphoning off enough votes from Al Gore to deny him a clear victory, Nader now found himself the target of a heated and growing chorus of naysayers.

Still, despite all the controversy, he had declared his intention to run and was trying to get on the ballot in all fifty states. That very morning, the *New York Times* had run an editorial that quoted many of his friends begging him not to run. Earlier in the week, former president Jimmy Carter had made a similar public plea. All to no avail. Was Nader being pig-headed? Did he not hear the clamors of distress from anxious Democrats who protested that it was simply too dangerous to have a candidate who would split the party vote?

Maybe he thought he'd get a chance to calm liberal nerves by speaking on that new liberal talk network. We can't know exactly what he thought when the phone call was over, for reasons that are about to become obvious. All we could say then and all we can say now is "Welcome to *The Randi Rhodes Show,* Ralph."

RANDI RHODES: Jimmy Carter made a statement the other day about Ralph Nader's candidacy and it was pretty straightforward so I just wanted to play you a little bit of Jimmy Carter and then we will speak to the independent candidate for president of the United States, Ralph Nader.

VOICE OF JIMMY CARTER: I have a friend named Ralph Nader. He is trusted enough by my family to have been permitted in Plains, Georgia, to umpire a softball game where I pitched on one side and my brother pitched on the other side. That's a lot of confidence. When I was president he gave me a lot of advice and tonight I want to return the favor by giving him some advice. Ralph, go back to umpiring softball games or examining the rear end of automobiles, and don't risk costing the Democrats the White House this year, as you did four years ago.

RHODES: That's a heavy-duty statement, Ralph Nader, and that came from the former president of the United States Jimmy Carter, who relied upon you for advice, so what do you make of that?

RALPH NADER: Well, I just respond with his motto—in 1976 when he ran for president, his motto throughout the country and the title of his book was *Why Not the Best?* Why not the best policy—

RHODES: [Laughs] Oh we like ourselves, do we?

NADER: Why not the best policies? Why not the best ways to involve the American people? Why not give more voices and choices in our presidential election, instead of having it locked up by the two parties, who increasingly are dialing for the same corporate dollars?

RHODES: But we had the Green Party and your candidacy, and now they don't want you, so you're an independent. They don't think you're the best.

NADER: No, the Green Party [won't make] the decision until June as to whether they want a candidate and under what conditions, and that's too late for the valid access deadlines.

RHODES: And—

NADER: One out of every three Americans calls themselves independent and [hasn't] really had an independent candidate for a long time.

RHODES: You know what? Another day, another time, I'm fine, good, let's do it. Let's put the best ideas on the table, whether they be Green, Reform, independent, [but] this time, we can't afford it, and you know it. So I'm thinking, now just hear me out, as a very open-minded liberal, I'm thinking, maybe Ralph does have this huge ego. He lives in Connecticut and lives small and he's really not into the whole know thing, except for the power part of life, *or*, maybe Ralph wants to be a king maker—do ya know what I mean? Maybe you're gonna make a deal with the Democrats and turn over any voters that you might have out there to the Democrats in exchange for, I don't know, trade commissioner or something that you're interested in.

NADER: You should know me better than that. There're no deals. When you run for president, you run all fifty states, you—

RHODES: But you said yesterday on *Crossfire* that you were gonna talk to Kerry—

NADER: Of course, talk to him [about] how to defeat George W. Bush. Do you really think the Democrats know how to defeat the Republicans? They've been losing for ten years to the worst part of the Republican Party, losing the House, the Senate, the—

RHODES: We won for two elections and then we lost the last one because the fix was in—I mean, it was a dirty election; I know, I was in Florida.

NADER: You're right there. The Democrats won the election—

RHODES: So what do you mean, ten years?

NADER: But they blundered. They didn't even know how to keep what they won. The Democrats are very similar on military policy, foreign policy, Federal Reserve policy, food and drug policy, Department of Agriculture—

RHODES: No they're not—

NADER: *Sure*, of course—

RHODES: The Republicans talk about [how] regime change was the Clinton administration's policy, but it was regime change from *within*. It was never military action on our part in Iraq. That was not the policy.

The policy was to get those people to forgive us for when the Republican President Bush the First told them, "Rise up and we'll get your back," and then they saw American helicopters that we sold to Saddam come and slaughter them—those are the people in the mass graves and everybody knows it. Or they need to know it. But, we can't afford you this year, Ralph.

NADER: You're quite right on what Bush 1 did, in terms of urging the Shiites and the Kurds to rise up against Saddam and then—

RHODES: *Slaughter* them.

NADER: He let Saddam slaughter them. But, remember that the Democrats had a very aggressive foreign military policy when they were in power, a huge military budget. Clinton was a draft dodger, so he wasn't willing to take on the Pentagon. He wasn't willing to take on the Congress on huge military expenditures. That starved many of the necessities back home among the American people which—

RHODES: Did it starve the police officers? Because we put 100,000 cops—or close to it—on the streets before Bush came in—

NADER: Yeah.

RHODES: Yeah, it didn't?

NADER: But don't worry, childhood poverty is increasing regardless of the two parties. Affordable housing problems are becoming more serious, consumers are going into more—

RHODES: Now they are. You know why? Because the states are starving. We have a president that literally stole the Treasury, and that's why we can't afford you. I wish we could, Ralph Nader, I wish we could.

NADER: Wait, wait. Why don't the Democrats stop the things they don't like from the Republicans, like the tax cut for the wealthy—

RHODES: *They're in the minority!*

NADER: Wait, wait. The war—

RHODES: *They're in the minority!*

NADER: Wait, wait, wait, the war resolution—

RHODES: Oh, Ralph, come on! You like to spew this stuff, but you're smarter than that—

NADER: Wait, wait, wait, the war resolution, the Patriot Act—

RHODES: Ralph, Ralph, how many—

NADER: Do you have listeners now?

RHODES: How ma—

NADER: Do you have listeners?

RHODES: Ralph, I've already—

NADER: Votenader.org is the Web site for people who want a more deliberate—

RHODES: Let me tell you something. I have probably, ya know, millions and millions of listeners. I've been on the air for years and years and years, which you may not know because you didn't do your homework, but the truth of the matter is, they don't want you to run, either—even your Green Party supporters—they can't afford you. That's why the Green Party is not endorsing your candidacy and you've become an independent. We can't afford you, Ralph. Now, if you want to do a little horse-trading, that would be smart politics. And if you wanted to be king maker, meaning you ran for a while and then you turned over your voters and you endorsed Kerry, and said to Kerry, "Ya know, you need a guy like me, ya need a guy like me on" name a policy that you're most passionate about and go fix it. And then, four years from now, you'll find out what the Democrats have known for ten years, and that is, they're in the minority in Congress and they can't vote out appropriations bills, they can't vote out these core projects, they can't vote out the stealing of the Treasury, the underfunding of education, the underfunding of Medicare. Come on, you know this!

NADER: Well, since you're filibustering, you should have mentioned that the Senate and the Democrats should have filibustered a lot of these things and blocked them. Filibustering is a tool that the Republicans know how to use better than the Democrats—

RHODES: They filibustered a couple of judges, and look what happened—

NADER: You're, you're—

RHODES: Look what happened!

NADER: Are you, are you—

RHODES: During the recess, they put 'em in and—

NADER: Are you interviewing or are you filibustering? You wanna give me a chance to speak?

RHODES: *No, no. I'm angry at you. I'm angry at you. I'm a genuine person who's really mad at your candidacy!*

NADER: Why are you denying millions of people the opportunity to vote for my candidacy?

RHODES: 'Cause we can't afford—

NADER: How arrogant—

RHODES:—it—

NADER: How arrogant can you be?

RHODES: *I'm not arrogant! I'm a patriot! We can't afford you! And real patriots have to stand up and question your candidacy!*

NADER: Wait a minute. Why are you denying millions of Americans the opportunity to have more choice—

RHODES: Because—

NADER:—and vote for my candidacy?

RHODES: How many ways do I have to tell you? We can't afford you.

NADER: Can you afford freedom? Can you afford choice? Can you afford civil liberties?

RHODES: Give me a Democrat president—

NADER: Is this, is this the way you want to start Air America? You want it to be "Hot Air America"?

RHODES: Oh no—

NADER: Log into the Web site—

RHODES: Ralph, tell me something—

NADER:—votenader.org.

RHODES: If you did get to be president, tell me who you would caucus with. Tell me who you could get to vote for your views and visions and your bills. Who is

an independent, other than Bernie Sanders and Jim Jeffords? Who you gonna count on? Let's say ya win, okay?

NADER: You can't win without a huge mobilization of people—

RHODES: Let's say you do. Let's say at seventy years old, from your little house—

NADER: Wait, wait, wait—

RHODES:—you are ready to do this.

NADER: Now you're getting nasty.

RHODES: I'm not—

NADER: You are ruining the first day of Air America—

RHODES: I'm not ruining anything. This *is* Air America.

NADER:—because you're not letting your guest have a chance to speak.

RHODES: I asked you a question.

NADER: You're not letting your guest have a chance to speak.

RHODES: So ya get there, ya make president, right? Ya make president. Who are you caucusing with? Democrats or Republicans?

NADER: How 'bout Ed Markey? How 'bout—

RHODES: That's your choice! Democrats or Republicans!

NADER: How 'bout Pelosi?

RHODES: Pelosi's a Democrat!

NADER: That would—

RHODES: Pelosi's a Democrat!

NADER: Listen, listen—

RHODES: [Speaking slowly] Pelosi is a Democrat minority leader.

NADER: Listen, if I win the presidency, that means the Democrats will win the Congress, and a lot of my friends are in the Congress. And, by the way, you've got a very bad interviewing technique, and you're not gonna get—

RHODES: [Laughs]

NADER: —an audience with overtalking.

RHODES: I'm not interviewing you!

NADER: Do not overtalk. The interviewer—does not overtalk—

RHODES: *I am not interviewing you! I am mad at you! Don't you understand the difference?!*

NADER: Fine, just close up and start screaming to your audience.

RHODES: [Laughs] Look, don't tell me how to do radio. I've done it for twenty years. You screwed up the last election, and now you wanna screw up this one, and I'm pissed!

NADER: Ya know, you oughta be ashamed of yourself because—

RHODES: *But I'm not!*

NADER: You agree with me—

RHODES: *You* should be ashamed of yourself!

NADER: You agree with me on so many issues. You really oughta be ashamed of yourself.

RHODES: I'm not ashamed of myself. I can't *afford* you.

NADER: Nobody stands—

RHODES: Wow, sometimes I—

NADER: —nobody stands for workers and—

RHODES: —sometimes I look at—

NADER: —poor people the way I do.

RHODES: —ya know, sometimes I look at a really, really fabulous pair of shoes and I can't afford them. I can't afford you. I'm not saying you're not fabulous. I can't afford you! Why you don't get this, I don't know.

NADER: Oh, you can't afford a living wage in this country. Why don't the Democrats ask for a $10 living wage?

RHODES: What I'm saying is, when you get there, let's say you're president, let's do this—

NADER: Yeah.

RHODES: Who you caucusing with?

NADER: Oh, all kinds of people in Congress. I'm very persuasive.

RHODES: Name them! Besides Ed Markey, Jim Jeffords—and I'll give you—

NADER: Kennedy, Feingold—

RHODES: *Kennedy!*

NADER: —Kennedy, Feingold—all kinds—Boxer from California.

RHODES: Oh see, Ralph, you really don't know politics. If you think that the Democrats are gonna vote with an independent president, you're out of your mind. They've got a national party—

NADER: I don't deal with someone who doesn't allow me to talk. And if you want your guest to close up on you on the first day of Air America—

RHODES: You just keep telling me—

NADER: You're overtalking. You're filibustering!

RHODES: They've heard you say that a thousand times, but you won't answer the question. Say, say he does—see, this is the problem, and I am pissed, and I don't, ya know, I'm not interviewing Ralph Nader, I'm mad at Ralph Nader! I've been mad at Ralph Nader since 2000. And I've got news for you— if Ralph Nader became the president of the United States, where does he go to get his bills passed? Does he go to the Republicans? Does he go to the Democrats that he just beat? Ya—ugh—ya know, this is why there's no prospects for Ralph, other than what Ralph is really doing. And what, Ralph, I think, is really doing, if he's smart enough—and Ralph's pretty smart—is, is he's gonna run and then he's gonna endorse Kerry and turn over those voters, which might be 3 million maybe, in exchange for trade commissioner, EPA, something that he wants to do! But he won't tell you that.

One Day at the White House

Washington, DC, date redacted, 2006

Air America Radio got passes to attend a special presidential press conference at the White House. Our guy Ramon has the transcript.

PRESIDENT GEORGE W. BUSH: Good evening. I want to thank you all for coming. Before I take your questions, I have two important announcements to make. Firstly, I know many of you are concerned about the ongoing situation in Iraq and America's "exit strategy." Today, it is my pleasure to announce that I have signed an executive order to bring our boys home. [Applause] One US soldier will be returning to the United States each day—for the next 150,000 days. Meaning, all of America's sons and daughters who have put themselves in harm's way to fight the global war on terror will be reunited with their loved ones—in just 410 years. *Numero dos.* I'm pleased to announce a change to this administration's current immigration policy as it pertains to the thousand-mile fence being built along the Texas-Mexico border. You see, here's the thing: What do people do when they see a fence? When people see a fence, they instinctively want to climb over it. And that's the thing we're trying to avoid. What we want is for people—un-American people—when they get to the border . . . to stop. And how are we going to get them to stop? Instead of a fence, we're gonna put up gazebos. Thousands of gazebos. Everyone loves a gazebo. Sometimes there's lattice on 'em. Think about it. Who doesn't love to sit on a gazebo? So now, when the illegal alien gets to the border—he's gonna see the gazebo and what's he gonna do? That's right. Have a seat. We're even gonna put out some pitchers of margaritas and nachos. Your migrant worker loves margaritas and nachos. While the illegals are getting drunk—we're gonna detain 'em and ship 'em back home. So, you see . . . immigration? *No problemo.* Okay. Now I'll take your questions. Rachel Maddow?

RACHEL MADDOW: Sir, that is the dumbest idea I have ever heard.

BUSH: I'm sorry, Rachel, I disagree. Dick Cheney's first idea was dumber. He wanted to put up a neon sign at the border that said, "No Vacancy." You know, like at a hotel. But, in order for the sign to be effective, it would have to be in Spanish—only that's impossible now that English is now our official language. Plus, no one could find a long enough extension cord.

MADDOW: You're right, sir, a giant neon sign is much dumber. Anyway, your poll numbers recently reached a historic low. Americans think you're incompetent, your priorities are out of whack, and Iraq is a disaster. Since you label anybody who criticizes the American presence in Iraq as unpatriotic—

BUSH: Rachel, let me interrupt. We both know I could artificially raise those poll numbers. I could make some meaningless gesture like capturing Osama bin Laden or lowering the price of gas or reducing the size of the federal deficit—but, that's not why I was elected president by the American people.

MADDOW: Sir?

BUSH: Rachel, I want to tell you something: This administration will not be making decisions based on "what the people want." If that was the case, the American people should have elected Santa W. Claus as their president. In the meantime, I'm going to continue to take advice and listen to the only person that matters: Karl Rove. Oh, and Jesus Christ. Next question. Randi?

RANDI RHODES: Speaking of Karl Rove, sir—

BUSH: Oh, I'm sorry. Did I say Randi? I meant to call on Candi. Is there someone here named Candi? Candi? Candi? Where's Candi?

RHODES: Mr. President, I'm going to ask my question. What did you know about Karl Rove's involvement in the leaking of classified information? When did you know that the name of a covert CIA agent, Valerie Plame, and her brass plate cover company, Brewster Jennings, had been given to the press?

BUSH: Randi, I think we both know that what Karl Rove does is Karl's business.

RHODES: But doesn't Mr. Rove serve at your pleasure, sir?

BUSH: Yes. And what a pleasure it has been to have this trusted advisor and Republican strategerist in my administration. This administration is stratergistly strategical. I am a *war president*.

RHODES: Karl Rove is the dirtiest political operative in this nation's history. He single-handedly spearheaded an ugly rumor mill that smeared two great Americans: Senators Max Cleland and John Kerry. He even morphed Senator Cleland's face into Osama bin Laden's face in a TV commercial! In addition, "Karl" may have committed an act of treason and continues to mislead this great nation *and* our brave troops by beginning every sentence with *Iraq* and ending it with *9/11*—which you yourself said were not related. I believe your exact quote was "We have no evidence that Saddam Hussein was involved in *the* September 11." Sir, Karl Rove is the devil.

BUSH: [Whispering] Randi, ixnay on the evul-day, okay? He's right over there. [Bush gestures with his eyes to Karl Rove, who stands along a side wall.] He'll hurt me. [Speaking normally] So! In answer to your question, Randi, Karl Rove has my utmost confidence and will continue to serve this administration until such time as he decides to stalk—I mean work—somewhere else. Next question. In the back—Mark Riley?

MARK RILEY: Mr. President, in his new movie, *An Inconvenient Truth*, Al Gore makes a persuasive and convincing case that global warming is real, is here, and is deadly.

BUSH: Marc, I've seen it . . . and here's my review. Have the camera come in tight. *"An Inconvenient Truth* is the feel-good global warming movie of the summer."* [Laughs] I'll probably see that quote in *USA Today*. That's a free plug. I should get some money for that.

RILEY: Be that as it may, Mr. President, the polar ice caps are 35 percent smaller than they were one hundred years ago. The temperature of the oceans have risen on average two degrees. And the number of days of frost every winter is in decline. Why hasn't your administration made protecting the environment a priority?

BUSH: Can I get serious for a moment? I am aware that things on the planet are getting hotter. I had some pizza the other night. The cheese burned the roof of my mouth. But hot melted mozzarella is not a reason to increase costly regulations on industry or a reason to spend money developing cleaner-burning fuels.

RILEY: Mr. President, if we don't act soon, thousands of miles of the US coasts, including cities like New York and Boston, will be under ten feet of water.

BUSH: Two overrated cities, in my opinion. Mark, here's my advice: When the cheese gets too hot, do what I do—blow on it a few times until it cools. Next question. Jackie?

JACKIE GUERRA: Mr. President, last year when you said that ordinary Americans making domestic calls were not having their phones tapped by the NSA in an effort to combat terrorism, was that a truthful statement?

BUSH: Jackie, we are fighting a global war on terror. Not a *skirmish* or some kind of *tussle*. It's a *war*. W—O—R. War!

GUERRA: Mr. President, that doesn't answer my question. Were you telling the truth about domestic wire-tapping?

BUSH: I've said all I'm going to say on that subject.

GUERRA: Why are you lying to the American people?

BUSH: I'm not lying.

GUERRA: We deserve an answer! And I'm not going to stop until—

BUSH: *Code blue! Everybody duck! She has a gun!*

[Secret Service agents restrain and remove Guerra.]

SECRET SERVICE AGENT: All clear! I repeat: We are all clear.

BUSH: Why doesn't everyone please calm down. That was an unfortunate incident. Thankfully, the Secret Service was able to deal with that threat in a timely and efficient way. Why don't we get back to the questions. David?

DAVID BENDER: Mr. President. That wasn't a gun. That was Jackie's tape recorder. See? I have one, too.

BUSH: David, you can't be too careful. Remember, we're at war with terrorists. Who are crafty. Who will stop at nothing to destroy the American way of life, including cloning Jackie Guerra, sneaking a weapon into a tape recorder, and killing hundreds of innocent civilians. That's why I'm against stem cell research, by the way. Now, why don't you ask your question?

BENDER: Mr. President, before the war with Iraq, you said that Saddam Hussein was developing weapons of mass—

BUSH: *Code blue!*

[Secret Service agents make their way toward Bender.]

BENDER: Stop! Stop! What are you do—

BUSH: It's okay, boys. Just a little joke. I'm kidding, Dave. G'head with your question.

BENDER: No one's going to hit me in the testicles with a baton, right?

BUSH: Of course not, Dave. G'head.

BENDER: Before the war with Iraq, you said that Saddam Hussein was developing weapons of mass destruction. We now know that was *not* the case. Were you fooled by bad intelligence or did you knowingly lie to the American people?

BUSH: We lied, Dave.

BENDER: Excuse me, sir?

BUSH: We lied, Dave. The only reason we attacked Iraq was to avenge the assassination attempt on my father. And to get access to cheap oil.

BENDER: Thank you, sir. That's the first honest thing you've said tonight.

BUSH: It was another joke, Bender. I thought you Jews had a sense of humor. Of course, the real answer is we were duped by bad intelligence. I have time for one more question. Thom?

THOM HARTMANN: Mr. President, since you have taken office, the deficit has ballooned to nearly 7 trillion—

BUSH: Oh, Thom, I'm sorry. They're giving me the wrap-it-up sign. But before I go, I want to urge all Americans who are watching tonight . . . to stay tuned for a special episode of *Desperate Housewives*. It's the one where you get to see a side shot of Teri Hatcher's booby. [Laughs] It's coming up next. Good night. And God bless America.

The Upside of Anger

Steve Earle spoke with caustic comedian Lewis Black about why yelling can be a good thing.

STEVE EARLE: Lewis, most people probably know you as the guy in the middle of the stage telling people what you think is wrong with everything and sometimes what you think is right with things. Do people that you meet ever ask you what exactly it is that you are so pissed off about?

LEWIS BLACK: Yeah, they do, and I always find that an odd question. I'm always kind of like "Would you expect me to be happy?" I wake up in the morning and by definition within 15 minutes, something bad has happened.

EARLE: People that know anything about me know that I don't like what's going on in the world. But I blame it on us. I think not being angry enough, sometimes people get complacent. I mean, people that *know* something is wrong and don't say anything? I think it's a public service sometimes to agitate people when they need to be.

BLACK: Well, it's not something I consciously set out to do. You don't think, "If I could make a living by screaming at people . . . " But who would have thought that you would have to remind people that they are allowed to be upset. You know, if somebody is sticking it to you, you should be allowed to yell.

EARLE: Absolutely. In a democracy, you should be allowed to yell as loud as you want to and about anything you want to.

BLACK: And they'll continue to ignore you, but at least you're yelling.

EARLE: Absolutely. And that is cathartic. There's not a doubt about it, yelling helps.

The Liberal Agenda

Here's the weekly fax from the Streisand Ranch in Malibu giving us a rundown of all our important liberal causes.

CONFIDENTIAL

Remember, liberal soldiers, these are your marching orders for the week.

1. Pay Iraqi journalists to plant pro-abortion, pro-gay marriage, anti-Bush articles in Iraqi papers.

2. Send the White House your own addendum to their "National Strategy for Victory in Iraq," entitled "Back-Up Plan for Humiliation."

3. Use the Freedom of Information Act to demand to see what Halliburton got Dick Cheney for Christmas.

4. Support public displays of the Ten Commandments only if they're displayed next to a stone tablet of Ginsburg's "Howl."

5. Praise the ACLU for suing Donald Rumsfeld over prison abuse. Then remind them it's OK to WIN a case once in a while, too.

6. Insist that the United States come out with one more unpopular dollar coin with a woman on it. Suggest the Sarandon silver dollar.

7. Get in someone's face—and nurture them.

8. Try to blame your latest emotional meltdown on global warming.

9. Shower with sand and brush your teeth with a twig.

10. When the waiter brings you water at a restaurant, ask him, "Could you send that to the Sudan, please?"

11. Today's phrase, just drop it into conversation: "Hope that little war we're about to have with Syria didn't get in the way of important coverage about what Lindsay Lohan is doing this week. Hey look, it's Lindsay walking across the street with a shopping bag! Wake up, sheeple!!"

FAXED by Babsi

Love Your Country When It's Right, Right It When It's Wrong

Randi Rhodes

It's been said that getting Democrats to agree on something is like herding cats. Say, that's hard work. But it's worth it!

Imagine a political party with so many ideas that some of them may actually be good ideas. I know you're saying, "But, Randi, a real foreign policy won't fit on a bumper sticker the way 'Bring 'em on' does." But remember, with Bush, all you get is the bumper sticker. We Democrats get to fight ourselves *and* Osama bin Laden! But wait there's more . . . you also get health care, world class education, renewable fuels, and your civil rights back! You may even get to vote! "Democrats can COUNT" makes a nice bumper sticker.

Coming up with real solutions for America requires knowing the actual damage we've suffered. We don't have that assessment yet because the most secretive administration in American history hasn't come clean about the really sad state of our union. We don't know what damage has really been done to our military, our treasury, our civil liberties, or our economy. Al Gore had to make a movie about global warming after the Bush administration changed NASA's findings on global warming to exclude GLOBAL WARMING! And that's just the tip of the melting iceberg!

Democrats have no subpoena power currently, so there is no way to know what Bush and company have done to us. Democrats can't agree on solutions to problems we don't yet know we have. We do know that once we uncover the actual damage that has been done to our military, our treasury, our environment, our free press, our civil liberties, and the Gulf Coast, there will be a reckoning, and someone will have to break the bad news to us. That job will fall to a Democrat. It will require openness and candor, and some Americans will attack him or her, but it will also mark a brand-new era of openness and prosperity for all Americans.

Liberals have been smeared as America haters. We don't hate America. We hate the lunatics who have taken it over. "Liberal" has been made a dirty word by conservatives precisely because liberal ideas work for ALL Americans. Liberalism unifies the country and creates peace and prosperity. And exactly for these reasons, conservatives have worked hard to make the word liberal an insult. Conservatives are not interested in creating a peace dividend. They are interested in war profiteering.

Conservatives fear open government, equality, a free press. Most especially, they fear and loathe participation in government by the country's own citizens. They like to steal and cheat in private without all the questions. Citizens should be seen and not heard! Secrecy is how they get away with enriching themselves at everyone else's expense. Who profits from war, tax cuts in a time of war, and a divided America? Not you. It's always easier to steal when no one is looking! Ask Halliburton, Bechtel, big oil and gas, OPEC, United Defense, Raytheon, Custer Battles, or whoever got the missing $9 billion in Iraq. Ask Dick Cheney. He'll tell you to go f**k yourself. Ask Rummy. You won't get an answer but your phone might get tapped, and I guarantee you will be smeared by Fox News. I have been called a traitor, an America hater, Osama bin Randi, Randi Hussein, and my personal favorite, Tokyo Rhodes, all because I had the nerve to ask questions and propose solutions that didn't involve defense contractors.

To help avoid questions that might, goodness gracious, lead to answers, conservatives create diversions. Like questioning Americans' patriotism by pointing to a burning flag or screaming when the flag is photographed draped over a real patriot's coffin. Remember, you are never to ask who is in the coffin or why.

And, of course, there are the gays. Gay Americans are the new black Americans. They are deviant and unnatural (as if being born gay or black is not part of nature). But don't forget that just because conservatives are currently concentrating on gayness, black folks are still to be feared! Black folks are better off living in a baseball stadium than they are in their own homes. They are simply animals in a corral, and this is a good result. Just ask the president's mother. Brown people should be assigned to corporations in order to remain in America. They are to work for less than the minimum wage, enrich the corporation, and get in the back of the line.

Everyone is diminished by this administration. And that's the intended goal! In fact, this administration has an entire catalog of tactics to make you feel weak and helpless. Their favorites are questioning your patriotism, homophobia, racism, and of course the best tactic of all . . . selling the TERROR. The only thing they have to sell is FEAR itself.

There has never been a discussion in America about what to do if we are attacked again, just as there was no plan on 9/11, when we were attacked. Nothing has changed. There is no plan for you or your city—ask New Orleans or Gulfport, Mississippi—there are just warnings and color codes.

Issuing color-coded terror alerts is not what I call leadership. Unless your intention is to lead America into a state of perpetual fear!

This administration has learned that in America, apparently color has an impact on the state of people's mind. They like yellow and orange and, of course, RED. Ask yourself if you believe that America will ever be blue or green? Green and blue are bad colors. Yes, color is a big thing in Bush World. Black, brown, blue, and green: bad. White, yellow, orange, and red: good.

There are no black or brown Republicans in the Senate or House of "Representatives." States must remain RED, and you must remain yellow.

So now that conservatives have you convinced that your children live in a dangerously yellow or orange world and you are not safe at night, at work, or living next to black, brown, or other people of the rainbow and that living near the beach is certain death, you must be ready to accept that the only thing that can save you is God himself.

Religion is the twenty-first-century Bush Preparedness Plan for the Homeland. Some Americans are living their lives waiting and hoping to die in the Rapture. Some Americans think death is better than life. Thanks to conservative Republicans, we have become a culture of death! We cause it and pray for our own. We used to think people like that were members of Hale Bopp or Jim Jones' Kool-Aid drinkers. But now a good slice of America is ready to die!

If you think death is better than life, George W. Bush is your president. If you think that you can live a life of greed, gluttony, and violence but as long as you "accept" the Lord, you will go to Heaven, he is your president. If you are ready for the Rapture, he is your president. Of course, if this is what you want, you could join al Qaeda instead. They want the same thing you do. However, this is wholly un-American. And that's why you CAN'T be a patriot and support this president. Instead you must realize that Americans who think Bush is going to bring the Rapture and are ready to go are loyalists!

In America our government derives its just powers from the consent of the governed. Meaning? They have to ASK US what they can do—not the other way around! Patriotism means pushing back against a criminal government that uses a climate of fear to spread a culture of death and torture around the globe.

In the twisted right-wing interpretation of our constitutional republic, citizens, constituencies, organized labor, and religions that are more hopeful than charismatic Christianity are mythical "little guys" to be attacked, diminished, and kept living in fear. They are not you or your neighbors. They are disloyal, godless elitists who must be marginalized.

What Liberals Believe
ACCORDING TO RANDI RHODES

- We believe our elected leaders ought to have been ELECTED. We also believe they should be neighbors, soldiers, police officers, schoolteachers, single working moms, straight, gay, black, white, American Indian, Arab American, first-generation American, and so on. In other words, we think the House of Representatives ought to be representative of Americans.

- We believe in a strong defense (not offense). We believe a peace dividend is worth more *than war profits for defense contractors and multinationals.* We believe that war IS hell on earth and that the earth cannot take much more war.

- We believe in diplomacy and spreading democracy by example not by bombing the s**t out of people until they say anything we want to hear or they bomb us back.

- We believe in secure borders and ports. We believe that the best defense to terrorism is intelligence gathering, not acts of aggression.

- We believe in effective crime prevention, which starts with ending poverty (the leading cause of crime).

- We believe in freedom and privacy for people and regulation and oversight for corporations.

- We believe in freedom of speech, freedom of assembly, freedom of religion, freedom from poverty, and most of all freedom from fear for PEOPLE not corporations! Corporations are NOT people . . . if they were, they would have colonoscopies and mammograms. Corporations must be regulated. They cannot say whatever they want to say (if the drug causes anal leakage, they have to tell you), they cannot assemble a plant in your neighborhood, they cannot promote religion, and they can not scare you out of your right to demand a decent wage and overtime pay!

(continued on opposite page)

The same exact things were said about the Loyalists v. Patriots in the Revolutionary War. Had we lost, we would have been hanged as traitors to the king. But we didn't lose. We WON, damn it! We are a free people who won the right to love our country when it is right and to right our country when it is wrong. We are free to believe in one God or ten, to own property, to think, and to remove a president and an administration that does not follow the law.

During the fascist regimes of Hitler and Mussolini, good people were made to believe that fascism was superior to democracy. They were loyalists and did nothing when their democracies were taken away one freedom at a time. We like to say it can't happen here, but it certainly can. Think of our democracy as a teenager. Young enough to screw up, but old enough to be responsible for it. The State needs PARENTING.

Just as being a parent is a difficult job, so is being a liberal. So call me a liberal. I wear the label as a badge of honor. I am governed the way I choose to be governed. I am the parent. The government is the teenager!

What we have now is a party that acts as if it's the only adult in the room, and it is asking Americans for something they should never give: Blind obedience (along with a crisp salute). That's exactly backward. But I do think that is why some people find it a "welcoming party." Join them and there's nothing more to do but send in your money! They'll do the rest.

Lazy people are often conservative people. They like being led. They themselves do not lead.

Following along with an authoritarian government is a guaranteed way to lose our democracy. In a democracy, every citizen needs to be ready to put up a fight, just like the Patriots of the American Revolution. You have to want it BAD! You have to be informed and ready to volunteer for your country. Showing up for your country means staying informed. Just like showing up for your kids! You have to know their secrets and what they're up to every minute or you're being a lousy parent.

Patriotism also means participating in the life of the country. You can always find a place that needs you. Think about working for a candidate, canvassing neighborhoods, working a phone bank to get out the vote, being a poll watcher or worker during election seasons. In nonelection seasons, identify problems, organize around them, write letters to representatives and senators, and if they don't respond, identify new representation. Become that representative! There is nothing more patriotic than running for office. Run for school board, city council, state or federal legislature. Volunteer for something. Anything that appeals to you. Start a young Democrats club, be a mentor, be a Big Sister or Big Brother, be a voice for something that you care about: clean water, legal aid, literacy, health care for all. Start a peace club and police recruiters at your mall or in your schools. Give money or time to Habitat for

What Liberals Believe (continued)

- We believe in ALL of our civil rights, including counting votes by hand. No corporately owned machines. Your vote is sacred and private and deserves to be counted by hand.

- Progressives believe in a fair tax code … not a tax code that favors one person over another.

- We believe that health care is a right to be enjoyed by ALL Americans because the purpose of government is to promote the general welfare of the people. There is no other reason to have a government except to promote the general welfare of the people.

- We believe that disaster relief comes first when people are dying. Nothing gets debated, passed, or voted on in Congress until everyone is safe and accounted for. Corporations who can help MUST help. There shall be no profit-taking after a disaster whether manmade or an act of nature.

- We believe that our planet is a living thing and needs to be nurtured and loved. We believe that science is not a myth and that it's not too "sciencey" to teach to our children.

- We believe that civil unions are to be encouraged. Any couple who can live together every day and be civil deserves everything this country can offer them and their family. Promoting family values means promoting families that look like yours and families that don't. Supporting same-sex couples is NOT the same as supporting polygamy or man-on-dog sex. These are choices, being gay is NOT.

- We believe love trumps hate. Hate is not a family value unless you are the Manson family, the bin Ladens, or George W. Bush.

- We believe in the separation of powers. There are THREE coequal branches of government. None of them pick the president of the United States. The states do. The people elect their representatives in the House and Senate.

(continued on next page)

What Liberals Believe *(continued)*

- We believe that no man is above the law, no man is beneath the law, and no man is the law. A "unitary executive" is just a fancy word for dictatorship.

- We believe all men are entitled to meet their accuser, know what they are accused of, and defend themselves in a court of law. There is no such thing as an "enemy combatant."

- We believe that there is no such thing as a "signing statement" that allows a president to ignore the laws passed by Congress and signed by the president.

- We believe there is no such thing as a warrantless search and seizure. These are myths that are repeated over and over again so that they can be made believable. They are never going to be true in a democracy.

- We believe our consent is necessary to govern. We believe that a president who doesn't pay attention to polling or read newspapers is not paying attention to the people of this country or the world.

Progressives believe in progress. Progress in schools, health, and the environment and the spread of prosperity and hope. These are examples of a strong democracy. Democracy should work for everyone who participates and even those who don't. Democracy can only be spread by works not words.

Remember, America can NEVER be destroyed by outsiders. Destroying America will be an INSIDE JOB. Liberals will never allow America to be destroyed.

Humanity and help rebuild the Gulf Coast. Choose something and do something even if it's just registering to vote and showing up informed on Election Day. Informed people vote Democratic. Ill-informed people vote against their own best interests over and over again because they don't know any better.

Conservative followers force themselves to believe that all of their leaders do the right thing when no one is looking. Liberals don't. Liberals believe in oversight, questioning, using any legal means to get to the facts: subpoenas, hearings, courts if necessary. Every man who knows the truth should be compelled to tell it. Every man who covers up the truth should be willing to trade his liberty for jail. These are the choices in a democracy. It's pretty black and white, but it's as hard as herding cats!

Labor Intensive

On April 22, 2006, onetime vice presidential candidate and now presidential hopeful Senator John Edwards talked with Jackie Guerra on *Workin' It* about the plight of America's working poor.

JACKIE GUERRA: It was really great to meet you the other night at the American Rights at Work Awards ceremony and to listen to you be so inspiring and actually make the war on poverty sound interesting.

JOHN EDWARDS: It *is* interesting; it's not hard to do.

GUERRA: One of the most obnoxious suggestions I often hear is that poor people are poor because they don't work hard enough. What's your response to that?

EDWARDS: It's a lie.

GUERRA: Don't mince words, brother.

EDWARDS: It's so obvious. Most folks who are at or near the poverty line are not only working—they work two or three jobs. They're responsible; they love their kids, and they are doing everything they know how to do to have a better life and, for their kids, to give them a better and easier life than they've had. They are just faced with such obstacles. They don't make enough money because pay is so low, they don't have health-care coverage, and they don't make enough money to pay for even the basic needs of life. So many families have to figure out which bills they can pay each month. This is immoral. Nobody should work full-time in our country and still live in poverty.

> "Most folks who are at or near the poverty line are not only working—they work two or three jobs."

GUERRA: But a lot of people say that it's not the government's job to help those who have less. Explain to me why we can all benefit from eradicating poverty.

EDWARDS: Well, first of all, families in this country who live in poverty are Americans just like all of us are Americans. All of us benefit from living in America—some in general ways and some in very specific ways. Whether it's a business, a charitable organization, or an individual, everyone gets benefits from living in the United States of America. So all we're suggesting is, why in the world should people who live at or near the poverty line be left out of that? It's not the government taking care of them; they want a chance to take care of themselves. So, things like raising the minimum wage, unionization in the workplace are enormously important. The most important antipoverty movement in American history is the organized labor movement.

GUERRA: Now, let me ask you this, Senator. You often hear that one answer to the question of poverty in the United States is raising the minimum wage, but the other side of that coin is [that] people often say, "Oh it's going to cost our country jobs and there'll be more outsourcing and it's going to hurt our economy." How do you address those concerns?

EDWARDS: History shows that it's just not true. It's a simple answer.

GUERRA: You mean it's a lie, it's another lie?

EDWARDS: Yes, that's exactly what I mean. The studies show that [in] places that have raised the minimum wage above the federal minimum wage, municipalities and states have actually seen their economies do better, not worse; their job creation has been higher not lower. And it all makes perfect common sense if you think about it. When you raise the minimum wage, you don't just affect the minimum wage, you affect those wages that are anywhere in the vicinity of the minimum wage, they all get lifted up. The second thing is, families are able to support themselves and make more money and can spend more money and put more money back into the economy, and the result of that is, you strengthen the economy and you create an environment for jobs.

> "The last thing our party needs is to start shifting and moving to figure out strategically what part of the political spectrum we need to occupy."

GUERRA: I want to switch gears just a little bit. The Democratic Party, Senator, used to be the party of average working Americans. I know, I'm the daughter of Mexican immigrants and when my parents came to the United States they named my brother and me after the Kennedys and immediately joined the Democratic Party as soon as they became citizens and could vote. But that whole concept and the idea of the Democratic Party seems to have changed in recent years—where do you think the party has gone wrong and what can we do to fix it?

EDWARDS: Well, I think first of all, the last thing our party needs is to start vacillating and shifting and moving, trying to figure out strategically what part of the political spectrum we need to occupy. I always think that's a bunch of nonsense. I always come back to this: I'm a Democrat because our party gives voice to people who don't have a voice. It's why I've always been a Democrat, it's why I am one today, and I think we cannot let the soul of our party slip away.

The Revolution Will Be Webcast

David Bender spoke with Joe Trippi, campaign director for Howard Dean, on July 24, 2005, about how the Internet has changed politics and the average person's ability to save the world.

DAVID BENDER: Well, Joe, you have had an extraordinary set of experiences that are recounted in this book that you've written, it's *The Revolution Will Not Be Televised*. Now let me ask you something, when you set out to write a book, did you have in your head the audience that you'd be writing it for?

JOE TRIPPI: I wanted to talk to the people, to the 650,000 folks out there who had worked so hard on the Dean campaign, but also give everybody else sort of a window to the future, in terms of how we could all connect together and build a movement together to make the country a better place and hopefully the world a better place.

BENDER: We spent some time together during the writing of the book, so I knew your thinking, and I understand a lot of what went into it was sort of recapping the experiences of the Dean campaign, but there's something much larger about it.

> "The Dean campaign was really the 'bottom' using the Internet to wreak havoc on a top-down political system that's not working for the American people."

TRIPPI: Right, it's actually in the subtitle, *Democracy, the Internet and the Overthrow of Everything*. It's about the ability for us to use technology and the Internet to strengthen our democracy, to get people more involved in changing things, and if we can, I think we can overthrow a lot of the bad stuff that's happening.

BENDER: One of the things I remember hearing you say in the past is that it's already happening and people are just waking up to it.

TRIPPI: Right. Well, Napster was the first sign of this, it wasn't the Dean campaign. Napster, the "bottom," was using the Internet to literally wreak havoc on a top-down recording industry that wasn't listening to its consumers. The Dean campaign was really the "bottom" using the Internet to wreak havoc on a top-down political system that's not working for the American people.

BENDER: You use this phrase a lot, "bottom and top." I want to be clear, you're talking about the large masses of people—consumers, in the case of something like Napster.

TRIPPI: Right. Everything in society is top-down, the corporations are top-down, the government is top-down, and political parties are top-down.

BENDER: And by "top-down" you mean small numbers of people making decisions for large numbers of people.

TRIPPI: Making big decisions for everybody. We get programming decisions from ABC, and we have very little control over it. We can turn it on or turn it off, but that's all we can do. The Internet and mobile technology and all these technologies that are coming along let us not just join the conversation, but connect with each other from the bottom and make decisions in the opposite direction. And that's what happened with Napster—the bottom decided, We're going to change the way music was distributed throughout the world.

BENDER: So, what a lot of leadership has been unaware of is that these changes are happening on their watch and they need to either respond to them or they're going to be washed away?

> "It no longer matters whether you're a major superpower or not.
> You're gonna see small countries be able
> to create movement in the global community."

TRIPPI: Absolutely wiped out. It no longer matters whether you're a major superpower or not. You're gonna see small countries be able to create movement in the global community. Finland is going to be head of the EU [European Union] presidency in the next couple terms. What happens when Finland says, "We've just assumed the EU presidency, and there's only two countries in the world that have not signed the Kyoto Treaty, the United States and Australia. As president of the European Union, today we ask each American to go to the EU Web site and sign the Kyoto Treaty on behalf of their country. Do not wait for your president, don't wait for your government, we're asking you to sign for yourself, for your country." And they talk about this, they hold a press conference, how many millions of Americans would go to the Internet and sign the Kyoto Treaty?

BENDER: That their government won't sign.

TRIPPI: I don't want to pretend that there's going to be any legal binding-ness to it, but the act of millions of Americans doing that may start to have a real effect on the administration to do something. My point is, Finland didn't have that ability to create that kind of global movement four years ago, five years ago, six years ago. I'm not saying they're going to do this, but it's that kind of change that you're going to see, where the bottom can actually come together and make change. I think issues like global warming are *only* going to be solved, are only going to be addressed, because millions and millions of people around the globe who are connected through the Internet, through technology, come together in a community that actually wants to do something and forces governments and corporations, particularly, to do the right thing.

Kos and Effect

On June 4, 2006, Markos Moulitsas Zúniga, author and founder of the leading progressive blog Daily Kos, talked with Angie Coiro in the San Francisco studios of Mother Jones Radio about the current state of blogs and where they fit in the political world.

ANGIE COIRO: I noticed in the [San Francisco] *Chronicle* this morning an article where they interviewed you and asked you for some political solutions to political problems. I'm guessing that there must be a bit of dissonance between what you got into blogging for and the position you find yourself thrust into now.

> "I don't necessarily want to be a leader in the progressive movement. I want to be able to help find those leaders, promote them, and give them the support they need."

MARKOS MOULITSAS ZÚNIGA: When I started blogging, this was really 2002; there were no illusions that anyone who was blogging was going to be any sort of a significant player in anything. At the time, the top blogs were getting a couple hundred visitors a day, and that was considered to be huge and influential. So it was a very, very small pond, and those of us who started blogging were very content to swim in that very small pond. There was never any illusion of any kind of influence. Of course, history has worked out a little bit different, and I don't think I've ever really come to terms with that. But at the root of it, what I feel like I'm doing is providing the infrastructure to allow leaders to emerge so that we can support those leaders. I don't necessarily want to be a leader in the progressive movement. I want to be able to help find those leaders, promote them, and give them the support they need.

COIRO: Some seek leadership and some have leadership thrust upon them. Do you think that you're using this position that you have to the fullest, whether you sought it or not?

ZÚNIGA: Well, I look at my life, and it's packed. It's not like I have a lot of space and time to really play with, so I don't think I could do more than I'm already doing. People always want me to do more and more and more, and I have to push back and say I have to have some balance. I've neglected my wife and my new son for a couple of years now, and I need to get to the point where I can start paying attention to them, to give them the attention they deserve. I also realize that I'm helping build a world and a country and a movement that will make life a lot better for my son in the future, and obviously that's what drives me every day.

COIRO: I think one of the hardest things, when you talk about blogosphere, is quantifying exactly how powerful blogs are. I notice that those of us who have Daily Kos up on our bookmarks and go to Atrios, and check all the others, sometimes when we talk to people who don't have those bookmarked, who don't look at them everyday, they look askance at us, "oh, you're one of those Internet weirdos." There's still a little bit of that. How far has the blogosphere penetrated the rest of the world?

> "I think the ability to build buzz and to motivate the ground troops is really the strength of the blogosphere and that's why it's so important to the party and the establishment in DC."

ZÚNIGA: I think you have to really keep in mind what the strength of the blogosphere is. It will never be a mass-market tool. It will never reach the masses because that's not what it's for, because people have to visit it, they have to take a conscious choice to spend time out of their day to go visit it. So what we're going to get is the hard-core activists in the progressive movement and the same on the other side of the political divide. So it's influential in the way that it really talks to the party worker bees, the people who are out in the street doing the hard-core work, those are the people who are going to be visiting these blogs. It's going to be influential in building buzz about candidates and in generating volunteers. It's going to be influential in some money raising, but the money is not that big a deal in the grander scheme of things. I think the ability to build buzz and to motivate the ground troops is really the strength of the blogosphere and that's why it's so important to the party and the establishment in DC.

COIRO: I mentioned some of the key 'net sites and the fact that you're one of the big ones, but there are other big ones. Isn't there a danger that we devolve into a situation where it's like NBC, ABC, CBS? They used to be the big three and they essentially all had the same information; they became the go-to guys. Are you in that kind of danger?

ZÚNIGA: I actually worry about that, to be honest. I have no intention to dominate the sphere and knock out competitors. One of the beauties of the progressive blogosphere that I don't see in other verticals is that we're very collaborative. Because we're all in it for the same reasons, and we're all part of the same movement. We all work together as much as possible, so it's not a competitive situation like you see in other places. But I also take heart in the fact that the blogosphere, so far, has been very, very fluid. There's a site called Technorati, and they have their list of the one hundred most influential blogs, and if you look at the list from nine months ago, compared to the list today, sixty-three of the sites that were on it nine months ago are no longer there. So there is a lot of flux. There are a lot of sites coming in and out. On the progressive side, just this last year, we've had Firedoglake kind of burst on the scene, and we've had Glenn Greenwald who has burst on the scene. So we have voices that are emerging and get pushed up, and voices that are stale or old and get pushed down. We see that churn in the blogosphere and as long as that's happening, I think we're going to be a very healthy medium.

COMPANY **Diebold Incorporated**   **SYMBOL** **DBD**   **FOUNDED** 1859

Hello, potential investors. Welcome to Diebold Election Systems! We're the world's leading manufacturer of electronic voting machines. With electronic voting, you have no hanging chads, no pesky recounts. Heck, there's no way to even have a recount. Nobody will be able to dispute an election again. How's that for democracy! And it pays dividends to stockholders.

The CEO and a prominent board member at Diebold are heavy contributors to Republican campaigns. So it's obvious that we know what we're doing. Nobody wants to see a replay of the disputed 2000 election. That exposed the weakness of vote-counting systems and almost resulted in a disaster: a Democratic victory. At Diebold, we're working hard to see that that never happens. So an investment in Diebold is also an investment in continued Republican hegemony.

With Diebold, you can be sure that elections turn out the way they're supposed to. Trust us.

CHAPTER
THE ASCENT OF

A Genealogy of Modern Voting Machines
The more scientists dig, the more voting machine species they discover.

Unearthed Ballot Fossils Reveal Path of Election Evolution

1. **Paper Ballot**
(Ballotus paperus)

2. **Lever Voting Machine**
(Ballotus leverus)

	Paper Ballot	Lever Voting Machine
WHEN SPECIES LIVED	4.4 million years ago	3.5 million years ago
LOCATION OF FOSSIL	Ohio	Florida
INFORMATION/ THEORIES	Piece of ballot found buried in Ohio landfill (probably uncounted).	Part of lever found in Florida lake. Giant comet doomed them.

No voting machine/ballot fossils found from this period, but recent discoveries of missing 2000/2004 ballot boxes in the ocean lead scientists to believe ballots, like man, originally came from the sea.

Like man, paper ballot rises from sea. Now more legible because it is less soggy.

Ballot evolves, loses fins, gains lever. Like man, begins to stand upright.

6 million years ago	5 million years ago	4 million years ago

THREE

VOTING MACHINES

and Their Evolutionary Predecessors

ome became extinct without progeny; others are direct ancestors.

3. Punch Card *(Ballotus punchus)*	4. Butterfly Ballot *(Ballotus chadus)*	5. Diebold Touch Screen *(Ballotus touchus)*
	BUSH GORE / YES NO	TOUCH ONE ■ BUSH ■ BUSH
26 years ago	**6 years ago**	**2 years ago to present**
Ohio	**Florida**	**Ohio**
Unearthed in Ohio woods, thought to be link to modern ballots.	Well-preserved 2000 Butterfly hanging chad found in tar pit in 2005.	Damaged touch screen found in Ohio dig. Died from predator attack.

By 1980, upright punch card machine begins to equal man in intelligence.	Ballot evolves, surpasses elderly Florida man in basic intelligence.	Diebold Voting Machine ® surpasses all man in intelligence. Man no longer needed for voting. Machine votes. Man extinct.
		VOTE BUSH. 
12 years ago	**6 years ago (2000)**	**2 years ago (2004)**

Congratulations!

KARL ROVE

for your extraordinary achievement

IN THE FIELDS OF

direct mail, press leaks, whisper campaigns, and character assassination

YOU ARE HEREBY HONORED AS AIR AMERICA'S

CREEP
of the
WEEK

NICKNAME: Turd Blossom

COLLEGE DEGREE: Rove did not graduate from college.

HATES: Special prosecutors

LOVES: Wedge issues, smear tactics, blacklists

CONSCIENCE: Missing since 1978

WHAT HE SAID ABOUT VALERIE PLAME IN 2003: "I didn't know her name and didn't leak her name."

WHAT HE SAID AFTER HE LEAKED HER NAME: "I've already said too much."

WHAT HE SAYS TO HIS STAFF IN HIS OFFICE WHEN HE THINKS NO ONE IS LISTENING: "We will f**k him. Do you hear me? We will f**k him. We will ruin him. Like no one has ever f**ked him!"[1]

[1] As reported by Ron Suskind in Esquire, January 2003

Siad Barre was a brutal, fanatical Somalian dictator in the same class as Idi Amin or Charles Taylor. Responsible for genocidal murder in Somalia, he was also an active member of an organization that calls itself the Family or the Fellowship. And you know what? This would just be a story about one more maniacal murdering dictator if it weren't for the fact that this organization Siad Barre was a member of is essentially run by Republican Senator Sam Brownback of Kansas, a poster child for the religious right and one of the Republican Party's 2008 presidential hopefuls.

In 2003, a writer for the Associated Press started unraveling a story about six US Republican congressmen who were then living together in a plush, Washington, DC, townhouse owned by a fundamentalist Christian group calling itself the Fellowship. Up until that point, the most the media had ever reported about this group was that it was made up of Republican politicos who organized an annual National Prayer Breakfast at the White House for President Bush.

But even with that connection to the White House, very few in the mainstream media actually took the time to figure out what the Fellowship was all about or what specifically it had to do with Senator Brownback, or with the evangelical movement, that is, until Jeff Charlotte of *Harper's Magazine* went undercover and did an exposé on the Fellowship that should scare the bejesus out of anyone who still cares about the future of America.

In 2006, virtually every Republican candidate who wants support from money evangelicals like Pat Robertson and James Dobson has to get the blessing of questionable types such as Sam Brownback and Charles Colson, whom you may remember from Watergate. It turns out not to be difficult to understand what the Fellowship is all about: It's about intolerance of anything that Sam Brownback decides should not be tolerated.

For example, the Fellowship decided that a group calling itself Americans United for Separation of Church and State was having too much success talking logic and reason to state legislators, so it helped organize a criminal investigation of that group through the US Department of Justice. The Fellowship has also worked

tirelessly to ensure that states don't stiffen criminal penalties for hate crimes against minorities and gays. The organization in addition supports a worldwide American "religious" offensive to spread Christianity in places like Iraq, Iran, and North Korea, not via God's word, not through the compassionate teachings of Jesus, but rather, using smart missiles, MI rifles, and raw military might.

Senator Brownback would do away entirely with secular government if he had his way and would instead support a style of government founded on his personal version of Christianity. I have often wondered if Senator Brownback's Jesus is the same Jesus I know from his Sermon on the Mount, a lesson in tolerance and compassion; the same Jesus who advocated peace over war, who taught that Christianity should exclude no one.

I have to wonder because this organization that calls itself the Fellowship has a history of low-profile meetings with the leaders of dictatorial death squads in Central America. And, of course, they almost single-handedly propped up the bloodiest dictator ever to cast his evil shadow on Somalia.

The Fellowship supports dismantling governmental regulatory rules, which would leave American workers, consumers, and its underclass at the mercy of a new corporate fascism that is a product of an alliance between big business and the religious right.

What Sinclair Lewis in the '30s warned us of has come to pass. He predicted that if and when fascism comes to America, it would have a cross in one hand and an American flag in the other.

Keep your eye on Sam Brownback as he mounts his bid to replace the man most of us believe can't be topped in terms of how bad a president he has been, because I gotta tell ya, Brownback could be an even worse president than W.

Two Houses Divided Cannot Stand

With his incisive comments about the relationship between Bush and Congress, Massachusetts senator Ted Kennedy showed that he hasn't lost a step after thirty-four years of public service. His talk with Al Franken on June 8, 2006, began with a comparison of the number of subpoenas issued by Congress during the Clinton and Bush administrations.

TED KENNEDY: [Congress issued] 1,100 subpoenas in the Clinton administration and three in the Bush administration, and that's a pretty clear indication of the priorities that this Congress has.

AL FRANKEN: How many in this administration?

KENNEDY: Three, with all the problems of torture, with detention, with rendition, with eavesdropping—

FRANKEN: Three!

KENNEDY: All of this is extraordinary; it's the unitary presidency. It's really a cockeyed view of the role of the executive, where all the power is in the executive. Once the president and the country went through the experience of 9/11, we got effectively "a war president," and we're now in a "war." His inherent power now overrides all statutes and all international agreements. What follows on that is the politics of fear. We've had that over the last five years. And it has been destructive of the public dialogue in terms of the debate on national and international affairs and it has convoluted what our founding fathers wanted in terms of the checks and balances between the executive and Congress. As you know, Al, it says "we the people"—the Constitution gave the power and authority effectively to Congress . . . it's we the people, it's the general welfare issue.

FRANKEN: The general welfare, yes.

> "Once the president and the country went through the experience of 9/11, we got effectively 'a war president,' and we're now in a 'war.' And what follows on that is the politics of fear."

KENNEDY: History teaches us that when we come together, we do the best for our country, and that was always the politics of hope, it's the politics of the future, and now we have the politics of division. We have seen it in the Congress with the federal marriage amendment, flag burning amendment, the estate tax repeal, as if these are the three burning items that are of concern to the people in my state of Massachusetts or across the country. People are concerned about the high price of gasoline, health care that's out of sight, education that they can't afford, jobs they're unsure of, pensions that are disappearing. There's been no increase in the minimum wage and pollution is rampant. Now double the number of children are dying from asthma because of pollutants.

> ## "The American people have to finally decide that they're being used and abused."

FRANKEN: Yeah, but aren't a lot of the kids dying from asthma from the flags that are burning?

KENNEDY: [Laughs] There you go. The American people have to finally decide that they're being used and abused. I mean, the Democrats haven't done as well as they should, we all understand it. But still, if you look at what we have achieved when we did have authority and power, we had a sound economy, we passed a higher education bill to educate kids, and we [looked after] Medicare and Medicaid. We went to the moon with President Kennedy, and we made a down payment on nuclear arms control. I mean, we were trying to deal. And most important is that we knocked down walls of discrimination in the '60s. Those are things we have done.

FRANKEN: You get portrayed by the right in their fundraising letters as this tremendously left-wing, divisive character, but the fact of the matter is that, for example, on immigration you and John McCain put together the bill which is basically the bill that passed in the Senate.

KENNEDY: That's right.

FRANKEN: I want to ask you something about this immigration bill because it seems to me the way to stop illegal immigration is the enforcement of the law at the workplace. Now what I want to ask about is, after the law passed in '86, the burden was going to be on the employer. But because there was so much counterfeiting of documents the employers were given a pass, and for good reason. Is it possible to do this kind of biometric documentation that is going to make it possible to really enforce this?

KENNEDY: First of all, you're absolutely right. You have to have an effective system between the employer and employee, and you're absolutely right in understanding what happened in '86. We had decided we didn't want a permanent underclass. We wanted to bring them out of the shadows and we did that with an amnesty, but we also were going to put into effect a tough employer sanction program, but it was never done. It was never effectively enforced by either Republicans or Democrats. Even during the time of the Clinton administration, I went down to the Labor Department and met with the department that was enforcing it, and it was really laughable. They weren't really doing anything at all.

FRANKEN: But wasn't that because of the documentation?

KENNEDY: Because you had so many false documents, and it was impossible to do. But no effort was really made. That has to shift, and biometrics is the big change where we can now have a degree of certainty. So you have to have legality and tough enforcement. And then you've got to recognize that we've got 4 million children of undocumented aliens that have come here. Those are American children and what are we going to do, deport their parents and make them orphans? A number of these kids are serving in the Armed Forces in Iraq and Afghanistan. They come back from serving over there and getting wounded over there and find out that their parents have been deported?

FRANKEN: Doesn't labor and don't American workers have a legitimate concern about the numbers that might come in on a guest worker program? And don't people have concerns about exploitation of guest workers? What can be done about that?

> "You've got to recognize that we've got 4 million children
> of undocumented aliens that have come here.
> Those are American children and what are we going to do,
> deport their parents and make them orphans?"

KENNEDY: Well, you've read history and you know. The greatest exploitations—well, slavery was the greatest exploitation, clearly, here in this country—but the second was the Presaro program in the late '50s and early '60s. That program effectively gave all the cards to the employers, and you had enormous exploitation of individuals, men and women. We got rid of that program in the '60s, and we cannot duplicate it. And we're getting exploitation today, because if you have an employer that knows they're employing an undocumented worker, they'll say, you work not just forty hours a week, you work fifty or sixty or I'm going to call the immigration service. At the same time, you're depressing wages, you're depressing working conditions, and that is hurting the American worker. Hopefully, you get a situation where a guest worker, with a limited stay, comes here with a guarantee that they've got the coverage of the Davis-Bacon protections.

FRANKEN: Davis-Bacon is the prevailing wage.

KENNEDY: Prevailing wage for construction, which is higher than the $5.15 minimum wage. And we've also hired 2,500 inspectors, whose only job is going to be to make sure that we're not going to have the exploitation. That's never been done before. That's a major difference. You know, we can't guarantee that this is going to be the end-all of this, but we've spent $20 billion in the last ten years on the border. We've got 300 times the number of border guards down there, and the total number of people that have come across has increased 300 percent. So what we need is a comprehensive kind of approach. What we really need is for

Mexico to invest. Over the next ten years, fifteen years, that's what's going to have to happen with the countries in Central America. We've got to involve them in this effort.

> "We've spent $20 billion in the last ten years on the border. We've got 300 times the number of border guards down there, and the total number of people that have come across has increased 300 percent."

Let me just mention one thing, there's $500 billion that's been paid into the Social Security that's never going to get reclaimed because of undocumented workers. There's $7 to $10 billion paid into the Social Security system every year from people that are undocumented that'll never be reclaimed. We don't want to diminish that, the Social Security fund is under enough pressure at the present time. But the fact is these people are never going to get that money back. We should be able to work out some way for helping to develop Mexico and to increase economic opportunity down there. That'll really have an important impact. People are coming over because they want to work hard and provide for their families. They attend church, and they love America. These are all qualities we admire in people, we respect the fact that people work hard and play by the rules, and that's what the great majority of them do, and we ought to understand it.

FRANKEN: Well, the opponents of this would say they don't play by the rules by coming in illegally, but I also have some problems with this comprehensive bill that has been passed in the Senate. I don't know, for example, how you're going to distinguish between people who have been here two years and people who have been here five years. That seems to be an invitation for counterfeit documents.

KENNEDY: Yeah, well, to be honest about that, it's the way legislation works.

FRANKEN: It was a compromise.

KENNEDY: It was not in the McCain-Kennedy bill. It was added, and we got a very substantial additional group of senators to cosponsor. The concept is basically this: People have a different feel for people that have been here for ten or fifteen years. They're your neighbors, people that go to church with you, versus somebody who's just come over the fence in the last forty-eight hours. And people want to deal differently with the people who have been here some time and have really demonstrated that they're playing by the rules versus someone that's just come over here, who we know nothing about. That's conceptually where it is, but I agree with you that it adds an enormously difficult kind of administrative challenge for people. I would have preferred that it had not been added on, quite frankly, but we did pick up a good deal more support for the reasons that I've just outlined, and that's unfortunately the way that sometimes a bill goes ahead.

Roping in the Red States

On April 19, 2006, former governor of Virginia, presidential hopeful, and Democratic fundraiser Mark Warner spoke with Al Franken on *The Al Franken Show* about how the Democrats can learn to win again.

AL FRANKEN: So what are you doing with yourself?

MARK WARNER: I am running around the country trying to do all I can to get Democrats elected to Congress, the Senate, gubernatorial seats. I was in Tennessee last week with Harold Ford, who would be a great United States senator; the week before I was with Claire McCaskill in Missouri. There is a real sense around the country that people know this administration, on almost every front, is messing up. From the level of corruption in Washington, to the failed policies in Iraq, to failed fiscal policies, to America's diminished stature in the world. I mean, the list goes on and on. And I've been trying to advocate as well [that] we need to not only point out those failings, we also need to lay out how Democrats would do things differently.

> "There is a real sense around the country that people know this administration is messing up."

FRANKEN: What do you have to say?

WARNER: That in Virginia, that two-to-one Republican state, we actually changed our education system, brought jobs back to some of our communities, and had an honest debate about finances.

FRANKEN: And that's what you call the Virginia Miracle.

WARNER: [Chuckles] Well, I'm not sure I'd use that term. But I'm pretty proud of the fact that we took a state that was in deep deficit, turned it to surplus, and we got jobs back to some of our communities that had not had a lot of hope for the last twenty or thirty years.

FRANKEN: And you left with 80 percent approval rating.

WARNER: Well, I left with 80 percent approval rating because we actually focused on results. I mean, one of the things that was pretty interesting is, good policy ends up being good politics and you get stuff done. And if you can actually find some way to bridge the partisan divide in two-to-one Republican states, people respond.

FRANKEN: I don't know if you are aware of this, but there is talk about you as a potential presidential candidate [in] 2008.

WARNER: I'm shocked, shocked.

FRANKEN: And I also want to know if you are aware of this: The last two Democrats elected president were Southerner governors.

WARNER: Well, people have brought that up along the way, too.

FRANKEN: And you've made the point that, that Democrats can't just focus on sixteen states and then hope for triple bank shot with Ohio, Florida, and—

WARNER: I think that's a crazy strategy, you do the Democrat party a disservice, and we do the country a disservice. But there are a whole lot of states where Democrats could be competitive, where Democrats currently are competitive.

FRANKEN: Well, you just talked about Tennessee, you talked about McCaskill, Missouri, those are states that Bush carried that I believe those Democratic Senate candidates can win.

WARNER: I do too, but when you write off half the country what you're basically saying, to that half of America, to the so-called red-state America, is "All right, we're not going to have ideas or candidates that are going to be competitive there." You are going to basically cede the field to the Republican party, which is increasingly out of the mainstream. I mean, you have a Republican party that wants to redebate questions around science versus politics.

FRANKEN: Now, you are pro-science, aren't you? You're one of these pro-science guys.

WARNER: As a dad of a daughter with juvenile diabetes, I sure as heck would say I'd be willing to utilize any kind of research I can to see if we can cure that disease and a host of other diseases. I can tell you, in a state like Virginia, and Missouri and Tennessee, there's an awful lot of what we used to call Reagan Democrats or moderate independents or moderate Republicans who are looking for a new home, but we got away from the ideas that would give them that home.

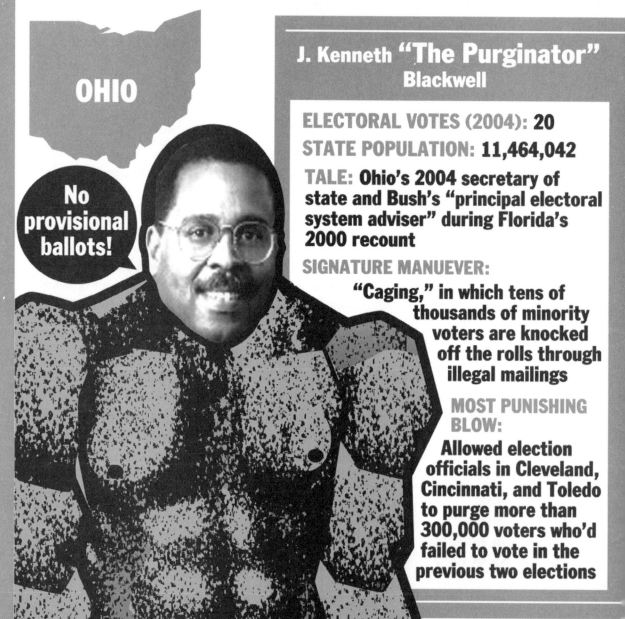

★ OHIO ★ TALE OF

MOST CORR

SMACK

OHIO

No provisional ballots!

J. Kenneth "The Purginator"
Blackwell

ELECTORAL VOTES (2004): 20

STATE POPULATION: 11,464,042

TALE: Ohio's 2004 secretary of state and Bush's "principal electoral system adviser" during Florida's 2000 recount

SIGNATURE MANUEVER:

"Caging," in which tens of thousands of minority voters are knocked off the rolls through illegal mailings

MOST PUNISHING BLOW:

Allowed election officials in Cleveland, Cincinnati, and Toledo to purge more than 300,000 voters who'd failed to vote in the previous two elections

UPT STATE
DOWN

Call me Congress-woman!

FLORIDA

Katherine **"The Recountinixer"** Harris

ELECTORAL VOTES (2000): 25

STATE POPULATION: 17,789,864

TALE: Florida's 2000 secretary of state and Bush's Florida cochairwoman in 1999

SIGNATURE MANUEVER:

"Scrubbing," in which Harris booted thousands of eligible, mostly African-American, voters off the rolls after they were erroneously added to the state's felons list

MOST PUNISHING BLOW:

Set deadline for election results and then rejected extension requests from counties performing hand recounts

THEY SAID WHAT??!?!!

During the 2006 debate in Congress on the gay marriage amendment, standing before an enlarged family photo displayed on an easel, Senator James Inhofe, Republican of Oklahoma, offered this tidbit, for reasons that remain unclear.

As you see here, and I think this is maybe the most important prop we'll have during the entire debate, my wife and I have been married 47 years. We have 20 kids and grandkids. I'm really proud to say that in the recorded history of our family, we've never had a divorce or any kind of homosexual relationship."

Sen. James Inhofe
2006

Seriously, he said that?

The **unrecorded** history, on the other hand, now that's a whole other story . . .

But now, after the gay marriage amendment has been defeated, look out! All the Inhofes are going to get divorced and marry the nearest gay person. (Thanks a lot, you dastardly liberals.)

And we believe everything you say, ever since you declared global warming to be the biggest hoax ever perpetrated on the American people.

Another In(hofe)sight: "The homosexual marriage lobby, as well as the polygamist lobby, they share the same goal of essentially breaking down all state-regulated marriage requirements to just one, and that one is consent. In doing so, they're paving the way for illegal protection of such practices as homosexual marriage, unrestricted sexual conduct between adults and children, group marriage, incest, and, you know, if it feels good, do it." *We want to party with you, cowboy!*

It's this kind of logic that makes us wonder why you were voted one of the dumbest senators in *Washingtonian* magazine's annual survey of congressional staffers.

We're sure that any gay members of your family would feel very comfortable coming out to you and the missus.

Disgraced House Majority Leader Tom DeLay's many, many scandals reached critical mass, and Ramon was there to get the Palm Pilot.

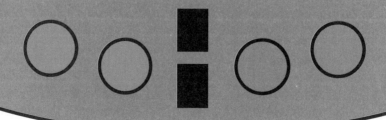

HAMMERTOM
TODAY'S SCHEDULE:

7 am Wake up. Read about myself on the front pages of the New York Times and the Washington Post. Prepare for the End of Days.

9 am Assemble defense team. Put wife and daughter on the payroll. Remember the best defense is a good offense.

11 am Gather staff for document-shredding-and-hard-drive-erasing party. No one must find out about the "Ooker-Hay Urder-May."

1 pm Call Michigan militia. Tell them to put Operation Activist Judge Safari on hold. Initiate Operation Protect the Hammer.

3 pm Distribute cyanide capsules and sidearms to staff. We'll just SEE who's loyal here.

7 pm Pray to God for advice. But tell him I'm going to have to drop him from the payroll. Just until this blows over, Lord.

The very best in global industry ... *working for you!*

COMPANY **Dow Chemical Company** **SYMBOL** **DOW** **FOUNDED** **1897**

Dow Chemical knows the value of product placement, and their products are everywhere: in the rivers, oceans, air, soil, plants, animals, and even you. So investing in Dow means you're investing in yourself and your world.

Dow Chemical is a giant in the field of plastics, chemicals, hydrocarbons, and herbicides. And Dow understands synergy. Did you know that Dow, one of the world's leading producers of dioxin, also makes Styrofoam? The same insulation used in the coolers that are used to transfer donated livers to the people whose lives were so intimately touched by dioxin? It's true!

Dow is also a leading producer of pesticides, and who better to produce weed killers than the makers of napalm and Agent Orange, a chemical that is still working today on US veterans and the residents of numerous Vietnamese villages. You see, Dow's plastics aren't the only things that last forever. Invest in Dow Chemical. Think of it as defoliating the world—for a smoother, shinier planet.

Hispanic Republicans: Hasta la Vista, Babies

David Bender

David Bender, host of *Politically Direct*, "received" the following "transcript" from a confidential source. It records a conversation that took place recently between Deputy White House Chief of Staff Karl Rove and an unidentified male (UM). It was recorded as part of a general sweep of all communications that contained key words relevant to the war on terror. Those words are highlighted in bold. The transcript originally surfaced as evidentiary material during the discovery process relative to the pending trial of a former cabinet aide.

UNIDENTIFIED MALE (UM): Hello?

KARL ROVE: It's Karl.

UM: Karl, how are—

ROVE: Cut the crap. We're f**ked and it's all your fault.

UM: What are you talking about? *What's* my fault?

ROVE: Don't play dumb with me, you sanctimonious son of a bitch. You set us up. You planned this and we walked right into it. All that hugging and kissing bulls**t. We're *friends* now. All is *forgiven* from 2000. You never fooled me for an instant. Maybe the Boy Blunder thought you were sincere, but I never bought it. Not for a goddamned second.

UM: Now Karl—

ROVE: Don't "now Karl" me. I've got to hand it to you, though. You've played this beautifully. How did you do it? What did you have to promise to get that cheesehead Sensenbrenner to introduce an immigration bill that was so tough it would even make J.Lo a felon?

UM: Karl, I didn't—

ROVE: Don't even bother to lie. I've still got a few friends on the Hill. Your fingerprints are all over that bill. Then, as soon as he introduced it, you made a beeline for the microphones and got up on your high horse with all that mushy crap about how *terrible* it would be if someone's poor little *abuela* was sent back where she came from. No, not *you*. Not the friend of the people. Not the champion of the little guy. Not a *genuine* compassionate conservative like you—

UM: Now, Karl, why would I want to do something like that?

ROVE: Why? *Why?* I'll *tell* you why. Because you want to run for president, that's why. You want *us* to take the heat by sticking with the base while you get to be Señor Statesman. You knew those maniacs like Tancredo would fire up the Minutemen and you'd look all moderate by comparison. Meanwhile, we're stuck with having to pander to those a**holes in order to keep that bitch Pelosi from taking over. This is a **ticking time bomb** for us. And you're loving it. You get to rise above the whole thing and then run against the lunatics in your own party.

UM: I've always supported the president. You know that, Karl. We're both in favor of a guest worker program. I've backed him up completely on that.

ROVE: Sure, that's what you *want* everyone to believe. That's the genius of your play, you get to have it both ways. You tell everyone how loyal you are to the president, but then you also get to go out and criticize those right-wing crazies like Dana Rohrabacher who want hospitals to gather up information on illegal aliens before treating them. We have to live with these nut-jobs. You get to talk about the importance of learning multiple languages while I'm stuck with a guy who can barely put a sentence together in English. You get to do photo ops with all the Latinos in your state. We have to go stand on the border and talk about building fences. *Fences!* Do you know what I had to do to talk Ken Mehlman off the ledge after that one? The poor bastard was in tears. We got more than 40 percent of the Hispanic vote in 2004. If those a**holes in the House get their way, we'll have *4 percent* next time, not to mention there'll be nobody left to cut a goddamned lawn in this country. We are *so* f**ked!

UM: C'mon. You're just being overly dramatic.

ROVE: *I'm* being dramatic? Have you seen the poll numbers? *I* have. Cross-tabs. Internals. Trend lines. I get this s**t on my desk every single day and it's going from bad to worse. Let me tell you what those polls say—they say that Hispanics are **terrorized** and that they're going to turn out in numbers like we haven't seen since Pete Wilson got kicked in the cojones in California when he did the same stupid f**king thing twelve years ago with that goddamned anti-immigrant ballot initiative. That one brilliant move made the Democratic Party a safe haven for Hispanics from San Diego to the Oregon border and it single-handedly turned Ronald Reagan's home state into the bluest state in the nation. And those people are about to become the margin of victory for every future election in this country. I don't need to tell *you* this—you've got them all over your state, too. They breed like . . . like *Catholics*.

UM: Uh, Karl, they *are* Catholics.

ROVE: You see?! We are *so* f**ked. Everybody except *you*, that is. You're the goddamned voice of reason. My lame duck is out there quacking like an idiot about guest workers and nobody takes him seriously anymore. Meanwhile Tom Tancredo is the new face of the Republican Party. I should have had his legs broken when he first started opening his big mouth about "border security." Like *he* knows anything about security. I *invented* security. Everybody knows **9/11** is mine. I own it.

UM: You don't really mean that, Karl. You wouldn't actually break a congressman's *legs*—

ROVE: I can't believe I let Cheney talk me out of it. He's such a wuss. I'm telling you, we're gonna lose the goddamned Congress and then I really *will* be indicted. I'll have subpoenas coming out of my ass.

UM: C'mon Karl. You're making too big a deal out of all of this. Why don't you just go out and get **bin Laden?** That will change the subject.

ROVE: Just go out and get **bin Laden?** That's easy for *you* to say. You know full well we've got an ironclad deal that gives him eight years in Pakistan in return for no **new attacks.** If we try to renegotiate with him now, he'll hold us up for a sheik's ransom. And I don't know where the hell I'd even *find* that many virgins . . .

UM: So what is it that you want me to say?

ROVE: I just want you to admit it. Just tell me the truth. You really love watching us squirm, don't you?

UM: [Snickering, then laughing]

ROVE: You motherf**ker! I'll get you, you bastard. I'll go after your wacko wife, your crazy brown-skinned daughter. You just wait—I'll make your life a living hell!

UM: [Laughing] Karl, Karl, Karl—calm down. You're going to have an aneurysm. Listen, I've got to run. By the way, Mother's here. She sends her best.

ROVE: F**k *you*, Jeb!

UM: *Adios, amigo.*

END OF TRANSCRIPT

Party Etiquette

In the summer of 2004, while performing at a John Kerry fundraiser, comedian Whoopi Goldberg made some jokes, including an off-color riff on the president's last name, that so enraged Republicans that the Democratic Party publicly distanced itself from her. Almost a year later, she talked to David Bender on *Politically Direct* about the incident that got her in hot water and why she doesn't care.

DAVID BENDER: You've been involved in a lot of political stuff in the last few years. How'd that work out for you?

WHOOPI GOLDBERG: Well, it was fine until my party abandoned me. There's no other way to say it. They just put their tails between their legs and they ran.

BENDER: Let's tell people what happened, just for those who might have been living in Bolivia and missed the whole experience. Last summer you did what you have done for as long as I have known you. You went out and stood up for the Democratic nominee, John Kerry. I believe it was the Democratic National Committee, at an event at Radio City Music Hall, and somehow, in some way, some people took exception to what happened there. Now I actually did a little homework. I went and read the transcript of it and I've got to say you were *so* mild.

> "My party abandoned me. There's no other way to say it.
> They just put their tails between their legs and they ran."

GOLDBERG: Yeah, there was *nothing*. The Democrats wouldn't release the transcript after it happened to vindicate me, and that was really shocking. You know, I've done a lot of stuff in my career. I will take responsibility for that which I did, but I didn't *do* this. And it shocked me and pissed me off and broke my heart that the Democrats allowed it to happen, that they allowed this mockery of freedom of speech to happen. And to this day I haven't heard much from anybody. They don't come around, nobody rings, and that's okay. That's okay.

BENDER: You're lucky, actually.

GOLDBERG: Well, at this point in time I suspect I am lucky, but it is the words of Bill Clinton that keep me going. He was talking to the Democrats and he said if you can't stand up for what you believe in, we're never going to win. And that is to me the truth.

BENDER: What do you think happened?

GOLDBERG: They got scared.

BENDER: Well, they got scared, but as I looked at it, it was waiting to happen. The Republicans had [planned it].

GOLDBERG: It was orchestrated.

BENDER: It was orchestrated from day one.

GOLDBERG: Yes.

> "It shocked me and pissed me off and broke my heart
> that the Democrats allowed it to happen, that they allowed this
> mockery of freedom of speech to happen."

BENDER: It didn't matter what was said that day.

GOLDBERG: No, it didn't, and that is where they all sort of bailed.

BENDER: Well, they were unprepared for it. It was the same way with the Swift boats. They were so incredulous that something like that could happen.

GOLDBERG: Yeah, but you know what, John Kerry had in his hands the ability to take care of that immediately. If John Kerry had said, "You know what? When I came back from Vietnam I sat in front of all these people and I told them what my experience was. I stood in the face of great difficulty, people called me a nonpatriot, called me all kinds of names, and, of course, we then saw My Lai come, and all these other atrocities come, and I stood there in front of everybody and said this is what I think you should know. As your president, I will do the same."

BENDER: Right.

GOLDBERG: And if he had just grown one cojone, he could have taken care of it.

BENDER: What happened to him? What happened to that guy who came back from Vietnam and showed such courage before the Senate committee? Where was he?

GOLDBERG: He was hijacked by a frightened group of people called the Democrats who believe in their own mind that their agenda is not worthwhile and therefore could not figure out how to fight for it. You see it in all the things that happened with Howard Dean, and all the little manipulations of people who, before we even began the campaign, were saying it's not going to be this person or this person, that's the guy we're nominating. Period.

BENDER: Right. The fix is in.

GOLDBERG: That for me was the first folly. I knew that no matter what else came that there was going to be a great change in our party. Now we are standing with our thumbs in our mouths going, "What next?"

BENDER: What do you think about Howard Dean as chair of the party?

GOLDBERG: Well, you know, I have really closed my eyes to the party. I haven't turned my back on them, but I no longer feel comfortable saying that I feel like I'm represented by them. Because again, like Clinton said—and I love Bill, you know—but until people can stand up for what's right in the face of whatever is flying at you, nothing is going to change, and we will be stuck with this kind of odd funk that emanates from our psyche.

BENDER: Whoopi, you had an experience that grew out of what happened at Radio City where immediately other people bailed out on you—Slim Fast, which by the way is the reason I now weigh so much.

GOLDBERG: Well you have to understand what happens when you scare big business . . . and I think because this is a Dutch company, it never occurred to them that this was an orchestrated [campaign], or that the people who ate Slim Fast were still the people who watched my TV show. They just saw me kick around the cutout of the president and heard that I had said all kinds of [things about him]. And so they just bailed instead of waiting to even hear what I had said. And no one said, "Oh wait a minute, that's not what went down." But David, you have to keep in mind that before I got off the stage at Radio City it was already on the Internet—it was on the Internet, it was around the world, and the setup was in. But you know what, it's not ever going to stop me from doing what it is I do.

BENDER: Well, that was Karl Rove who had his finger on that button. Talk about the nuclear option. They were ready to blow up Hollywood.

GOLDBERG: Yes.

BENDER: Very specifically, they had that in mind?

GOLDBERG: Yes, but you know they didn't go after *them*. They went after the biggest, blackest thing they could find.

The very best in global industry...*working for you!*

COMPANY **Wal-Mart Stores, Inc.**   SYMBOL **WMT**   FOUNDED **1962**

When the first Wal-Mart opened in 1962, its founder, Sam Walton, just wanted to have low prices, open a few more stores, become the biggest private employer in Mexico, and shake the world's economy whenever his company switched suppliers for dog food.

From these humble aspirations, Wal-Mart became America's number one retailer. If you have toothpaste, the odds are one in four that you bought it at Wal-Mart. If you have disposable diapers, the odds are one in three. And when you throw one of those diapers away, it's probably filled with something that started out at a Wal-Mart. You see, Wal-Mart just wants to make life easier. That's why they're removing all other local retailers, who only sow confusion. By 2017, those tiresome choices will vanish and Wal-Mart will change its name to The Store.

How can we afford to offer these discount prices, you ask. Our employees pitch in by earning discount wages. That also attracts them to Wal-Mart's low, low prices. Competitors have to drop their wages, driving their employees to Wal-Mart's low, low prices. The more you shop at Wal-Mart, the more you have to shop at Wal-Mart.

Of course, some people resist being assimilated—labor unions for instance. But Wal-Mart doesn't need unions, because employees can speak up for themselves. This is particularly important for the many children who work for Wal-Mart's suppliers overseas and are at the tender age when they need to learn self-reliance. That's the American way, after all. And to love America, you have to love Wal-Mart—big, bright, and enterprising. (Anyway, you have to love Wal-Mart because it's all that's left.)

Attack of the Killer Corporations
Thom Hartmann

A new aristocracy is taking over not just the United States of America but also the world. It's based on influences from a modern synthesis of old-time laissez-faire "free market" economics and modern libertarian thought that derives mostly from a cult formed in the 1950s by Ayn Rand. The proponents of this economic system, such as Thomas Friedman, Milton Friedman, John Stossel, George W. Bush, and the editorial page of the *Wall Street Journal,* put forward the myth of the "free market" and suggest that government should not play any sort of a regulatory part in this mythical free market. The result, they say, is that people's natural greed will motivate them to make decisions that will ultimately be the best for themselves as well as for all of society.

A key piece of this plan is that the elite need not pay the price of admission to a free society, to paraphrase FDR's statement about taxes.

There are two main problems with this way of looking at business. First is the obvious fallacy of believing that corporations will always work in the public interest. One has only to look at the laundry list of environmental and social disasters perpetrated by corporations to see how naive an idea that is. The second is the core notion of a free market that exists independent of government. The fundamental problem with the concept is that there is no such thing as a free market without government.

NO GOVERNMENT, NO MARKETPLACE

Government creates and facilitates markets, much as the rules of baseball, a baseball infrastructure (stadium and diamond), and baseball umpires facilitate playing the game of baseball.

For a market to exist, there must first be a legal concept of private property and private property ownership. This requires laws that define what ownership means, what can be owned and what cannot be owned because it's part of the public commons (do you own the sky over your house?), and how ownership can be passed from person to person or from generation to generation.

This requires laws defining property, ownership, and terms of exchange. It requires legislatures to enact and fine-tune these laws as times and circumstances change. It requires courts to interpret the laws and adjudicate them. It requires police to enforce them and prisons to hold those who defy them. It requires a national monetary system to provide a stable means of exchange. And in the event of international exchange, it requires treaties and international agreements to facilitate trade and protect parties in nations that may have differing laws regarding ownership, definitions of property, taxes, and systems of contract enforcement.

Thus, without "government interference," there can be no marketplace at all, and nobody can play the game of business.

Given this simple reality, there have historically been two schools of thought about how governments should create and mediate marketplaces so that business can exist.

HE WHO HAS THE GOLD MAKES THE RULES

The first school of thought suggests that society—particularly those people who have at various times been referred to as the masses, the working class, peons, or serfs—exists to serve the marketplace, and the marketplace itself is owned by a small ruling elite (referred to by the *Wall Street Journal* as the investor class). People who subscribe to this notion are generally advocates of laissez-faire economics, as this is the core tenant of that system, which reached its peak in the United States during the Robber Baron era and led directly to the Republican Great Depression. The most famous advocates of this system are Presidents Herbert Hoover and Ronald Reagan and former head of the Federal Reserve Alan Greenspan.

COMPASSIONATE CAPITALISM

The second school of thought—common through Europe for much of the past two centuries, and ascendant in the United States during the era of the Golden Age of the American middle class, starting with Franklin Delano Roosevelt and ending with Ronald Reagan—suggests that society creates marketplaces by lawmaking for the ultimate purpose of advancing the health and welfare of the larger society itself. It's fine if somebody wants to start a business and make money, so long as they play by rules that not only don't harm society, but also in some way improve or strengthen it. Republican Theodore Roosevelt was a strong proponent of such a system, as were FDR, Harry Truman, Dwight D. Eisenhower, Lyndon Johnson, and the economist John Maynard Keynes.

This second school of economic thought was responsible for the rise of the great industrial democracies of Germany and Japan after World War II, as well as for building the United States into the world's mightiest economic and industrial powerhouse.

While the first school of thought—laissez-faire "free market" or "the world is flat" economics—brought us the Great Depression and have, since Reagan's presidency, hollowed out much of the American middle class, it nonetheless has powerful and wealthy proponents—proponents who are gaining almost feudal-like power over the country and indeed the rest of the world.

FREE MARKET FEUDALISM

This isn't the first time this has happened. The economic historian Marc Bloch is one of the greatest twentieth-century scholars of the feudal history of Europe. In his seminal book on the subject,

Feudal Society, he points out that feudalism is a fracturing of one authoritarian hierarchical structure into another: The state disintegrates as local power brokers take over.

In almost every case, both with European feudalism and feudalism in China, South America, and Japan, "feudalism coincided with a profound weakening of the State, particularly in its protective capacity."

Whether the power and wealth agent that takes the place of government is a local baron, lord, or corporation, if it has greater power in the lives of individuals than does the representative government, the culture has dissolved into feudalism.

Bluntly, Bloch states: "The feudal system meant the rigorous economic subjection of a host of humble folk to a few powerful men."

This doesn't mean the end of government, but, instead the subordination of government to the interests of the feudal lords. Interestingly, even in feudal Europe, Bloch points out, "The concept of the State never absolutely disappeared, and where it retained the most vitality men continued to call themselves 'free'."

The transition from a governmental society to a feudal one is marked by the rapid accumulation of power and wealth in a few hands, with a corresponding reduction in the power and responsibilities of governments that represent the people.

YOU GET WHAT YOU DON'T PAY FOR

Once the rich and powerful gain control of the government, they turn it upon itself, usually first eliminating its taxation process as it applies to them. Says Bloch: "Nobles need not pay taille [taxes]."

Or, as Glenn Simpson noted in an article in the *Wall Street Journal,* "General Electric Co., for example, reported paying an effective tax rate of 19 percent last year on world-wide income, compared with 26 percent in 2003."

Corporations are taxed because they use public services and are therefore expected to help pay for them—the same as citizens.

Corporations make use of a workforce educated in public schools paid for with tax dollars. They use roads and highways paid for with tax dollars. They use water, sewer, and power and communications rights-of-way paid for with taxes. They demand the same protection from fire and police departments as everybody else, and they enjoy the benefits of national sovereignty and the stability provided by the military and institutions like NATO and the United Nations, the same as all residents of democratic nations.

In fact, corporations are heavier users of taxpayer-provided services and institutions than are average citizens. Taxes pay for our court systems, which are most heavily used by corporations to enforce contracts. Taxes pay for our Treasury Department and other governmental institutions that maintain a stable currency essential to corporate activity. Taxes pay for our regulation of corporate activity, by assuring safety in the workplace, guaranteeing a pure food and drug supply, and limiting toxic emissions.

Under George W. Bush, the burden of cleaning up toxic wastes produced by corporate activity has largely shifted from a polluter-funded Superfund and other programs to taxpayer-funded cleanups.

Every year, millions of cases of cancer, emphysema, neurological disorders, and other conditions caused by corporate pollution are paid for in whole or in part by government-funded programs from Medicare to Medicaid to government subsidies of hospitals, universities, and research institutions, which are funded by tax dollars through the National Institutes of Health and National Institute of Mental Health.

NO TAXATION WITHOUT . . . WELL, JUST NO TAXATION

Because it's well understood that corporations use our tax-funded institutions at least as heavily as do citizens, they've traditionally been taxed at similar rates. For example, the top corporate tax rate in the United States was 48 percent during the Carter administration, down from the peak of 53 percent during the Eisenhower and Kennedy years.

Today it stands at 35 percent, but in May of 2001 then Bush administration Treasury Secretary Paul O'Neill suggested there should be no corporate income tax whatsoever. This was the opening salvo in a very real war to have working people bear all the costs of the commons and governance, while the wealthy corporate elite derive most of its benefits.

And, as George H. W. Bush pointed out when he was president, this isn't just an American phenomenon. It's a New World Order.

"The corporate tax-cutters of recent years stretch from Portugal, where the rate has dropped 10 points to about 17 percent," notes the *Wall Street Journal* in a January 28, 2005, article, "to Austria, down 9 points to about 25 percent."

As Cato Institute adjunct scholar Richard W. Rahn noted in Reverend Sun Myung Moon's *Washington Times,* "The idea and practice of the corporate income tax has been dying slowly for the last two decades."

The December 1, 2004, *Washington Times* article, titled "End Corporate Income Tax," reflects a powerful and growing movement not just in the United States but across the world. So-called free trade agreements and supranational institutions like the WTO have given multinational corporations control of the economic lives of nations that were previously democracies. Holland, Ireland, Germany, Portugal, Belgium—the list goes on and on.

DON'T LET IT HAPPEN HERE

In a feudal state, as Bloch reminds us, the nobles need not pay taxes. And as Mussolini showed us, the newest form of ancient European feudalism has been reinvented and renamed. He called it "fascism"— a word that has been defined by *The American Heritage Dictionary* as "fas-cism (fash'iz'em) n. A system of government that exercises a dictatorship of the extreme right, typically through the merging of state and business leadership, together with belligerent nationalism."

We are quickly shifting toward a corporate-run state in countries all over the world. It appears "free" and even allows elections, albeit only among candidates funded and approved by corporate powers, held on voting machines owned by those corporate powers, and marketed in media owned by those corporate powers.

But this bears little resemblance to the democratic republic envisioned by our nation's founders.

If our elected representatives—and those of other "free" nations—don't wake up quickly and reverse course, we will soon again be in a feudal world. And it's up to us—We the People—to help them awaken.

when will
BIG OIL
be happy?

The Oil Industry's Slippery Game

In January 2006, ExxonMobil, the world's largest oil and gas corporation, announced that it had achieved record profits in 2005. In 2005, ExxonMobil made the most money of any corporation in any year in the history of the world: $36 billion. That's enough money to feed, clothe, and house 1 million families of four in the United States for an entire year.

And 2006 has been even better for the oil industry. In April, ConocoPhillips, ExxonMobil, and Chevron announced $15 billion in profits for the first quarter alone. Those profits would have been even higher, except some idiot lost a men's room key at a Mobil station in Pacoima. Because you don't just have to replace the key, you have to replace the whole lock.

So, what accounts for the oil industry's record profits? You know, other than the price of a gallon of gas skyrocketing toward the cost of a Starbucks Macchiato. Some say there's an increased demand for oil worldwide, others say it's a result of a decreased supply from OPEC, still others say it has to do with market tensions resulting from instability in the Middle East, specifically Iran. There are even a few people who think it has something to do with Scientology.

What's the answer? It's hard to know. There are credible experts who believe there's enough natural gas in the ground to last another 100 years and that the rise in gasoline prices is just an old-fashioned money grab—the result of collusion on the part of the oil exporters (Iran, Kuwait, et al.), the oil companies (ExxonMobil, BP, et al.), and a Republican White House that has turned a blind eye to price gouging. However, there are also credible experts who believe the supply of natural gas is dwindling so rapidly that we will run out in twenty years and that the rise in gas prices is a necessary evil that will force consumers to buy more fuel-efficient cars, the oil companies to develop more efficient fuels like ethanol, and the government to invest in alternative energies like wind, solar, nuclear, and others.

Given all of that, which side should you believe? Well, more on that later. But first, some facts that *aren't* in debate.

THE TIES THAT BIND

Since 1990, the oil and gas industry has donated $190 million to finance US elections. Of that, 75 percent went to either Republican candidates or the Republican Party. Since 2003 alone, the top ten oil and gas companies have spent $33 million lobbying Congress and donated another $3 million to Republican candidates. In George W. Bush's two presidential elections, oil and gas companies gave Republicans 79 percent of their $61.5 million campaign war chests.

The deep-rooted connections between the White House and the oil industry have been well documented. President George H. W. Bush and his father, Prescott Bush, both helmed oil companies. The current President Bush also ran a now defunct oil business. He also loves those little toy Hess trucks. Vice President Dick Cheney was at the helm of Halliburton, a leader in the oil service business for five years. Secretary of State Condoleezza Rice was a director at Chevron until 2003. A *New Yorker* article in 2003 described the Saudi ambassador to the United States as "almost a member of the [Bush] family." And, at a Mobil station near you, not only can customers buy a stick of beef jerky from the cashier, they can also donate a dollar to the Jeb Bush for President 2008 Committee.

Even more disturbing than these intimacies are the vast paybacks the oil and gas industry has gotten from the Republican-controlled White House and Congress over the last five years. In a staggering piece of legislation known as the 2005 Energy Bill, signed by President Bush on August 8, 2005, the oil and gas industry was on the receiving end of a $6 billion prize. The $6 billion was in the form of tax subsidies that permit the oil industry to write off the vast preponderance of costs associated with deep-sea oil exploration and with making their plants more efficient and less polluting. The oil companies were also forgiven the royalty payments due to Uncle Sam for oil pumped out of wells on federal lands. And, the bill protects the makers of MTBE (a gasoline additive linked to cancer) from costly litigation. Meaning that if you get cancer as a result of exposure to MTBE, you'd better hope they do a hilarious episode about the subject on *Grey's Anatomy*, because that's the only relief you're going to get.

On February 14, 2006, the *New York Times* reported on an additional $7 billion giveaway to the oil industry buried in the new Department of Interior budget. Over the next five years, Big Oil will be able to pump $65 billion worth of oil and natural gas from federal territories in the Gulf of Mexico without paying a nickel of royalty money to the federal government. And if the energy exploration company Kerr-McGee wins a recently filed suit, the oil and gas industry will be able to skip out on an additional $28 billion in royalty fees. "It's one of the greatest train robberies in the history of the world," said Representative George Miller, Democrat from California. "And a f**king disgrace," he did not add.

Perhaps the most egregious example of a quid pro quo comes from Texas Republican Representative Joe Barton, chairman of the Energy and Commerce Committee. Barton is an eleven-term congressman who, in the time he's been in office, has taken nearly $2 million in campaign donations from the oil and gas companies, making up one-sixth of all the money he has raised for running for Congress. On September 26, 2005, Representative Barton introduced the Gasoline for America's Security Act of 2005. And with a name like that, you'd suspect it was a bill that would, well, provide gasoline for America's security. Well, you couldn't be more wrong if your name was W. Wrongy McWrongenstein.

At the heart of the plan, passed by the House on October 7, 2005, was a two-pronged gift to Barton's oil industry benefactors. First, the government would subsidize the repair of oil refineries along the Gulf Coast that had been damaged as a result of Hurricane Katrina. So far, it seems like a good idea. However, what the bill failed to mention was that many of those refineries had already been closed by the oil industry years earlier in an effort to decrease gasoline production and increase prices. Next, the bill would permit the federal government to just give the oil companies land—including wildlife refuges and closed military bases—where they could build new refineries. Oh, and the bill also permitted energy facilities to burn garbage as fuel and call it conservation.

And that's not all that Texas Republican Joe Barton, chairman of the House Energy and Commerce Committee, has done for his oil industry cronies. He's voted in favor of drilling in the Arctic National Wildlife Refuge, he's against raising corporate average fuel economy (CAFE) standards for automobiles (to make cars more fuel efficient), and he voted no on a bill that would decrease greenhouse gas emissions. He also nicknamed one of his kids Octane.

DRIVING THE POINT HOME

So—back to the question: Which side do you believe? Is the high price of gasoline a necessary evil that will shock Americans into taking conservation more seriously, or is it merely a result of greedy oil companies grabbing for bucks? The truth is that we won't know the truth for quite some time, and by the time we do, it will be too late.

That's why it's imperative for all Americans to switch to driving more fuel-efficient cars and hybrids. That's right, no more Hummers! We know, it will be harder to spot the assholes on the highway, but don't worry, they'll still have those stickers on their rear windows that say "coed naked lacrosse." Also, commuters should carpool when possible—and even shower together. But that's just for fun. You can also encourage your representatives to support legislation that funds research and development of alternative fuels. And, with whatever time you have left after you put your kids to bed, support efforts to find a diplomatic solution that will decrease tensions in the Middle East.

Sure, it seems like a lot of work, but so is getting up at 4 a.m., feeding your horse, hitching it to the buggy, and getting to the office on time via the only form of transportation that will be left to you.

Bush loves going out on the stump speech circuit selling America's brain-dead media on the idea that America's economy is thriving during his war years.

And most American journalists simply print and report what the little shrub has to say without a truth check, without intelligent analysis, and most of the time without even tough questions.

Chances are, most American journalists sit and stare at the shrub's economic stump speech delivery—like monkeys watching television—almost incapable of digesting or dissecting what they see.

All that truth-squading and tough analysis is a step that most reporters simply choose to skip. So, damn near everything that the little shrub has to say about the economy moves unchallenged from George's lips to America's ears.

Fortunately, sometimes the American public understands—they get it even when the American media doesn't.

Noted writer and economist Paul Krugman put it this way: "The problem isn't that people don't understand how good things are. It is that their personal life experience is telling them that all that fairy-tale talk coming out of Bush's mouth can't be true, based on the life they are living."

Michael Mussa, who was a member of Reagan's Council of Economic Advisers for two years, came up with what we call the *Misery Index*. Basically, it's a combination of the rate of unemployment and the rate of inflation.

According to Mussa, that Misery Index for Americans reached a twelve-year high under George Bush. In fact, that Misery Index hit a stellar 9.8—within that first year following Bush's appointed presidency.

Even though the media may miss the obvious, it is apparent that the typical American is not all that gullible when it comes to matters of his or her pocketbook.

According to the American Research Group (the same group whose findings Bush likes to cite when they say something favorable), 63 percent of the people they polled in late 2005 described the economy as bad, very bad, or terrible. Sixty-one percent of those same people expect the economy to be worse in a year, while only 17 percent of those polled expect it to improve.

Apparently, the average American can see through fantasy photo opportunities like the one where Bush appeared at a North Carolina plant and bragged that the plant had increased its workforce by 1,000 workers over four years. Well, the rest of the story—which took only a little investigation to find out—was that North Carolina has lost about 180,000, or 23 percent, of its factory jobs since the boy genius took the helm of the presidency.

Maybe the reason 43 percent of Americans believe the economy is in an economic recession is because 37 million Americans are now officially living in poverty—that's a six-year high, according to the US Census Bureau.

You see, George Bush really does live in a bubble just like the one his father inhabited when he was president. Unfortunately, America's media now occupies space in that same bubble.

From inside that Bush bubble, it is probably difficult for reporters following the economy photo-op speeches to get to the truth. And that's a problem because the truth tells us that:

- Bush tax cuts have cost the economy almost $1 trillion since 2001.
- Bubble Boy Bush has an $8 trillion deficit—a deficit that is higher than that of any other industrialized country on the globe.
- Personal savings for the average American lingered around negative 7 percent for most of this last year.
- Credit and mortgage debt are both higher than they have been in five decades.
- Hourly wages adjusted for inflation have fallen by almost 3 percent under the leadership of our bubble-insulated president.

Historians describe Calvin Coolidge as a president who was so insulated from the realities of the lives of Americans that he babbled and blathered about how robust his economy was right up to the very beginning of the Great American Depression.

He lived in a bubble, too.

Being Right While Being Left

On November 13, 2005, David Bender of *Politically Direct* spoke with Democratic presidential hopeful and Wisconsin senator Russ Feingold about being Jewish, about being a Democrat, and about being right about the war.

DAVID BENDER: You went down to Alabama and you were well received?

RUSS FEINGOLD: I got the ultimate compliment—at the end of one of the [newspaper] articles [they said], "You know he didn't seem like too much of a Yankee."

BENDER: But don't you hear a lot of people saying that the national Democratic Party is out of touch with their values? Isn't there a real cultural gap, and how do you bridge that gap?

FEINGOLD: Well, it really is interesting. There are two types of messages. In places like Alabama and Mississippi, what we did hear from people at roundtable and listening sessions was that Democrats really do have to talk about our families and, yes, some of the value issues. They're troubled by the way the party seems to be uncomfortable with talking about those things. On the other hand, in many other parts of the country, in California and Illinois, Democrats and others are saying, "You guys don't seem to have a spine, you don't seem to have a message. You're not tough enough." These are two different types of concerns. And we can talk about many issues, and we should. We should talk about Supreme Court nominees. I happen to be opposed to the death penalty. But every discussion should [include] the core issues that every family in America is facing: health-care cost for businesses and families, job loss due to lousy, unfair trade agreements, and the desire all over America to have a serious program for energy independence. There is no audience in America that would not think, "Hey, he's talking about the values that matter and the issues that matter to our families."

BENDER: How do you keep them from changing the subject to what Dean famously called during the campaign "God, guns, and gays?"

FEINGOLD: Well, you have to obviously show respect for people's religions, you have to show respect for Americans' right to own a gun. I happen to be one that believes the Second Amendment is an individual right. Many Democrats don't like that but I've always believed that. I think it's protected by the Constitution. I think Democrats make a big mistake by going down this road, by letting people think somehow that we think that having a gun for hunting or even for self-defense is wrong. But the point is that you show respect for the other values, but you [also have to] talk to people about the value of community. And the value of community is us coming together locally and nationally to make sure everybody has health care, to make sure everybody has a fighting chance to keep their job and they don't have to pay ridiculous gas prices because of a foolish energy policy.

BENDER: Senator, you and I are both Jewish Americans.

FEINGOLD: Correct. My little sister is the first female rabbi in the state of Wisconsin.

BENDER: Mazel tov.

FEINGOLD: Very proud of that.

BENDER: It was a wonderful moment for me when Joe Lieberman was nominated for vice president. I did not agree with everything he stood for, and I didn't support him when he ran for president. It's not axiomatic that you support a Jewish candidate if you're Jewish, but conversely, do you think it will still be difficult for non-Jews to be comfortable supporting a Jewish candidate for President?

> "I think Lieberman showed you can put up a candidate that is not only Jewish but is very religious."

FEINGOLD: I think that no matter what it is, when it's new—whether it be the first woman candidate for president or the first African-American candidate or the first Latino candidate—I mean, there will be a few people who unfortunately may not vote for somebody. But you know my experience in Wisconsin—and my name is clearly Jewish, there's no question that I'm Jewish, and I am very proud of it—it's been amazing. Once in a blue moon somebody says something about it, good or bad, but it appears not to have been an issue. I've been reelected three times statewide and treated better than anyone could ever have been expected to be treated. I think we have to assume the American people are a good people, a tolerant people. I think that's who they are in the end, despite what some people think. I think Lieberman showed you can put up a candidate that is not only Jewish but is very religious—and I'm very embarrassed of how devout he is compared to some of the flaws I have in that regard. [Laughter] I think people liked that he had that quality and the fact that he was Jewish was just another example of something that people admired, the religious conviction that he had.

BENDER: On that issue of the personal and the political, I spent fourteen months on the campaign trail with Howard Dean, and one of the things that was interesting was that his wife did not campaign with him, and many people said that hurt him. You're currently single. Is it difficult to talk about family values if you don't bring your family out on the campaign trail with you?

FEINGOLD: Well, I've had a lot of experience with this both as a state senator and a US senator, and I concluded early on that it was just absurd to drag my family to things unnecessarily. When my girls were little they liked to go to parades when I was in the state Senate because they'd give them stuff. At one point I wanted to keep moving and my daughter insisted that I buy her a toy from a vendor, and the crowd booed me till I bought her something. So that was [fun] for her. Of course my spouse, Mary, was with me. [I told her], "Hey it would be great if you'd come," but she did her own thing, and it just made no sense to force her to just stand there. Spouses that want to do that, great, but I think we're coming to a point in this country that people are going to no longer want to see people dragged around as spouses just for the sake of that. I think they want to know that someone is a decent person, they want to know that they treat people well. But forcing somebody to just go to every event for the sake of a campaigning, it seems phony to me, and I'm glad that I've never been a part of that.

BENDER: You were the first senator in open session to actually question the Iraq policy and to raise the idea that perhaps we should—not cut and run, as the Democrats are always accused of advocating—but rather set a target date to consider withdrawal. Were you ahead of the curve on that? Are people now catching up?

FEINGOLD: Well look, I go to every Wisconsin county every year and hold a town meeting, seventy-two listening sessions a year, so sometimes I hear stuff earlier. I realized that there was enormous concern. But when I went back in May and June and especially in August, there was a deepening despair about this Iraq situation which I had opposed from the beginning. I found even people who had supported the war, whose children were in Iraq, saying "for god's sake, Senator, is there no plan to finish this?" and "When can the troops come home?" So I decided to break the taboo that the president put on everybody, sort of a hex, which was if you say the troops are going to come home at some point, you're against the troops.

> "I found even people who had supported the war, whose children were in Iraq, saying, 'for god's sake, Senator, is there no plan to finish this?" and "When can the troops come home?'"

BENDER: You're endangering them in some way.

FEINGOLD: And it's ridiculous. And I think what's happening, and I hope I had a little something to do with it, [is that] Democrats are becoming emboldened. Of course, the American people want an endgame, a positive endgame if possible. Even the president has said we won't stay one day longer than we should. Democrats are starting to find their voice on this. But it needs to be a very firm voice and I'm still concerned that the Democrats have a little more guts, in talking about how this war has been a mistake, but also how it's being conducted has been a mistake.

BENDER: There is now an effort to find out about the intelligence leading up to the decision to go to war. Can you explain why it is that the Republicans have apparently been stonewalling for quite some time in terms of this issue?

FEINGOLD: I think it's pretty obvious to everyone that it was manipulated, and I think it's why they dragged their feet. In my mind, [Iraq is] one of the greatest failures in American foreign policy in modern times and possibly one of the most outrageous efforts to distort the truth, which I sensed at the time. It just didn't add up for me, either the arguments about the connection to Osama bin Laden or the claim that somehow there was an imminent risk of weapons of mass destruction. I had this feeling that every piece of evidence was being manipulated in a way to come to a predetermined conclusion, so this is a very important inquiry for the American people.

> "In my mind, [Iraq is] one of the greatest failures in American foreign policy in modern times and possibly one of the most outrageous efforts to distort the truth."

BENDER: If it is proved at some point that this evidence was deliberately manipulated and if that [manipulation] rises to the president, the vice president—and clearly they were involved with all discussions. Dick Cheney went to the CIA to find out what the intelligence was and by all accounts, a lot of people responded to give him what he wanted. If that is determined to be true, does that rise to the level of a high crime or a misdemeanor? Is that an impeachable offense if someone does that?

FEINGOLD: Well, this is a big *if*, and *deliberate* is really vague, but I would say if you were able to demonstrate that people, elected officials of the United States government, deliberately distorted evidence that led to a war, I would say even the ancient English founders of the concept of high crimes and misdemeanors might have been thinking about that kind of thing.

Greeted as Liberators

A TIMELINE OF THE AMERICAN ADVENTURE IN IRAQ
IN THE WORDS OF ITS REALLY RESOLUTE PERPETRATORS

FEB. 12, 2002 "As we know, there are known knowns. There are things we know we know. We also know there are known unknowns. That is to say we know there are some things we do not know. But there are also unknown unknowns, the ones we don't know we don't know."—Donald Rumsfeld, at a Department of Defense news briefing when asked about evidence that Saddam Hussein had weapons of mass destruction (WMD) or ties to terrorist organizations

FEB. 7, 2003 "It is unknowable how long that conflict [the likely invasion of Iraq] will last. It could last six days, six weeks. I doubt six months."—Donald Rumsfeld, to US troops

JAN. 28, 2003 "The British government has learned that Saddam Hussein recently sought significant quantities of uranium from Africa."—President Bush, State of the Union address, making a claim that the administration knew at the time to be false

MAR. 16, 2003 "I think things have gotten so bad inside Iraq, from the standpoint of the Iraqi people, my belief is we will, in fact, be greeted as liberators. . . . I think it will go relatively quickly . . . (in) weeks rather than months."—Dick Cheney, on NBC's *Meet the Press*

SEP. 8, 2002 "We don't want the smoking gun to be a mushroom cloud."—Condoleeza Rice, on the possibility that Iraq has nuclear weapons

FEB. 27, 2003 "The idea that it would take several hundred thousand US forces is far off the mark."—Donald Rumsfeld

2002

AUG. 26, 2002 "Many of us are convinced that Saddam will acquire nuclear weapons fairly soon."—Dick Cheney

OCT. 11, 2002 Congress authorizes force, if necessary, to disarm Iraq.

FEB. 25, 2003 "Something on the order of several hundred thousand soldiers are probably, you know, a figure that would be required. We're talking about post-hostilities control over a piece of geography that's fairly significant, with the kinds of ethnic tensions that could lead to other problems."—General Eric Shinseki, chief of staff of the Army, to Senate Armed Services Committee four months before retiring

MAR. 19, 2003 Bush declares war on Iraq. Operation Iraqi Freedom is launched.

MAR. 2002 "F*** Saddam. We're taking him out."—President Bush, to Condolezza Rice and three senators

SEP. 7, 2002 "From a marketing point of view, you don't roll out new products in August."—White House Chief of Staff Andrew Card, on why the Bush administration waited until after Labor Day to sell to the American people a preemptive strike against Iraq

FEB. 27, 2003 "Some of the higher-end predictions that we have been hearing recently, such as the notion that it will take several hundred thousand US troops to provide stability in post-Saddam Iraq, are wildly off the mark."—Paul Wolfowitz, deputy defense secretary, to House Budget Committee

When military experts suggest that you will need 300,000 troops to accomplish a mission—let's set aside for the moment the mission's underlying validity—the best thing to do, by far, is belittle and dismiss those experts. That shows you're for real! Here is a Bush administration guide to imposing your will on a messy world that calls out for firm, decisive, corporate-style management.

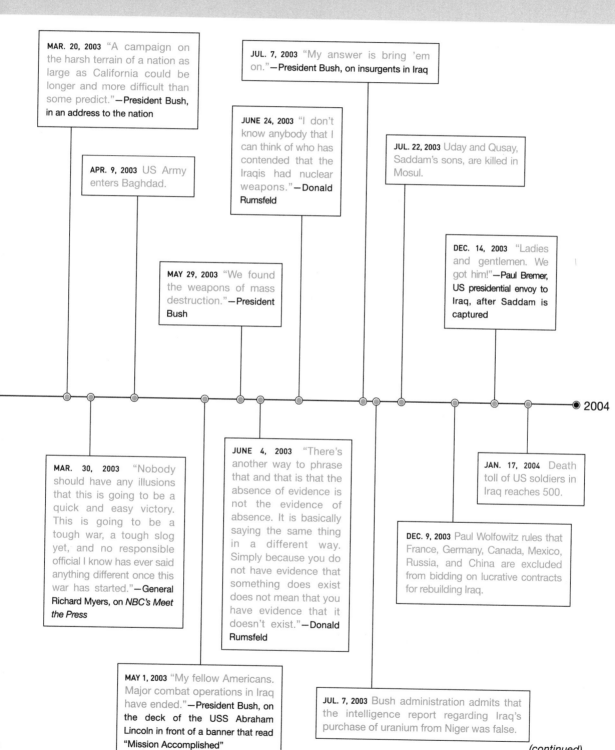

MAR. 20, 2003 "A campaign on the harsh terrain of a nation as large as California could be longer and more difficult than some predict."—President Bush, in an address to the nation

JUL. 7, 2003 "My answer is bring 'em on."—President Bush, on insurgents in Iraq

APR. 9, 2003 US Army enters Baghdad.

JUNE 24, 2003 "I don't know anybody that I can think of who has contended that the Iraqis had nuclear weapons."—Donald Rumsfeld

JUL. 22, 2003 Uday and Qusay, Saddam's sons, are killed in Mosul.

DEC. 14, 2003 "Ladies and gentlemen. We got him!"—Paul Bremer, US presidential envoy to Iraq, after Saddam is captured

MAY 29, 2003 "We found the weapons of mass destruction."—President Bush

2004

MAR. 30, 2003 "Nobody should have any illusions that this is going to be a quick and easy victory. This is going to be a tough war, a tough slog yet, and no responsible official I know has ever said anything different once this war has started."—General Richard Myers, on NBC's Meet the Press

JUNE 4, 2003 "There's another way to phrase that and that is that the absence of evidence is not the evidence of absence. It is basically saying the same thing in a different way. Simply because you do not have evidence that something does exist does not mean that you have evidence that it doesn't exist."—Donald Rumsfeld

JAN. 17, 2004 Death toll of US soldiers in Iraq reaches 500.

DEC. 9, 2003 Paul Wolfowitz rules that France, Germany, Canada, Mexico, Russia, and China are excluded from bidding on lucrative contracts for rebuilding Iraq.

MAY 1, 2003 "My fellow Americans. Major combat operations in Iraq have ended."—President Bush, on the deck of the USS Abraham Lincoln in front of a banner that read "Mission Accomplished"

JUL. 7, 2003 Bush administration admits that the intelligence report regarding Iraq's purchase of uranium from Niger was false.

(continued)

A TIMELINE OF THE AMERICAN ADVENTURE IN IRAQ
IN THE WORDS OF ITS REALLY RESOLUTE PERPETRATORS

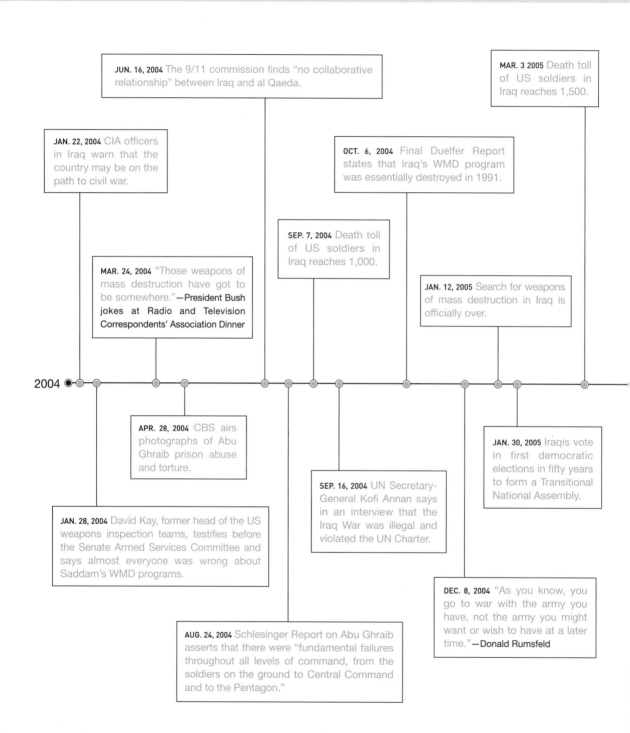

JUN. 16, 2004 The 9/11 commission finds "no collaborative relationship" between Iraq and al Qaeda.

MAR. 3 2005 Death toll of US soldiers in Iraq reaches 1,500.

JAN. 22, 2004 CIA officers in Iraq warn that the country may be on the path to civil war.

OCT. 6, 2004 Final Duelfer Report states that Iraq's WMD program was essentially destroyed in 1991.

SEP. 7, 2004 Death toll of US soldiers in Iraq reaches 1,000.

MAR. 24, 2004 "Those weapons of mass destruction have got to be somewhere."—President Bush jokes at Radio and Television Correspondents' Association Dinner

JAN. 12, 2005 Search for weapons of mass destruction in Iraq is officially over.

2004

APR. 28, 2004 CBS airs photographs of Abu Ghraib prison abuse and torture.

JAN. 30, 2005 Iraqis vote in first democratic elections in fifty years to form a Transitional National Assembly.

SEP. 16, 2004 UN Secretary-General Kofi Annan says in an interview that the Iraq War was illegal and violated the UN Charter.

JAN. 28, 2004 David Kay, former head of the US weapons inspection teams, testifies before the Senate Armed Services Committee and says almost everyone was wrong about Saddam's WMD programs.

DEC. 8, 2004 "As you know, you go to war with the army you have, not the army you might want or wish to have at a later time."—Donald Rumsfeld

AUG. 24, 2004 Schlesinger Report on Abu Ghraib asserts that there were "fundamental failures throughout all levels of command, from the soldiers on the ground to Central Command and to the Pentagon."

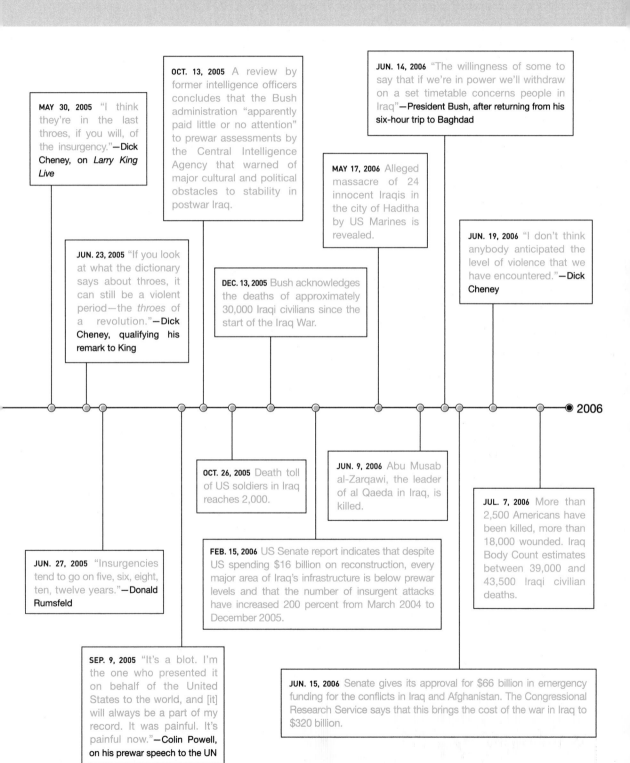

MAY 30, 2005 "I think they're in the last throes, if you will, of the insurgency."—**Dick Cheney**, on *Larry King Live*

OCT. 13, 2005 A review by former intelligence officers concludes that the Bush administration "apparently paid little or no attention" to prewar assessments by the Central Intelligence Agency that warned of major cultural and political obstacles to stability in postwar Iraq.

JUN. 14, 2006 "The willingness of some to say that if we're in power we'll withdraw on a set timetable concerns people in Iraq"—**President Bush**, after returning from his six-hour trip to Baghdad

MAY 17, 2006 Alleged massacre of 24 innocent Iraqis in the city of Haditha by US Marines is revealed.

JUN. 23, 2005 "If you look at what the dictionary says about throes, it can still be a violent period—the *throes* of a revolution."—**Dick Cheney**, qualifying his remark to King

DEC. 13, 2005 Bush acknowledges the deaths of approximately 30,000 Iraqi civilians since the start of the Iraq War.

JUN. 19, 2006 "I don't think anybody anticipated the level of violence that we have encountered."—**Dick Cheney**

2006

OCT. 26, 2005 Death toll of US soldiers in Iraq reaches 2,000.

JUN. 9, 2006 Abu Musab al-Zarqawi, the leader of al Qaeda in Iraq, is killed.

JUL. 7, 2006 More than 2,500 Americans have been killed, more than 18,000 wounded. Iraq Body Count estimates between 39,000 and 43,500 Iraqi civilian deaths.

JUN. 27, 2005 "Insurgencies tend to go on five, six, eight, ten, twelve years."—**Donald Rumsfeld**

FEB. 15, 2006 US Senate report indicates that despite US spending $16 billion on reconstruction, every major area of Iraq's infrastructure is below prewar levels and that the number of insurgent attacks have increased 200 percent from March 2004 to December 2005.

SEP. 9, 2005 "It's a blot. I'm the one who presented it on behalf of the United States to the world, and [it] will always be a part of my record. It was painful. It's painful now."—**Colin Powell**, on his prewar speech to the UN

JUN. 15, 2006 Senate gives its approval for $66 billion in emergency funding for the conflicts in Iraq and Afghanistan. The Congressional Research Service says that this brings the cost of the war in Iraq to $320 billion.

The very best in global industry... *working for you!*

COMPANY **Honeywell International Incorporated**   SYMBOL **HON**   FOUNDED **1906**

For one hundred years, Honeywell has been exploding with growth. Why? Evolution! In 1906 a young engineer named Mark Honeywell formed the Honeywell Heating Specialty Company, makers of hot-water heat generators. This idea of making Americans comfortable with heat evolved into the idea of making Americans comfortable by blowing up people who weren't Americans.

Honeywell became so successful at building cluster bombs that in 1990 it spun off its defense business into Alliant Techsystems, which helped produce a very special bomb that consists of 202 bomblets—bomblets! Isn't that cute? How could you not want to be part of a tradition that adds a touch of whimsy to the theater of war?

Today, Honeywell makes parts for these bomblets. Each one contains 300 steel fragments that spray over an area the size of a football field. At least 5 percent of these bomblets do not explode on impact, effectively becoming land mines. When children see these brightly colored objects, they are naturally drawn to them. In Afghanistan, people could easily mistake them for food packets. But whereas even processed food goes bad eventually, Honeywell bomblets retain their power to explode long after they've become part of the landscape. This is the type of long-lasting, multipurpose product that makes for a wise investment choice.

Honeywell keeps us cool in summer, warm in winter, and safe all year-round. If you can think of a company that has done more to protect America from the scourge of peasant women and children, then go ahead and throw your investment away. But if you want to stick with a winner, then stick with Honeywell, where huge profits come home with every body bag.

The Secret AAR Energy Task Force

It started with a great idea. If Dick Cheney could get away with secret meetings to plot America's energy policy (with his energy-industry buddies), we at Air America Radio would hold our own secret meeting. We would gather the best and the brightest from the alternative-energy movement and plan guerilla actions to protect our planet. The meetings were held at an undisclosed location, and the names of the participants were never released. Of course, we didn't know about the whole NSA wiretap program then or that all our movements were being tracked by Pentagon satellites. Ramon preserved some notes from the files when the mainframe was wiped out.

— Get rich dude to buy ALL the Hummers in the world and take them OFF the road. Remove the tires, make them into mobile homes for poor. A family of four could live EASILY in each one... Hummer farms across from the Crawford "ranch" and right between Rummy's and Cheney's weekend spreads in Maryland. Expensive, but worth it.

— Create public service announcements for kids starring 'Pesticide Pete,' a NASTY-looking cross between Freddy Krueger and that toenail-fungus character on TV commercials. Infiltrate TV stations around the country. Plant the Pesticide Pete spots in cartoon shows so kids learn to stay off chemically treated grass and demand organic snacks.

— Off-the-Grid(dle) Day. Take used cooking oil from fast-food restaurants and convert to hybrid fuel. Let truckers fill up for free... leverage the voice of THOUSANDS of early converts. ▓▓▓▓▓▓ warns of unexpected side effects like pungent french-fry smell on interstates. Hmmm... possible McD's underwriting?

— Operation Blowhard. Install windmills along the beach at Kennebunkport, cut off the Bush compound's electrical lines. Videotape Barbara Bush making a public statement endorsing wind power. Contingency plan: Take her dogs hostage to get her to do it.

— Do these hemp cargo pants make my butt look fat?

Congratulations!

RICHARD PERLE, PAUL WOLFOWITZ, AND DOUGLAS FEITH,

ALSO KNOWN AS "AMERICA'S OWN AXIS OF EVIL"

for your achievements

IN THE FIELD OF

opening the gates of hell

YOU ARE HEREBY HONORED AS AIR AMERICA'S

CREEPS
of the
WEEK

Did all three advocate regime change in Iraq prior to 9/11? Indubitably. Perle, Wolfowitz, and Feith believed that a "regime change" in Iraq would stabilize the region, protect the United States, safeguard US access to oil, protect Israel, and be beneficial to the Iraqi people.

After 9/11, did all three claim that a connection existed between Iraq and al Qaeda? Repeatedly.

To support this far-fetched claim, did all three rely on faulty intelligence about Saddam's WMD program? The only question is whether they actively manipulated that intelligence or were profoundly incompetent.

Did all three say that a war with Iraq would end quickly? Again, afraid so. *So far, the Iraq war has lasted more than 3½ years. More than 2,500 US soldiers have died. More than 18,000 have been injured in combat. The Iraqi civilian death toll is approaching, by conservative accounts, 40,000. In June 2006, the average number of Iraqis killed rose to 100 per day.*

Did all three advocate for a small ground force (40,000 or so) to invade Iraq? Well, yes.

Did all three believe that profits from Iraqi oil would pay for the war? Yes. *Hasn't happened. Never will. Read my lips. Never will.*

Were the "Axis of Evil" right about anything? Uh, let's see . . . No.

The Freedom Thieves

Mike Malloy and Kathy Bay

George W. Bush's concept of freedom mystifies me. When George W. Bush talks about his devotion to freedom, it is obvious he is not referring to the freedoms guaranteed by the US Constitution. In fact, he has serious, stated problems with the US Constitution, the fundamental political document upon which our fragile democracy has balanced for 230 years. (Or, as Bush reportedly referred to it, "that goddamn piece of paper.") Maybe it contains too many big words or unclear language for our toy president. Perhaps this most important political document would be easier for him to comprehend and revere if it were written in the style and simple meter of one of his avowed favorite books by one of his favorite authors, the late Theodore Geisel, as in "Stop! You must not hop… [on the people's right to assemble peacefully]."

RED FISH, BLUE FISH, OLD BUSH, NEW BUSH

It is no news flash, then, in light of Bush's unceasing attack on human rights, that freedom, a concept most of us thought we clearly understood after 200-plus years of struggle, has been under a vicious assault for the past six years. In this relatively brief period we have, for example, seen the creation of something called "First Amendment zones"! Astonishing. The entire *nation* was a First Amendment zone before this pod of Bush freaks assumed control. Now, that so-called "zone" has been reduced in some instances to the size of a kids' soccer field when Bush or one of his thugs come to speak. Once-Constitutionally protected protesters are now fenced off in these "zones," surrounded by wire or gates or militarized SWAT teams or armed toughs recruited from the suddenly abundant private "security" corporations. All of this is overseen by the local police and the Secret Service for any indication that the enclosed crowd might move to force its way out of the barricaded enclosure and into the streets, the stadium, the auditorium, or wherever the Bush neo-fascists might be speaking.

This is so mind-bendingly different from the American way I learned about growing up in unionized, working-class, Democratic Toledo, Ohio, in the 1950s. Neither Bush nor any member of the extended Bush Crime Family believes in the guaranteed freedoms of the first ten amendments to the Constitution that my fifth-grade civics teacher identified as the Bill of Rights. She insisted we students memorize and recite them until they were etched permanently in our ten-year-old minds.

Freedom of religion (or the freedom to reject it all as superstitious bat squeeze)? Only if you practice right-wing, fundamentalist, the-world-is-soon-gonna-end, kill-'em-all crusader Christianity.

Freedom of assembly? Welcome to your first "First Amendment zone" experience and be careful not to step beyond the yellow police tape unless you want to discover what the verb *Tazered* means.

The right to confront your accuser as well as the right to examine the evidence against you? Two words: Jose Padilla.

Freedom from cruel and unusual punishment? Helloooooooo, Gitmo dog cages and Abu Ghraib water boards.

Freedom of the press? Arrest those reporters at the *New York Times* who disclose the many abuses of all the *other* freedoms and supposed protected rights, like fair and speedy trials, habeas corpus, due process, and the true basis of freedom that Antonin Scalia and Clarence Thomas insist does not exist: privacy.

"FREEDOM AIN'T FREE"

Bush has further shown his *contempt* for freedom by authorizing the wholesale, unrestricted wiretapping of US citizens (in spite of prohibitions and restrictions clearly defined by the Foreign Intelligence Surveillance Act, or FISA, laws.) This is a clear and unquestioned destruction of the Fourth Amendment to an extent unprecedented in US history. In light of the Bush Crime Family's unceasing assault on individual freedom, there is very little that erupts from the simple brain of a typical conservative that is more irritating than the vapid mini-slogan "Freedom isn't free." Or, as the followers of Rush Limbaugh so often put it, "Freedom *ain't* free!"

As Bush has shown he believes, the real meaning of freedom is the freedom of corporations to make a profit by any means necessary, in both the domestic and global markets, with no restrictions regarding health, safety, labor laws, income tax obligation, or environmental concerns.

Therefore, after the stolen presidential election in 2000, the Bush Crime Family's first order of business was appointing a cabinet whose members would guarantee that their brand of corporate freedom would flourish. Enter Cheney, Rumsfeld, Powell, Rice, and Ashcroft. All that was missing was the key element these flying monkeys needed: An event that would justify unleashing their bastardized brand of freedom on the entire world. Something terrible and traumatic enough to make the unthinkable possible—to make the American people not only accept a loss of freedom, but embrace it.

Bush hit the trifecta on September 11, 2001, and began using Orwell's *1984* as a how-to guide. Quickly came the flood of government warnings to watch out for terrorists everywhere. Words like *evildoer*, *crusade*, and *axis of evil*—all previously relegated to Marvel comic books or medieval monasteries—entered contemporary language. Longshoremen on the Maine coast were urged to watch out for swarthy, cold-blooded killers lurking in lobster beds. Mail carriers would skulk as well as deliver mail. All Muslims were suspects. Librarians were directed to report to the local authorities those who checked out "suspicious" books. A post office employee in Chicago called the FBI when some foreign-looking college students requested postage stamps without images of American flags on them. The compliant corporate media spewed forth a steady stream of fear-inducing images and candy-colored terror alerts, and for the first time news tickers ran a constant subscript of global threats at the bottom of our TV screens. The citizenry was quickly and sufficiently saturated with red, white, and blue nationalism and paralyzed with fear. As planned, Bush's approval rating skyrocketed. The stage was set. Now Bush's minions could move to implementing the real domestic objective: the USA Patriot Act.

Bush's first attorney general, the religious fanatic, statue-draping, oil-anointing, gospel-singing Crisco Kid himself, John Ashcroft, is a classic example of the Bush Crime Family's duplicity and a kick in the groin to the historic civil rights traditions of the Justice Department. Devoted to the Orwellian credo that "freedom is slavery" and the Dominionist Christian phantoms of seven-headed beasts, multibreasted whores, and foul-smelling demons erupting from

> "I'd rather people buy our automobiles instead of our atomic weaponry."
> —Gore Vidal on *Politically Direct*

Babylon, Ashcroft demonstrated his contempt for freedom early in his phony tenure. As the nation's chief law enforcement officer, he championed the USA Patriot Act, a law written years ago by the dregs of the Nixon-Ford administrations—American fascism's midwives, Henry Kissinger, Donald Rumsfeld, and Dick Cheney—and kept safely hidden until the moment of perfect opportunity: the attacks of 9/11. Passage of the act was a dagger to the heart of American freedoms and signaled the imminent arrival of what Benito Mussolini fondly called "corporatism." Further, Ashcroft oversaw the subsequent creation of the enormous, secretive, incomprehensible, and criminally inept Department of Homeland Security. The list of abuses under the Patriot Act—and now Patriot Act II—are legion, but some of the most appalling include the loss of privacy concerning your Internet surfing habits, your medical records, and—with a nod to long-dead Red-baiting Republican Senator Joe McCarthy—lists of individuals known to belong to suspect political organizations.

The Republican-dominated Congress whisked it through both the House and the Senate without meaningful opposition or discussion from muted Democrats, with the notable exception of Senator Russ Feingold of Wisconsin. An entire Patriot Act industry was spawned, complete with banking and data mining/information technology businesses that protect your personal information by delivering it into the hands of government officials who know what is best—and safest—for you, your family, and America. To date, it is certain that no terrorist has been netted as a result of the increased police power granted by the act. Had there been even one arrest, we would have been inundated with prime-time, nonstop press conferences and briefings. TV talk shows foaming with equal amounts of right-wing hysteria and Bush worship would run 'round the clock. And all of it would be interspersed with video of a disheveled, wild-eyed, swarthy, Middle Eastern–appearing suspect staring blankly into the camera.

The ramrodding of the Patriot Act was merely the opening shot from a man who believes the Department of Justice was unnecessary since only God is fit to judge man. Ashcroft further distinguished himself as hideously anti–civil liberties by ordering the jailing of hundreds—if not thousands—of law-abiding men of Middle Eastern descent in the aftermath of 9/11.

As it has turned out, however, Ashcroft was merely the preview of coming attractions to the Department of Justice. After Crisco Man metamorphosed almost overnight from US attorney general to K Street lobbyist, Bush appointed his very own personal lawyer, Alberto Gonzales, as the first US attorney general who is on record as an advocate and enabler of torture. Once Ashcroft had sufficiently trashed freedoms for American citizens, Gonzales was called in for the wet work against foreign nationals.

Gonzales has shown himself to be a perjurer as well as a garden-variety liar. His Senate confirmation hearing was riddled with coy deceptions, half-truths, disinformation, and outright lies—all designed to speed his confirmation so the real business of curtailing, blunting, and, in some cases, ending individual freedoms at home and abroad could proceed. Bush's utter contempt for international laws and treaties banning torture, coupled with his authorizing the so-called *rendition* of suspects to countries where torture is commonplace—or to secret US-run prisons in those countries—is piling atrocity upon atrocity, contempt upon contempt. This, truly, is an administration totally out of control and desperately in need of being ended if the concept of individual freedom in the United States, and our image as a beacon of justice, fairness, and equality abroad, is to survive even in truncated form.

At this writing, the latest revelations of the Bush Crime Family's ongoing and determined assault against freedom are the National Security Agency's collection of data relating to hundreds of millions of private phone calls made by tens of millions of American citizens. What's more, the personal banking records of, again, perhaps millions of us are now considered to be another resource for government data mining and surveillance. This is further evidence of the unstoppable criminality of a regime determined to maintain power.

Snooping into bank and phone records not enough? Then there is always this: "Spy Cameras Watch America from Space," a June 2006 Associated Press article that detailed the suspected manipulation and illegal use of spy satellites against US citizens. Or "Federal Source to ABC News: We Know Who You're Calling," as reported nervously by ABC News itself, which described the surveillance of phone conversations conducted by reporters for the various news-gathering organizations, most notably the *New York Times* and the *Washington Post*. And now the Internet bloggers—the last "true" free and independent/noncorporate press—are beginning to feel the lash as Bush's flying monkeys at the FCC attempt to regulate Internet content and reporting.

DOWN WITH BIG BROTHER

That tough-talking Texan from New Haven, Connecticut, repeats like a mantra chosen specifically for the demented "We're at war against a determined enemy who hates our freedoms." But our true freedom, the freedoms promised in our founding documents and fought for during the past 200 years, the freedoms we thought we had secured by struggling against any attempt to subvert them, by refusing to exchange them for a false sense of security, are being threatened not by a foreign enemy but by a cabal of political operatives put in office specifically to undermine and destroy not just the reality of individual freedom, but the concept itself. The rope around the neck of freedom in the US continues to be drawn tighter as the horrific events of 9/11 recede into history and the determined efforts of uniquely American fascists—Republicans, Bush supporters, neoconservatives, Christo-fascists, corporatists, whatever name it is by which they are identified—continue to force their way into the present and insist the future belongs to them. Bulls**t. The future is theirs in the same way that evil can triumph: Only if good people do nothing.

The Hart of the Matter

Former senator and onetime presidential hopeful Gary Hart spoke with Rachel Maddow on March 27, 2006, about the war in Iraq and what the Democrats could have done to prevent it.

RACHEL MADDOW: Senator Hart, I wanted to get your reaction to the news this morning on the front page of the *New York Times* about the latest Downing Street memo, the latest memo that said the Bush administration, the president himself, was determined to go to Iraq regardless of what they found in terms of weapons and regardless of what the UN did. What's your reaction to that?

GARY HART: Well, I'm not surprised. I sensed in late '02 and early '03 that the administration had made a decision early on, shortly after 9/11 if not before, to depose Saddam Hussein. The so-called Project for a New American Century had been advocating publicly since '95, and in a letter to Bill Clinton in '98, that America go to war with Iraq and get rid of Saddam Hussein. So this plan—scheme, if you will—long predated 9/11 and I think all of the terrorism arguments were hollow from the beginning.

MADDOW: They wanted to depose Saddam Hussein for geopolitical strategic reasons.

HART: Yes.

MADDOW: And now it seems like they have no plans for US troops to be gone anytime in this administration, I don't feel like anytime in our generation. And that means that their geopolitical aims of having US troops there on a permanent basis and a giant billion-dollar embassy and all that stuff—it's all going to come true! At great cost to us, and we never assented to it!

> "I get angry at my own party. I think the Democrats, before they voted for or against a resolution, should have asked a lot of questions about the long-term."

HART: Well, there's no question about it, and I get angry at my own party. I think the Democrats before they voted for or against a resolution should have asked a lot of questions about the long-term. And it was not really done. I think it's the opposition party's duty to raise all the questions and demand answers before supporting any policy of this sort and they didn't—leading Democrats—didn't do that. I've been trying to get the press to ask the question about [how long the troops will be there] for a year, year and a half, and only in the last week or two did they begin to ask the questions, and it caused the president to say, "Troops are going to be there after I leave." So why couldn't those questions have been asked a year or two ago? We were pouring concrete, welding steel, we were creating permanent military bases in Iraq. So it's almost as if despite everything, the plan is going forward, that is, a permanent American presence in Iraq.

MADDOW: With it never being sold to the American people, never being explained to us.

HART: Yes, and it also raises a Constitutional crisis in this country, because Congress has not been doing its job. If you listen to the Republican leaders they keep chanting, "Support the president, support the president." When you join the Congress, you do not take an oath to support the president. You take an oath to protect and defend the Constitution of the United States and to oversee the operations of the Executive Branch. And this Republican Congress and its Democratic allies have not been doing their job.

MADDOW: Do you feel that strategically the Democrats should have a unified position on Iraq right now? 'Cause they don't.

HART: Well, obviously they should, but they don't. And I can't for the life of me figure out why some leading Democrats still continue to support the war, even after two-thirds to three-quarters of the American people have abandoned support for the war. Some Democrats, although I haven't heard anything recently from them, are for increasing troop levels. And it just dumbfounds me; it makes no sense at all.

MADDOW: And aside from that call, you get a panoply of vaguely antiwar positions, from pull out as soon as possible, to pull out yesterday, to strategic redeployment—a whole bunch of different ideas. There isn't a solitary plank. I feel, strategically, the Democrats ought to unveil a plank on everything about two weeks before the November elections.

> "When you join the Congress, you do not take an oath to support the president. You take an oath to protect and defend the Constitution of the United States and to oversee the operations of the Executive Branch."

HART: I couldn't agree more. But if you review the history of the Democratic Party, we're a coalition party, which means that you have to form consensus. The Republicans are a much more corporate party in the sense that their beliefs, their core beliefs, are much more shared and common. Democrats are all over the lot. It's a virtue and it's a curse in a way; the virtue is it's an open tent, the curse is it's awfully hard to get people to agree on things.

MADDOW: I think, though, the Democrats, when you pick big principles, can be unified, we just don't have a message machine that makes us sound like we're unified.

HART: Well, in my book coming in September, called *The Courage of Our Convictions*, I advocate a manifesto for Democrats based on our historic principles, and I think that's what's needed. I don't think you can get unity on individual policies, whether it's health care or education or the war in Iraq, until you restate what your principles are and get everyone to agree on that. And we haven't done that.

MADDOW: Senator Hart, your book *The Shield and the Cloak: The Security of the Commons* is about fighting terrorism, it's about national security, it's about the American role in the world. What's the shield and what's the cloak?

"The last time I checked there were about forty tyrants in the world. Are we really going to depose all of them? Including Kim Jong Il? I don't hear anybody advocating invasion of North Korea or Zimbabwe. We're not in the tyrant-deposing business."

HART: The shield, of course, is the military. I make two arguments here, one is that security in the twenty-first century is going to be a much broader concept than it was in the twentieth, that is to say, prevention of exchange of nuclear missiles with the Soviet Union. It must include energy, it must include the environment, it must include livelihood. We must understand security to be more than simply the security of our borders or prevention of terrorist attacks. And second, we cannot achieve that kind of security without international cooperation. America cannot be secure if the rest of the world is insecure. So instead of going in alone, we're going to have to reform our alliances and perhaps create new ones.

MADDOW: Now the Bush administration says we can't be safe unless we intervene in other countries to depose tyrants. And they've characterized or caricatured people who are opposed to that sort of strategy as being isolationists.

HART: Two responses. First of all, that is pure rhetoric, there are alternatives [to] unilateral invasions, and second, the last time I checked there were about forty tyrants in the world. Are we really going to depose all of them? Including Kim Jong Il? I don't hear anybody advocating invasion of North Korea or Zimbabwe. We're not in the tyrant-deposing business.

MADDOW: I don't know that America's ever been in a worse position in terms of our international standing. How do we rebuild that? How do we regain our credibility after straight-facedly lying about our intentions, our goals, our methods, and everything else for five years now?

HART: It'll take a generation. It's like relationships between individuals, you have to build confidence, you can't buy it, you can't sign treaties to create confidence, people have to trust you. And we're going to have to rebuild that trust. You know, we won two world wars and the cold war based on international cooperation with our allies. And we've just thrown that away. We thumbed our nose at our allies, it wasn't just that we left them, but we called them "Old Europe" and "cheese-eating surrender monkeys" and all kinds of things—I'm dumbfounded by it. All during the cold war, all we heard from the right wing was "NATO, the Alliance, we need to stick together," and all that kind of stuff, and then they just totally threw it overboard.

MADDOW: In your book you define a much broader role for police and intelligence forces in fighting terrorism. Also, you ask for a fifth branch of the military to be formed for special ops.

HART: Well, there's a revolution in military affairs that's not well understood. The nature of warfare is changing. It is not going to be great armies in the field wearing uniforms and marching to bands and all the rest of it. It is going to be grungy Rangers and Delta Force kicking down doors and shooting it out, almost with daggers in their teeth—that's the warfare of the future. If you want to see what it looks like, watch *Black Hawk Down* or watch the footage from Fallujah. It is low-intensity urban conflict between and among clans, tribes, and gangs, and the warriors of the future are not the 101st Airborne Division, it is the Special Forces. Some of them don't even wear uniforms, they have scraggly hair and beards, they eat scorpions and drink snakes' blood and kill people hand-to-hand. That's the warfare of the future.

MADDOW: Finally, Senator Hart, if there is a Democratic president elected in 2008 and they want you to come back and sit in the Cabinet, are you gonna say yes?

HART: I'm a public servant and I won't define ways to serve the country but . . . I have no ambition.

MADDOW: Sure. [Laughs]

8

How to Make Billions Without Actually Delivering Results

There's No-Bad in No-Bid

Join America's Halliburton experts at this all-day workshop in which Iraqi enrollees will learn that "no results" is the new results. Learn how to secure no-bid contracts, complete only 20% of the promised construction, and then secure more no-bid contracts. Also learn to:

- Avoid competition
- Avoid accountability
- Have fun!

Halliburton is a close friend of Vice President Dick Cheney and is a regular contributor to Fox News.

Course 408T
Sec. A
Members' fee $39/ Others' fee $49
(Halliburton will not refund your fee if it fails to complete your class.)

How to Secure a "Cost-Plus" Contract in Iraq

Sick of controlling your expenses as a way to ensure your business makes a profit? Wish you could be reimbursed for ALL of your expenses and then get an extra percentage as a profit? Take this course to:

- Avoid expenses
- Avoid accountability
- Have fun!

Course 409T
Sec. B
Members' fee $39/ Oth⟨
(Halliburton will not refu⟨ if it fails to complete yo⟨

How Naked Yoga Can Release You from Society's So-Called Business "Rules"

Sick of the restrictions of clothing and accepted business practices? Halliburton offers a course on naked ⟨

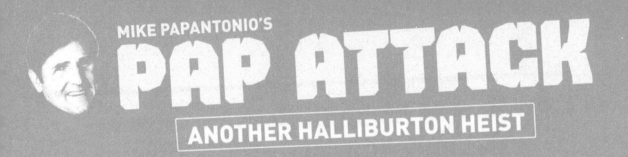

Deadeye Dick Cheney is a master when it comes to suppressing facts that would round out the picture of just what a malevolent, miserable miscreant he really is.

Whether it's a story about his getting all liquored up and mistaking his six-foot fellow hunter for a bird and nearly blowing his damned head off, or a story about his personal role in releasing the identity of CIA undercover operatives (isn't that a treasonable offense?), or a tale of his cutting deals in secret meetings with the oil industry giving them permission to gouge Americans at the gas pumps, Diabolical Dick knows how to keep the truth from getting out.

For instance, most people may not have followed a story in the *New York Times* that explained how Cheney has gotten away with lining the pockets of his personal cash cow Halliburton yet again. This scam required the help of the Pentagon—but hey, when you're a war pimp vice president willing to pump billions into the military industrial complex, Pentagon favors come easy.

In this latest Cheney story on February 27, 2006, the *New York Times* explains how the Pentagon ignored its own auditors' protests that Cheney's personal war-profiteering machine, Halliburton, had squeezed another quarter billion dollars out of the disastrous war in Iraq. Auditors initially found that $260 million worth of charges on no-bid contracts were either inflated or unsupported by paper trails. No one could actually show what Halliburton had done to earn the money.

But in the end, it's my guess that a telephone call from some Cheney crony to the right Pentagon general cleaned up all that fuss about bothersome invoices and needless rules and regulations that other contractors are forced to adhere to. In fact, Halliburton not only scurried away like a rat with a quarter billion dollars worth of cheese, the company was actually awarded about $60 million worth of bonuses for their nonexistent work—compliments of American taxpayers. Ain't capitalism great?

But if you think this story of rats and cheese and corrupt capitalism is bad, there's a corruption story I can tell you that dwarfs even that. It's the rather nauseating tale of how George Bush's Coalition Provisional Authority, specifically Bush's right-hand man in Iraq's reconstruction, L. Paul Bremer, allowed about $9 billion to completely disappear without so much as an invoice or paper trail—the money simply vanished without a trace!

This $9 billion could have been used to buy better equipment, such as better body armor for our troops—but instead, under the leadership of Bush, Cheney, and Bremer, it simply disappeared without an explanation, and without anyone being prosecuted and going to jail.

Instead, Bush actually awarded Bremer the highest honor a president can give a civilian, the Presidential Medal of Freedom.

And to people who can lose $9 billion, maybe a quarter-billion-dollar Pentagon giveaway to Cheney's private cash cow is mere chump change.

Congratulations!

Alberto Gonzales

for your exemplary efforts

IN THE PRACTICES OF

circumnavigating the law, violating individual freedoms, and fostering a climate of military recklessness

YOU ARE HEREBY HONORED AS AIR AMERICA'S

CREEP
of the
WEEK

NICKNAME: **Gonzo**

IMMIGRATION STATUS: In an interview with Wolf Blitzer in 2006, Gonzales admitted that three of his four grandparents "may well have been" illegal immigrants to the United States. *Back then it was fine, but today, now that's another story.*

WHAT HE CALLED THE GENEVA CONVENTION'S RULES FOR THE TREATMENT OF ENEMY COMBATANTS: "Obsolete."

THE DEFINITION OF TORTURE, GONZO-STYLE: [Limited to] "injury such as death, organ failure, or serious impairment of body functions."

WHAT GONZALES SAID WHEN ASKED IF THE NATIONAL SECURITY AGENCY WAS MONITORING THE CALLS OF AMERICANS WHO ARE NOT HAVING CONVERSATIONS WITH TERRORISTS: "I can't give you absolute assurance."

WHAT HE TOLD A GROUP OF NEWSPAPER EDITORS IN 2002: "You have a right to know what is going on in government. But we also believe such rights are not absolute."

REACTION TO CONGRESSIONAL LEADERSHIP'S UPROAR OVER GROSS OVERREACH OF AUTHORITY: Pouted, threatened to resign unless the president backed him up.

Defense Department Disgrace

Martin Mubanga was arrested in Zambia in 2002, taken to Guantanamo, and later released without charge in January 2005, after 33 months in captivity. On May 22, the 32-year-old Londoner told Laura Flanders about his time at Gitmo.

LAURA FLANDERS: You described a situation where your cell was searched by six or seven military police and a Qur'an was thrown to the ground. Can you explain why that was so offensive to you?

MARTIN MUBANGA: In our religion, firstly, the Qur'an is believed to be the word of God, who we refer to as Allah. Basically the Qur'an is supposed to be treated with respect and most people believe that the Qur'an should be placed in a high place in a house. It's never to be placed on a floor, on a dirty floor, or to be treated or to be mishandled in any way.

FLANDERS: What did those six or seven military police do?

> "At the time, there was a story going around that I was supposed to be a top-notch fighter, as they said, and they tried to provoke me in many ways to see what I could do."

MUBANGA: At the time, there was a story going around that I was supposed to be a top-notch fighter, as they said, and they tried to provoke me in many ways to see what I could do. This was one of the methods that was used to see if I would fight and on this particular occasion they threw the Qur'an on the floor.

FLANDERS: So, they came in, they threw the Qur'an on the floor, then what happened?

MUBANGA: Well, as I was saying, there were two on either side of me, holding my wrists as I was kneeling down, and they had me in wristlocks. And one of the three that were searching [my room] took my Qur'an and instead of replacing it to its place, he threw that on the floor . . . Rahul [Ahmed, a former Guantanamo Bay detainee, who was returned to Britain on March 9, 2004] from Tipton witnessed this and he was in the cage next to me. And he remonstrated the soldier, the MP who did this, which they ignored. They wanted to see if they could provoke a strong reaction from me. And obviously, I was not able to do anything at that time.

FLANDERS: So what happened after that?

MUBANGA: If you report it to the commanding officer on the block or to the captain, it's just words. They say that they will look into the matter and discipline will be taken, but you will not be informed of any particular action that has been taken. So you know, even after that, another brother from Saudi [Arabia], who is also a British resident from South London, tried to organize various brothers to take a stance and try to get the general—at the time who was General Miller—to have placed at each and every bloc, a notice stating that no MP should touch or search the Qur'an. This, however, was refused point blank by General Miller and the hierarchy in Guantanamo Bay. Subsequently, this brother and other brothers thought that they should do some sort of actions to show their anger and to try and reverse this decision, which resulted in many people being "earthed."

> "If you report it to the commanding officer on the block
> or to the captain, it's just words."

"Earthed" is basically when a minimum of five military policemen dressed in riot gear, with riot shields, would come in and manhandle you and put you to the floor. On occasion, you would be pepper-sprayed, you'd be tied and carried out. In this protest that took place, some brothers would be beaten for refusing to go to interrogation, for refusing to go to shower, or for refusing to come out of their cell for the search. All they asked for was that our Qur'an, the book of our religion, be treated with respect and that it not be searched or touched or desecrated in any way.

FLANDERS: What other repercussions were there for detainees who tried to stand up for respectful treatment of the Qur'an?

MUBANGA: The officials or the hierarchies would punish us by shaving our hair or shaving our beards. There was a particular bloc Quebec Bloc and Romeo Bloc, which is in Camp Three of Delta Camp, where they would give shorts to brothers. In our religion, you are not permitted to pray while your knees are uncovered. There should be a minimum amount of bodily parts that should be covered while praying. And they failed to respect this particular ruling in our religion by giving our brothers shorts to wear for 24 hours. And on other occasions, you could lose your clothing and your mattress and your bedding for failing to comply with camp rules. And all of this could have been avoided if they showed respect for our religion, its concept, and its rulings.

FLANDERS: You had plenty of time to figure it out . . . can you say now why you think the soldiers were behaving as they were? Were they just bigots? Were they receiving orders? Did they believe that they would get information from you if they pressured you around your religion? How do you make sense of it?

MUBANGA: From my personal opinion, it's about politics. Bush and those with him in the American government and around the world were just looking for scapegoats and someone to blame. And they had to put someone in the picture. Having gone to the methods, or rather the extremes that they had gone to, they had to be seen to be getting a result.

FLANDERS: Would you say that the soldiers themselves were motivated by a hatred of religion?

MUBANGA: In my personal opinion, I would say that some of the soldiers were naïve, some of the soldiers were receiving orders, and some had hatred for the religion. There were a few who were quite simply following orders, and rightly or wrongly they would follow those orders because they saw no alternative other than themselves being remonstrated or reprimanded. You know, there were a few who had a hatred for the Islamic religion and the Islamic way of life and people from the East and had a general ignorance toward the religion and anything that was not American. I mean, there were quite a few MPs who had the attitude that simply because they were born in America, they were better than everybody else.

"The officials or the hierarchies would punish us by shaving our hair or shaving our beards."

FLANDERS: Is it possible they genuinely thought that you were in some way responsible for killing Americans? Was that what they said to you, that they thought you were a killer, that they felt you were a high-placed terrorist? Would this explain their behavior?

MUBANGA: There were a few MPs who had that opinion of me. I think far more failed to understand why I was in Cuba. Many MPs would come to me and ask about my story and ask why I was there. Quite a few saw me as being similar to themselves, being from the UK. But they had a very negative attitude toward brothers from the East—from Saudi, from Yemen, even from Russia and China, brothers who were classified as "Eastern Muslims" or "Muslims from the East."

FLANDERS: How has this affected you physically, psychologically?

MUBANGA: Well, coming back to the UK, there are things that I still have to get used to and that will take some time. But I am trying to put aside those things which are causing me some pain and are causing me some distress and some discomfort. Basically, I feel it's my duty to speak out about the things that happened to me and happened to other people at this moment in time, in Cuba and around the world.

FLANDERS: Do you have physical injuries from your time?

MUBANGA: I have slight injury from my time, but I wish not to discuss it, but there are some things that aren't quite right. And I am currently seeking medical assistance for those things.

FLANDERS: And what about the effect on your political feelings and opinions or attitudes toward the United States, toward your religion, toward this whole so-called war on terrorism?

MUBANGA: As far as I am concerned, I have never been against the United States. However, I am not in agreement with Bush and those who are with him. I think it's fair to say that we stand at opposite sides of the fence! I don't feel that they are the right people to be in power. I don't feel that they will bring about any true justice or that their motives are pure. And I feel that the power should be in someone else's hands, someone more worthy.

FLANDERS: Were you a very religious person before you were picked up?

MUBANGA: I suppose it would depend on what you would define as being religious, but definitely, my experience in Guantanamo Bay has made me understand my religion more and appreciate my religion more and made me turn to my faith that much more.

FLANDERS: Martin, is there anything else you would like to say to Americans in particular who might be listening to this, trying to make sense of what is being done in their name in Guantanamo, in this week of discussion about *Newsweek*?

> "I have never been against the United States. However, I am not in agreement with Bush and those who are with him."

MUBANGA: What I would say basically is that we have to ask ourselves, as individuals, why things are being done and why certain stories are arriving at this moment in time. I think basically that there is more to this story than meets the eye.

FLANDERS: You spoke outside the US embassy on Friday; can you describe the scene there? How many people were protesting?

MUBANGA: There were a few hundred there protesting. Basically, I feel that the message was clear and the feelings of those who participated were clear. And I feel that there would have been many more except that people are afraid. And people don't want to be in detention without trial as could be the case here. And even here we have one Muslim brother, Ahmed [Babar Ahmed, a computer programmer who has been accused by the United States of using Web sites to raise funds for the Taliban and other terrorists], who is facing extradition to the United States without any evidence being presented. So I think quite clearly that people are intimidated and are afraid to speak out. But there are some who are willing to put that on the line, as it were.

CONDI ®

CONDi ®

"A Special

Dream Embassy®
in Iraq

The only project currently on time and on budget, all for YOU!

Walls are 15 feet thick!

It's so big it's visible from outer space!

BOOM

This toy is approved for Middle Ages

It's possible that George Bush genuinely does not understand.

It's conceivable that he is intellectually incapable of grasping the details of the science involving stem cell research.

After all, Bush's very own Harvard MBA professor, Yoshi Tsurumi, gave us the distinct impression in an interview that in all the years he had taught at Harvard, he had never been in the presence of a duller wit or more empty intellect than George W. Bush.

That is not exactly a news flash to most of us. I mean, early in the Bush first term, it was easy to laugh about Bush bumbling around the White House like an entertaining but ridiculous cartoon character.

But then, we saw that this absence of intellectual curiosity made him vulnerable to manipulation by war pimps like Paul Wolfowitz, Richard Perle, Rumsfeld, and Rove. And all of a sudden, the giggles and laughter went away, and we began to realize that the cartoon character occupying the White House looked less like a funny, likable Homer Simpson and more like a scary, wicked Count Olaf.

Now we see that same cartoon character being manipulated again by engineers of America's religious zealot movement. And as a result of that manipulation, America's body count will continue to rise.

Not casualties of a war based on lies, but casualties of a flat-earth ignorance that denies the importance of stem cell research.

George Bush, Jerry Falwell, and Pat Robertson spent weeks ghoulishly placing themselves in the limelight of Terri Schiavo's tragic death, preaching about the horror of it all.

But the real horror is knowing that without stem cell research:

- 250,000 Americans with all types of paralyzing spinal cord injuries will never have a chance to put their bodies back together.
- 19 million Americans with diabetes will more than likely always live with the horror of suffering an incurable, killer disease.

- Almost 400,000 Americans with multiple sclerosis will continue to see their bodies die in tiny, horribly incremental ways.
- The list of lives that will not be saved and improved with stem cell research is endless.

The Swedes know that, the Australians, the British, and the South Koreans know that.

In fact, 64 percent of the American public knows that.

This issue has more Americans realizing that there is nothing cute, likable, or entertaining anymore about that creepy cartoon character who is, unfortunately, ready to veto that critical research in this country.

This is the kind of issue that requires intellect and rational thinking, not more of the same lame-duck cartoon act.

THEY SAID WHAT??!?!!

Early in 2001, Dick Cheney called some of his favorite people together to craft an energy plan for the United States. He and his secret society of "experts," who were mostly energy-industry executives, gathered in the kinds of shadowy, undisclosed meetings that came to stand for Dick's brand of open government. What were they doing? Who was in there? It was all a deep, dark mystery. No amount of protest, no legal action, could force him to disclose the details. But we knew all along they were going to recommend an energy binge, didn't we? Sure we did. And our worst fears were confirmed when he gave a speech in late April.

Yeah, that's right! Why try to conserve a resource that you're running out of? Where's the logic in that?

Conservation may be a sign of personal virtue, but it is not a sufficient basis for a sound, comprehensive energy policy

Dick Cheney
April 30, 2001

To say nothing of the fact that you and your oil-patch buddies never got rich selling Americans *less* oil, right, Dick?

You're not still mad at us for suggesting you get a wind-powered pacemaker, are you? Is that what this is all about?

What did the veep propose instead? A classic short-sighted GOP solution: Drill in the Arctic National Wildlife Refuge and build more carbon-producing power plants.

When it comes to personal virtue, we look to you for guidance, big fella. Tell us again about the personal virtue involved in shooting a buddy in the face and then going back to the ranch for dinner while he's in the emergency room.

In an effort to return civility to the discourse in Washington, DC, Cheney also tried to blame the Clinton administration for the nation's "energy crisis."

It's so unfair how some people point out that while you were pushing to jack up energy production, you still had more than 400,000 unexercised stock options in Halliburton and were quietly collecting hundreds of thousands of dollars in deferred compensation, even though you said you'd cut all your ties with your old company. As if you'd let a little thing like money influence you.

Encouraging conservation doesn't sound nearly as butch as "drill 'em and kill 'em," does it?

Congratulations!

DR. BILL FRIST

*for your rare ability to
treat the Hippocratic oath*
AS MERELY A SUGGESTION

*and grandstand
in moments of crisis*

YOU ARE HEREBY HONORED AS AIR AMERICA'S

CREEP
of the
WEEK

CREEP
of the
WEEK

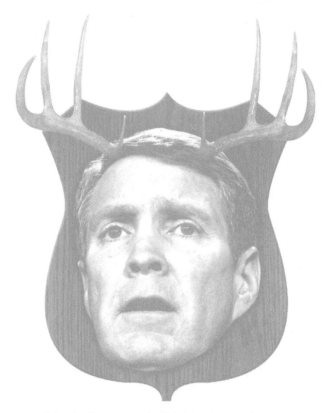

VOTING RECORD: Dr. Frist voted for the first time in his life when he was thirty-six years old.

WHAT DR. FRIST DID WHILE IN HARVARD MED SCHOOL IN ORDER TO STUDY THE HEARTS OF CATS: Adopted kitties from local Boston-area shelters, treated them like pets for a few days, then killed them and experimented on their organs.

WHAT DR. FRIST BLAMED FOR THE BUTCHERY: Stress

WHAT HARVARD MED SCHOOL GRAD DR. FRIST TOLD GEORGE STEPHANOPOULOS WAS THE FAILURE RATE OF CONDOMS: 15 percent (*Not to nitpick or anything, but the Centers for Disease Control and Prevention (CDC) says it's 2 to 3 percent.*)

HOW DR. FRIST DIAGNOSED THAT TERRI SCHIAVO WAS NOT IN A PERSISTENT VEGETATIVE STATE, DESPITE A DIAGNOSIS BY HER ON-SITE TEAM OF DOCTORS: By watching some home movies of Terri for about an hour.

WHEN ASKED IF AIDS COULD BE TRANSMITTED THROUGH TEARS OR SALIVA, DR. FRIST SAID: "I don't know." According to the CDC, tears and saliva have NEVER been shown to result in the transmission of AIDS (emphasis added).

WHAT DR. FRIST DID TWO WEEKS BEFORE HOSPITAL CORPORATION OF AMERICA (HCA)—A COMPANY OWNED BY HIS BROTHER AND FATHER AND THE LARGEST FOR-PROFIT HOSPITAL CHAIN IN AMERICA—ANNOUNCED A LESS-THAN-STELLAR QUARTER: Sold his shares. (*Two weeks later, the stock was down 15 percent. Dr. Frist's stake in the company was upward of $25 million.*)

AMOUNT OF MONEY HCA PAID THE FEDERAL GOVERNMENT AFTER AN INVESTIGATION REVEALED IT HAD GROTESQUELY OVERBILLED FOR MEDICARE PATIENTS: $631 million. *Added to previous fines, the total paid by HCA is 1.7 billion, aka the largest fraud settlement in history.*

WHAT SENATOR FRIST PROPOSED TO OFFSET GAS PRICE GOUGING: Give every American family $100—about the equivalent of two tanks of gas. (*Perhaps because they only know how to approve giveaways to Big Oil, Senate Republicans helped kill that idea*).

The very best in global industry... *working for you!*

COMPANY **Altria Group**   SYMBOL **MO**   FOUNDED **1985** (started as Philip Morris in 1847)

Philip Morris made his first cigarette in 1854. Today, the company is called Altria and makes cigarettes, beer, and Kraft Foods. There's a name for people who use Philip Morris products—they're called *everyone.*

With so many products available, your investment is secure. Should someone quit smoking Philip Morris cigarettes, he or she is sure to replace that destructive habit with Oreos, Cheez Whiz, and Lunchables. So, when you invest in Philip Morris, you're safe in the knowledge that people are defenseless against America's two greatest weapons: processed food and nicotine.

Although it's too late to get in on the ground floor, it's never too late to become part of the Altria/Philip Morris family. Remember, no one ever went broke investing in cigarettes and alcohol.

The very best in global industry...*working for you!*

COMPANY **Halliburton Company**   SYMBOL **HAL**   FOUNDED **1919**

If you are looking to invest in a full-service company, you could do no better in fullness or service than Halliburton. Just ask Dick Cheney. As secretary of defense in the early 1990s, he decided to privatize such military services as washing clothes for the troops.

The Pentagon paid Halliburton $3.9 million for a study on how best to privatize washing the boxers of enlisted folk. Not completely convinced that it would be wise to send out the skivvies, they then paid Halliburton another $5 million to do a follow-up study. The Halliburton study convinced them to outsource the military unmentionables, so they guaranteed a profit to Halliburton to provide the services.

There's no job too tough for Halliburton if it guarantees a return on your investment. This company calls counterterrorism a growth opportunity. Take the task of cleaning up Iraq. It was a job that nobody else wanted. Or, more specifically, it was a job that nobody else was allowed to bid on.

Halliburton also provides oil and gas services in more than one hundred countries around the globe. Some of these countries are so anti-American that they forced Halliburton to compete with local companies for contracts. This type of thing would never happen in the United States—at least not to Halliburton—but it is a tribute to their fortitude that they still manage to operate under these conditions. And when the day comes when we take one small step onto the surface of the red planet, Halliburton will be there for you, as long as no other companies—Martian or otherwise—are given the unfair advantage of being allowed to bid for the contract.

Big Money, Bad Science

Robert F. Kennedy Jr.

As Jesuit schoolboys studying world history, my classmates and I learned that Copernicus and Galileo self-censored for many decades their proof that the Earth revolved around the Sun and that a less politic heliocentrist, Giordano Bruno, was burned alive in 1600 for the crime of sound science. With the encouragement of our professor, Father Joyce, we marveled at the capacity of human leaders to corrupt noble institutions. Lust for power had caused the Catholic hierarchy to subvert the church's most central purpose—the search for existential truths.

Today, flat-earthers within the Bush administration—aided by right-wing allies who have produced assorted hired guns and conservative think tanks to further their goals—are engaged in a campaign to suppress science that is arguably unmatched in the Western world since the Inquisition. Sometimes, rather than suppress good science, they simply order up their own. Meanwhile, the Bush White House is purging, censoring, and blacklisting scientists and engineers whose work threatens the profits of corporate campaign contributors or challenges the ideological underpinnings of their radical anti-environmental agenda. Indeed, so extreme is this campaign that more than sixty scientists, including Nobel laureates and medical experts, released a statement in February 2004 that accused the Bush administration of deliberately distorting scientific fact "for partisan political ends."

GLOBAL MISINFORMING

The Bush administration's first instinct when it comes to science has been to suppress, discredit, or alter facts it doesn't like. Probably the best-known case is global warming. Over the past six years, the administration subverted nearly a dozen major government studies on global warming, including a ten-year, peer-reviewed report from a high-ranking government panel commissioned by the former president Bush in 1993 in his own effort to dodge what was already a virtual scientific consensus blaming industrial emissions for global warming. The list also includes major long-term studies by the federal government's National Academy of Sciences, the National Oceanic and Atmospheric Administration, and NASA, and a 2002 collaborative report by scientists at all three of those agencies. In short, some of the finest minds of the scientific world who have spent their professional lives studying climate change have weighed in on the subject and then been ignored.

In May 2002, a State Department report to the United Nations drafted by the Environmental Protection Agency (EPA) pointed out that man-made pollution clearly contributes to climate change and described some of the negative impacts that global warming would have on the United States in coming decades. Seeking to discredit the report—which apparently slipped through the gauntlet of Bush's censors—the president called it "a report put out by the bureaucracy." In September 2002, administration censors released the annual EPA report on air pollution without the agency's usual update on global warming, that section having been deleted by Bush appointees at the White House. On June 19, 2003, a State of the Environment report commissioned by the EPA was released after the pro-pollution types in the Bush administration excised language about global warming. The deleted passages included a 2001 report commissioned by the White House. In its place was a reference to a propaganda tract financed by the American Petroleum Institute.

In July 2003, EPA scientists leaked an analysis that the agency's leadership had withheld for months showing that a Senate plan to reduce the pollution that causes global warming could achieve its goal at very small cost. Bush reacted by launching a ten-year, $100 million effort to prove that global temperature changes have, in fact, occurred naturally, another delay tactic for the fossil-fuel barons at taxpayer expense. As Princeton University scientist Michael Oppenheimer notes, "With a president who does not believe in evolution, it's hard to imagine what kind of scientific evidence would suffice to convince him to take firm action on global warming."

NASA scientist Jim Hansen is widely considered to be the world's leading researcher on global warming. In 2004, Hansen drew the ire of the White House when he publicly ridiculed the administration, remarking to an audience at the University of Iowa, "I find a willingness to listen only to those portions of scientific results that fit predetermined inflexible positions. This, I believe, is a recipe for environmental disaster."

Shortly thereafter, Hansen and his colleagues at the Goddard Institute for Space Studies received an e-mail notifying them of a "new review process" and explaining that "the White House [is] now reviewing all climate-related press releases." They soon found out the censorship wouldn't be restricted to press releases, but would apply to all communications with the press by NASA scientists. Ever since, Hansen has been shadowed by a NASA communications representative in all his media interviews. "In my more than three decades in the government I've never witnessed such restrictions on the ability of scientists to communicate with the public," says Hansen.

But despite the leash around his neck, Hansen doesn't hide his discontent with the Bush administration's attempts to rewrite the science on global warming and muzzle its professional scientists. Nor does he adhere to the preferred opinion that uncertainties exist regarding the causes or severity of global warming. Hansen warns that the planet may be as little as a decade away from reaching the tipping point, beyond which global warming will reap catastrophic impacts on Earth's life-support systems and alter our future climate irreparably.

One of the wizards behind the curtain with the heaviest editing hand during Bush's first five years in office was Philip Cooney, the chief of staff at the White House Council on Environmental Quality. Cooney reviewed and altered scientific reports for Bush before they reached Congress and the public despite his lack of a science degree. Rick Piltz, a former government scientist with the US Global Change Research Program (renamed by Bush the US Climate Change Science Program), explains how Cooney changed phrases like "Earth is undergoing rapid change" to "may be undergoing change." "Uncertainty" becomes "significant remaining uncertainty." A line explaining that energy production contributes to warming simply disappears. "He was obviously passing it through a political screen," says Piltz. "He would put in the word 'potential' or 'may' or 'weaken,' or delete text that had to do with the likely consequence of climate change, pump up uncertainty language throughout."

No longer able to stand the manipulations of climate science perpetrated by Bush's henchman, Piltz resigned in protest in March 2005 and blew the whistle on Cooney under the guidance of the Government Accountability Project, a whistleblower protection group. In June, the *New York Times* published a front-page story revealing Cooney's editing of numerous global warming reports. Two days later, Cooney left the White House. Four days after that, he took a job with ExxonMobil.

PURCHASING POWER

The energy and extractive industries are among the special interests pushing hardest for Congress and the White House to obfuscate the threat from global warming and muzzle government scientists. This carbon-intensive industry sector has funneled more than $98 million to GOP candidates since 2000. Their investment has paid off in spades, not only in delaying a strong government response to global warming, but in beating back Bush's campaign promise to regulate mercury emissions as well.

As a favor to the utility and coal industries, America's largest mercury dischargers, the EPA sat for nine months on a report exposing the catastrophic impact of mercury on children's health, finally releasing it in February 2003. Among the findings of the report: The bloodstream of one in twelve US women is saturated with enough mercury to cause neurological damage, permanent IQ loss, and a grim inventory of other diseases in their unborn children. Despite this troubling fact, the Bush administration still refuses to curb mercury emissions, even though the technologies to do so are readily available.

The attack on science is not limited to global warming and air pollution. It permeates all government agencies. Roger Kennedy, former director of the National Park Service, told me that the alteration and deletion of scientific information is now standard procedure at the Department of Interior as well. "It's hard to decide what is more demoralizing about the administration's politicization of the scientific process," he said, "its disdain for professional scientists working for our government or its willingness to deceive the American public."

Science, like theology, reveals transcendent truths about a changing world. At their best, scientists are moral individuals whose business is to seek the truth. Over the past two decades industry and conservative think tanks have invested millions of dollars to corrupt science. They distort the truth about everything from tobacco, pesticides, and dioxin to ozone depletion, acid rain, and global warming. In their attempt to undermine the credible basis for public action (by positing that all opinions are politically driven and therefore any one is as true as any other), they also undermine belief in the integrity of the scientific process.

Now Congress and this White House have used federal power for the same purpose. Led by the president, the Republicans have gutted scientific research budgets and politicized science within the federal agencies. The very leaders who so often condemn the trend toward moral relativism are fostering and encouraging the trend toward scientific relativism. The very ideologues who derided Bill Clinton as a liar have now institutionalized dishonesty and made it the reigning culture of America's federal agencies.

The Bush administration has so violated and corrupted the institutional culture of government agencies charged with scientific research that it could take a generation for them to recover their integrity. Says Princeton University's Oppenheimer, "If you believe in a rational universe, in enlightenment, in knowledge, and in a search for the truth, this White House is an absolute disaster."

The very best in global industry ... *working for you!*

COMPANY	**Archer Daniels Midland Company**	SYMBOL **ADM**	FOUNDED 1902

As one of the world's largest grain and oilseed agribusiness companies, Archer Daniels Midland sees itself as an extension of the farm—a farm that would band together with all other farms to stamp out farms. By providing only one marketplace, ADM is helping farmers simplify their lives. If there's one thing farmers hate, it's frills.

While its competitors Cargill and ConAgra find their playgrounds in the developing world, ADM sees more domestic opportunities for earnings. Why worry whether poor people in Africa are consuming when poor people are consuming every day right here in America? At least 43 percent of ADM's annual profits are from products heavily subsidized or protected by the American government. So, in essence, if it weren't for ADM, a substantial percentage of the American government would be out of work.

And let's not forget ADM's dedication to clean air and water. The company has given the United States $351 million to clean up the environment—specifically, the environment surrounding ADM-owned facilities. Why call them "fines" when you can call them "contributions?"

Archer Daniels Midland: If you break down the phrase *price fixing*, it actually sounds like a good thing.

Battlefield Earth

After the release of his book and film documentary on global warming, *An Inconvenient Truth*, former vice president and eco-warrior Al Gore spoke with Rachel Maddow about the woes of our planet.

RACHEL MADDOW: Our next guest has been called many names, lots good, some not good. He's been called congressman, senator, vice president, democratic presidential nominee—we sometimes call him the Should-Be President of the United States. Here on the Rachel Maddow Show we have recently decided to add another couple of potential names to the list. We're considering the term Political Rock Star; we're also considering Cynic Slayer.

AL GORE: Wow, I'm gonna change my business card.

MADDOW: Cynic Slayer! It's kind of nice isn't it?

GORE: Thank you, I love that.

MADDOW: You'll get the Dungeons & Dragons vote. [Both laugh]

MADDOW: I saw you last night here in New York City at Town Hall and when you walked on the stage, I felt like the audience all but started taking off their undergarments and throwing them on the stage. The Political Rock Star thing! I can't imagine it's been like this for all of the last six years!

GORE: Oh, come on.

MADDOW: Well, at least you must be thrilled with the response to your film, *An Inconvenient Truth*.

GORE: I am. Mainly because it increases the odds significantly that more people will hear this message and see this message in a shorter period of time. We face a planetary emergency, the climate crisis is so dangerous, and it can be solved. The key is to get people to look at it clearly, understand it clearly, and then demand action—take action themselves—but also demand action from the political leaders in both parties. I'm happy with the reaction the movie is getting and the book is getting a similar reaction. It's also titled *An Inconvenient Truth*, and I hope everybody will see the movie and buy the book and go to the Web site, climatecrisis.net, and be a part of the solution to this crisis instead of a part of the problem.

MADDOW: The reaction to the film, to the book, and to your real resurgence into the public eye around this issue has been very strong among Air America listeners and among people who, like me, are very sympathetic to the cause. It's also been very strong on the right; there are "I Love Carbon Dioxide" romantic lullabies being aired by the Competitive Enterprise Institute. But I wanted to ask you specifically about what President Bush has said a couple times this week, which is that we need to figure out whether we have caused global warming or whether natural causes have led to it. What is he talking about? Do you know?

"If you have the entire global scientific community on one side and the largest polluter on the other side, and you have to choose between whose scientific view you're going to take, who would you pick?"

GORE: Well, that's the ExxonMobil view, and if you have the entire global scientific community on one side and the largest polluter on the other side, and you have to choose between whose scientific view you're going to take, who would you pick? Well, it seems to be an easy choice, but this White House, unfortunately, chose the polluter. I do want to say one thing, Rachel, about the differing reactions to the movie. To me the most interesting reaction is that there's been a surge of support from the Republicans and the conservatives and a series of articles and columns written by people who say, "I was a skeptic but now I'm not"—

MADDOW: Yeah.

GORE: —and eighty-five conservative evangelical ministers publicly broke with Bush and Cheney on this issue; several corporate CEOs who supported them have now broken with them on this issue. You're seeing some remarkable things—even, dare I say it, from Bill O'Reilly, who yesterday endorsed the movie, in effect. He said, "Al Gore is right on this issue," and a lot of others are, too.

MADDOW: Did that make you doubt yourself? [Laughs]

GORE: Well, I mean in all honesty I have argued for some time that this should not be seen as a political issue, but as moral issue and those of us, like you and me, who have long been advocating the scientific view of this, ought to do our best to welcome converts, to invite people on the other side of the political fence to join us in this. The stakes are just too high.

MADDOW: One of the ways you've tried to move people on this issue is to get rid of some of the despair and talk about the environmental success story of the effort to save the ozone layer. People put forward this idea that we could get rid of chlorofluorocarbons [CFCs], and one of the things I was really struck by is, as you've explained, the industries, the chlorofluorocarbon polluters, did push back on the whole ozone layer thing, but they didn't push back ultimately so hard that they stopped progress. What's the difference between the CFC industry and how much they pushed back on chlorofluorocarbons versus the ExxonMobils of today and how hard they're pushing back on global warming?

GORE: Interesting question. I think that the role of CO_2 is obviously much larger in our economy than CFCs, and I think that's part of the reason. The oil companies and coal companies are much richer and more powerful than the chemical companies were and I think that's also part of it. But I think the biggest change in the last twenty years, since we've had the ozone debate, is that the conversation of democracy has changed. The influence of special interests and lobbyists has grown dramatically, even as the influence of the average citizen wielding knowledge and strong opinions has shrunk. And we've gotta fight back, and Air America is a big part of the push back, and the Internet is part of the push back. I think we see in a lot of areas that harmful consequences come when the people's voice is diminished and the voice of the special interest is increased. Because they're almost never motivated by the public interests. In fact, their interests are almost always in direct contradiction to the public interest. So, in addition to the climate crisis, we have a democracy crisis, and we have to fix both of them at the same time. Unfortunately, the climate crisis is urgent, it is grave, and we do not have time to fool around with a lot of unnecessary partisanship and dueling before we fix this. We have got to start fixing it immediately.

"I think the biggest change in the last twenty years, since we've had the ozone debate, is that the conversation of democracy has changed. The influence of special interests and lobbyists has grown dramatically, even as the influence of the average citizen wielding knowledge and strong opinions has shrunk."

MADDOW: I understand that in building activists around this issue, you have to get people to change their own behaviors, not only because our individual behavior matters, but because that can also be galvanizing to us as activists about the way that we can change things. But are there big enough solutions out there that we could make a difference in the next five years, in the next ten years? Do we need to be doing stuff on a massive scale?

GORE: Yes we do, and there are solutions out there. But right now they are, I have to be candid, outside the boundary of what is considered politically realistic and feasible in our system. But that's just another way of saying we have to get the knowledge of this crisis to more people, so that we can expand the boundaries of what's politically possible. The political system can seem like it's moving at a snail's pace, and it usually does, but it has one thing in common with the climate system: it's nonlinear. It can move slowly and then cross a tipping point and then move swiftly and adopt a brand-new pattern. In 1941, for example, it was absurd to think America could build 1,000 airplanes, but by 1943 that was a really low number. And after 9/11, if the president had not only rallied the country [as he was] standing on the rubble and invaded Afghanistan to go after Osama bin Laden, both things he did well, but also said, "Okay look, we're going to keep going after the terrorists, and while we're at it, we're going to get independent of oil and coal and we're going to stop relying on this unstable part of the world, the Middle East, and we are going to save our environment by shifting to renewable energy," I think that at such a moment the people would follow, and I think that we are going to see many opportunities, unfortunately, in the months and years ahead when leadership can make a difference. After Hurricane Katrina, millions experienced a wake-up call on global warming. We're nearing a new hurricane season, and I hope the scientists are wrong, but if they aren't, it may be a bad one. But we cannot just sit back and endure this without creating the potential for much larger changes than now seem possible. And I think the people are ahead of the politicians. I think that we are close to a galvanizing moment when the people are going to demand that politicians, in both parties frankly, start offering meaningful solutions.

"I think that we are close to a galvanizing moment when the people are going to demand that politicians, in both parties frankly, start offering meaningful solutions."

MADDOW: I was a committed AIDS activist for a very long time and when you announced you were running for president in the year 2000 in New Hampshire, I personally interrupted your announcement by shouting and I had a banner about AIDS drugs for Africa. That kind of confrontation has really worked for the AIDS movement and it resulted in a whole lot of meetings. If Condoleezza Rice is declaring that she's running for president in 2008 in New Hampshire, what is the new me, the climate-change activist who's interrupting her, shouting? What does that banner say? What do you want people to be asking for in very specific terms?

GORE: I think confronting candidates personally with passion and well-reasoned appeals over and over again, and convincing them that you're not going to go away until they respond in a thoughtful and thorough way, is a time-honored and tested approach. If enough people do it, then the politicians are going to respond.

A Prayer for the Planet

Jim Wallis, editor in chief of *Sojourners* magazine and author of *God's Politics*, was a guest of *Eco-Talk* on March 16, 2006, and told Betsy Rosenberg about the Evangelical Climate Change initiative and how evangelical leaders are calling for action to defend the environment.

BETSY ROSENBERG: Recently a group of more than eighty-five evangelical leaders expressed what they called a biblically driven commitment to curb global warming. Why are these outspoken faith-community voices coming to the fore now?

JIM WALLIS: Actually mainline Protestant churches have been outspoken about the environment for a decade, at least Presbyterians, Lutherans, Methodists and so on. They've been saying some good things for a long time. But it hasn't gotten any attention because the religious right has gotten all the coverage in the media for their very narrow range of issues. For about ten years some of the most exciting new environmental initiatives have been coming from younger evangelicals. A new generation of evangelical Christians on college campuses and other places have been talking about this, and we've been covering them in *Sojourners,* but again they weren't getting any wider media attention until about two years ago. [That's when] Rich Cizik of the National Association of Evangelicals (NAE) and others in that broader mainstream evangelical group began to have a conversion, or an epiphany if you will, on the environment. They said that global warming was a religious issue. There was an article in the [*New York*] *Times* about this, which came out two years ago. The global warming politics changed in this town overnight, because the global warming constituency is not part of the Bush base, and so they were being ignored. And all of a sudden here's the NAE saying global warming is a religious issue and the White House actually called them that day to ask what policies don't you like? So now, two years later, this initiative is about to be launched and the religious right rears its ugly head and the usual suspects—James Dobson, Chuck Colson, Richard Land, and nineteen others—write a letter telling the National Association of Evangelicals not to sign the initiative [because] "we're part of the NAE" they say, "and we disagree, we're divided, we're for economic growth, and we're worried about the poor." It's the first time James Dobson ever showed any worry about the poor that I can recall. A couple of years ago that would have really tamped us down, it would have vetoed this and crushed it. But this time there was a pushback. Eighty-nine evangelical Christian leaders came out with this very powerful statement, a full-page ad in the *New York Times,* saying, in fact, that the environment is a Christian concern and a deeply evangelical issue. So the religious right has lost control of the issue of the environment. They tried to say this is not one of our issues. In fact their letter said let's stick to our core issues, abortion and gay marriage. This shouldn't be one of our concerns, and they lost. They lost that battle, and now the environment is a central evangelical Christian concern. That's a very big deal.

ROSENBERG: You identify yourself with nineteenth-century evangelical Christians. Many of us tend to confuse evangelism and fundamentalism. What are the distinctions?

WALLIS: Fundamentalism has really usurped what it means to be evangelical in America. In the nineteenth-century evangelicals were reformers, the evangelists were abolitionists; they fought to abolish slavery. The revivalists were also reformers. People looked at them as social progressives. So today, when I'm on these Christian college campuses, which I am almost every week, it's clear that the new altar call is around poverty, the environment, Darfur, sex trafficking, and HIV/AIDS. It's a whole different set of issues than simply abortion and gay marriage. There is a battle now going on among evangelicals.

ROSENBERG: Hallelujah.

WALLIS: A number of very significant evangelical leaders who represent lots and lots of people—educators, pastors, academics, evangelists—signed this thing about the environment, and they often refer to this as creation care. The environment is thought to be, in their language, God's creation, so what they're saying, what *we're* saying is, care for God's creation.

"The environment is thought to be, in their language, God's creation, so what *we're* saying is, care for God's creation."

ROSENBERG: How might this change politics and policies in Washington?

WALLIS: Well, one thing is that the political facts are changing on the ground. About half of the evangelical constituency—about 23 percent of the [American] electorate are evangelical—are religious right and pretty core. the good news is about half of them aren't. Half of them are moderate or progressive, and they're in play politically. If the right message comes from another side of the spectrum, they're going to be responsive. So if there's a candidate who talks about poverty as a moral issue, and the environment and human rights and Darfur and a broader range of questions, these voters are willing to vote in different ways.

ROSENBERG: And global warming is a moral issue?

WALLIS: Absolutely, but it's not just moral, we're saying it's a biblical issue, it's a religious issue, it's a matter of our faith.

When the Supreme Court faced the question of whether government buildings could display the Ten Commandments, Justice Antonin Scalia was stoked. Ramon got hold of his Palm Pilot.

THE PITBULL
TODAY'S SCHEDULE:

6 am Early morning workout; run to top of hill, lift tablets over head and yell, "People of America, I give you these commandments to use in the name of George W. Bush!" Then smash them on the sidewalk.

8 am Call president. Ask to speak to "Burning Bush." Enjoy laughter.

9 am Re-read Ten Commandments. Resist temptation to covet thy neighbor's wife, house, or butt. Especially the butt.

10 am Court in session. To impress other justices, change your walking staff into a serpent.

10:30 am Write decision. "If we remove the Ten Commandments from public buildings, the next thing you know, we'll have to remove the bizarre Masonic imagery from the dollar bill. And that's un-American."

2 pm Suggest that mandatory school prayer could help get this issue resolved.

4 pm Threaten ACLU counselors with a plague of locusts and, if necessary, the death of their first-born sons.

10 pm Get out binoculars. Covet neighbor's wife. Shame. So much shame.

George W. Bush: Evangelist in Chief

Americans traditionally have embraced political leaders who demonstrate a faith in a higher power. And presidents are no exception. Voters rest easier, or so it seems, knowing that the man with his finger on the button during times of national crisis also takes the time to clasp his hands together and bow his head while he searches for guidance and wisdom. Or a hand signal from Karl Rove.

And yet, Americans don't want their leaders to be too religious. Which explains the failed presidential bids of Alan Keyes, Pat Robertson, and Reverend Al Sharpton. Also, these three are sorta crazy. And two of them are black. But, you get the idea.

For a president, going to church on Sunday, speaking at a prayer breakfast, and lighting the national Christmas tree all fall under the umbrella of "tolerable" and "appropriate" religious activities. However, holding a prayer huddle before a cabinet meeting or making the sign of the cross over the budget probably would not be considered appropriate.

GOD IS HIS COPILOT

But George W. Bush is different. By any standard of measure, he's the most outwardly religious of all our presidents. During a 2000 presidential debate, he was asked to name his favorite philosopher. Bush said, "Christ. Because he changed my heart."

In an interview with Fox News in October 2004, Bush confirmed that he regularly reads passages from *My Utmost for His Highest*, a sixty-five-year-old collection of homilies by a Protestant minister. Bush said it's a way for him "on a daily basis to be in the word." Bush also told Sean Hannity that he will—when called upon—perform the miracle of turning stale bread into croutons.

Although he was born Episcopalian, Bush attended a Presbyterian church in his youth and joined a Methodist church after he got married—his heart wasn't changed until Jesus gave him the strength to stop drinking on the morning of his fortieth birthday. Too bad that same strength couldn't stop him from invading Iraq.

The record is clear: President Bush believes he's been touched by God. Richard Land, a leader of the Southern Baptist Convention, recalls that on the day Bush took the oath of office for his second term as Texas's governor, Bush said, "I believe that God wants me to be president."

When he assumed that preordained office, Bush made his faith an intricate part of his administration and its decision-making process. According to Bush's former speechwriter David Frum, "attendance at Bible study was, if not compulsory, not quite uncompulsory" for White House staff.

At the National Prayer Breakfast in February 2003, Bush told a group of religious leaders, "Events aren't moved by blind change and chance. Behind all of life and all of history, there's a dedication and purpose, set by the hand of a just and faithful God."

And yet, the president's deep-seated faith in Christ wouldn't be considered problematic by most of the country were it not for one eensy teeny wittle problem: The fact that he is actively imposing Christian theology on the rest of us—and using taxpayer money to do it.

OR MAYBE GOD IS IN THE DRIVER'S SEAT

In January 2001, Bush announced the formation of a new administration office, the White House Office for Faith-Based and Community Initiatives. The office's chief is sort of the czar for Christian missionary work. In the speech in which he outlined this outfit's mission, Bush said, "When we see social needs in America, my administration will look first to faith-based programs and community groups, which have proven their power to save and change lives."

Funding community-based outreach programs is a good idea. More of the money and services get to the people who need it, as opposed to funding a larger organization's infrastructure. Only, here's the thing: Taxpayer money is being specifically earmarked for faith-based religious organizations that in many instances discriminate against whom they serve (gays) and preach a religiously tainted pseudoscience (like condoms don't work—but more on that later). But surely the president wouldn't earmark millions of taxpayer dollars to support discrimination and pseudoscience. Surely there would be a mechanism put in place to screen out bigots and the like. In the mission statement, the president added, "We will encourage faith-based and community programs without changing their mission." Oops.

In 2005, President Bush allocated $170 million to programs that teach kids that the *only* way to avoid pregnancy and sexually transmitted diseases (STDs) is through abstinence. In the past ten years, the federal government has spent $1 billion advocating abstinence. These programs—and there are thousands of them—teach kids that condoms are ineffective at preventing pregnancy, that homosexuality is not normal, that abstinence should be the societal standard, and that the best sex happens in marriage. Obviously, the president has never spent a weekend in Thailand with Harvey Firestein. Former Surgeon General Jocelyn Elders, MD, calls abstinence-only programs "child abuse" because they deny young people the tools necessary to fight STDs and unwanted pregnancy.

In yet another boon to the religious right, President Bush in 2001 reinstated the controversial Mexico City Policy (which was initiated by President Ronald Reagan in 1984 and rescinded by President Bill Clinton in 1993). This policy—also known as the Mexico City Gag Rule—demands that international charitable organizations that accept donations from the US government and operate health clinics in the third world not perform abortions or discuss abortion as a viable method of family planning. In a White House memorandum, the president said, "It is my conviction that taxpayer funds should not be used to pay for abortions or advocate or actively promote abortion, either here or abroad." This, despite the fact that rape is the most frequently reported crime around the world, according to the United Nations. The gag rule isn't just a nuisance that aid workers must cleverly circumvent—it's criminal.

GOD IS ALSO A DARNED GOOD DISTRACTION

Then, in a February 2004 speech, with the rest of the country's problems solved, the president said, "Today I call upon the Congress to promptly pass, and to send to the states for ratification, an amendment to our Constitution defining and protecting marriage as a union of man and woman as husband and wife." The White House press secretary at the time, Scott McClellan, added, "The president believes very strongly that marriage is a sacred institution, and that we should do what is needed to protect and defend the sanctity of marriage."

If "sanctity" was what the White House was really concerned with, wouldn't they also have called for a Constitutional amendment banning bachelor parties, massage parlor happy endings, and those Las Vegas drive-through wedding chapels? And why not an amendment banning Larry King from walking down the aisle, too? He's done it eight times. Ten if you count the two weddings he just wandered into out of habit.

Then, in May 2006, with the president's poll numbers in the mid-30s, gas prices near $3.50 a gallon, the insurgency in Iraq gaining strength, the deficit near $7 trillion, and the midterm elections just a few months away, a Senate committee approved a Constitutional amendment banning same-sex marriage. And how does the president feel about this? "Our policies should aim to strengthen families, not undermine them," said Bush in June about courts that allowed same-sex marriage. "And changing the definition of marriage would undermine the family structure."

The president's faith in Christ in and of itself isn't what's wrong with him or his administration. People seem to forget that a belief in God isn't the sole province of the right wing of the political spectrum. People of faith who are liberals believe in God, too. They pray for strength and wisdom, advocate community service, and support freedom and democracy. What they lack, however, is the temerity to suggest with absolute certainty that God wants them to be the Evangelist in Chief.

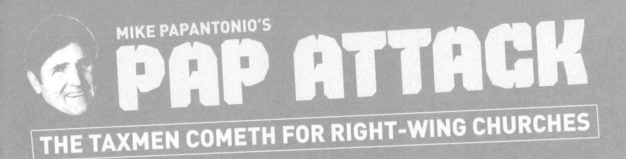

Conservatives love to beat up on the IRS. It's damn near impossible to carry on a conversation with *true* knee-jerk neocons and not have to listen to them tell you about the evils of the Internal Revenue Service. Stay tuned this year, though, and watch how all the right-wing windbags really ratchet up their attacks on the IRS, because the IRS is defying Karl Rove, George Bush, and even their lockstep Republican Congress in an effort to investigate tax fraud abuses of 501(c)(3) nonprofit organizations.

When I first looked at this story, I suspected that the IRS had a Republican political agenda in the way they were targeting 501(c)(3) groups. I was wrong. In fact, it turns out, the IRS may be one of the most important vehicles for saving religion and preserving democracy. They have begun to seriously draw the line between politics and religion by revoking the tax-exempt status of churches and religious organizations that are devoting church money, church facilities, and church manpower toward building a new Republican theocracy.

In order to be able to collect billions of dollars and not pay taxes on that money, the rules are simple:

Don't endorse particular candidates or specific political positions. A religious organization cannot distribute voter guides of any kind. In other words, a religious group cannot recommend their slate of political candidates or political party positions. A church also is not permitted to mobilize its staff or its congregation in an effort to promote a political candidate or a political party. Abide by those conditions and you are tax exempt.

It's a pretty good deal by any standard. But it's a deal that some churches apparently don't appreciate. In Pennsylvania, for example, Senator Rick Santorum and about 150 clergy members could not bring themselves to play by the rules. Those Pennsylvania pastors laid their 501(c)(3) tax exemptions on the line by posting a Web site notice called the Pennsylvania Pastors Network where that church-based organization tried to hire ten full-time political organizers to help churches mount a get-out-and-vote campaign.

It doesn't take a trained theologian or even a trained bottom-feeding politico like Rick Santorum to follow the money on this one and understand that it's all about politics. It is not New Testament religion. It is Karl Rove religion, pure and simple.

And that's fine if those clergy members want to move from preaching the word of God to preaching the word of Karl Rove. But it's also fine with most Americans if all the churches involved in that abuse of the law lose their tax-exempt status.

Looking back, every one of us should be grateful that the IRS had enough courage to fine Pat Robertson's Christian Broadcasting Network cash cow in the mid-1980s.

And it makes perfect sense that they went after Jerry Falwell's old-time gospel hour, the PTL Club political action committee, when it became evident to all of us that this tax-exempt money was just being laundered into politics.

In America today, churches and other religious groups own about 25 percent of all the real estate in the country.

The assets of the Roman Catholic Church alone exceed the holdings of America's five largest corporations combined.

The average American family pays more than $1,000 extra in taxes every year to make up for revenue lost to churches and religious groups.

And I suppose most of us are not bothered too much by that, because it's easy to see how organized religion is taking up the slack for a Republican government that has abandoned charity and decency in its treatment of the least of our society.

But at the same time, the overwhelming majority of Americans draw the line when it comes to the church playing politics with their money.

And if 150 clergymen in Pennsylvania want to use taxpayers' money to elect Rick Santorum, the numbers show that most Americans would not even blink if the IRS did exactly what we have given them the authority to do: Revoke their exemptions and draw a clearer line between religion and politics. A line that even political bottom-feeders like Karl Rove are afraid to cross.

Who Put Religion in My Diplomacy?

Rachel Maddow talked with former secretary of state Madeleine Albright on May 15, 2006. Albright has been an outspoken critic of the war in Iraq and of the Bush administration's handling of it. Not least among her concerns was Bush's unwillingness to listen to foreign-policy experts outside of his administration, most notably the farce of a meeting in which members of previous administrations were summoned to the White House to find out that their opinions were not required, only their presence at a photo op.

RACHEL MADDOW: I'd like to talk about religion and foreign policy and to talk about your own personal conversion in the way you have thought about religion and foreign policy—it's personal, and therefore it's gripping, but it's also, I think, going to change the way that people talk about religion. We tend to think of religion as something that, in the modern age, we were all going to grow out of, but that hasn't turned out to be the case.

MADELEINE ALBRIGHT: Well exactly. I mean, I'm the kind of person trained in international relations that used to say, in looking at a conflict, "This is complicated enough, let's not bring God and religion into it." But I think on the contrary, in order to try to resolve some of those conflicts, we have to figure out how to find the common threads of the various religions to see whether we can come up with some solution.

MADDOW: The common wisdom, as you mentioned, about religion in foreign policy and international politics is that it is divisive, and that it's kind of like a clash of irrationalities, and there's no rational way out for people who are in conflict over a difference in religion. How can religion be a positive force in international relations? How can religion bring out the best in people, in terms of the way we get along despite our differences?

> "I think the secretary of state actually needs religious advisors, because you have economics advisors and arms control advisors and environmental advisors, so I think we need some religious advisors."

ALBRIGHT: Well, I think that the main thing, interestingly enough, is that as one reads through the holy books of old, of the three monotheistic religions, it is evident that they're very similar in language. I mean you can find the bloodcurdling parts, but there also are parts where they're exactly the same in terms of peace, charity, social justice, treating others well, and I think we need to emphasize those. And our diplomats, who are very smart and trained in all kinds of things, need also to be trained in the religions of the places where they are going to be posted. And I think the secretary of state actually needs religious advisors, because you have economics advisors and arms control advisors and environmental advisors, so I think we need some religious advisors.

MADDOW: You know, one place that I have seen what you're talking about in action recently was in the letter from the Iranian president, Mahmud Ahmadinejad, to President Bush, which was in the last week or two. And in reading through that letter, which I found fascinating, he's saying, "Listen, you're a follower of Jesus Christ, I'm a follower of the Qur'an and the teachings of Muhammad, and I see from our common religious monotheistic base that we ought not be conducting ourselves this way, and you ought not be conducting yourself this way as the US [president]." What do you think the American response should be to the Ahmadinejad letter?

ALBRIGHT: Well, it's interesting because the letter is full of just terrible things, too, I mean in terms of invective against the US and saber rattling.

MADDOW: The part where he says, "Suppose the Holocaust happened," that's a little troubling.

ALBRIGHT: Little things [laughs], where he totally disregards history. But what I think is interesting is, I don't believe that there's a clash of civilizations, but there *is* a battle of ideas and I think there are things in that letter as well as what others have been saying, some around Osama bin Laden, that have to be taken seriously and responded to. So, I'm not suggesting that President Bush become President Ahmadinejad's pen pal, but that there should be a serious speech given by a very high-level administration official that takes on some of the same ideas and puts them into the best perspective.

> "I don't believe that there's a clash of civilizations, but there *is* a battle of ideas."

MADDOW: I read in the *New York Times* on Saturday that you were among a group of former secretaries of state and secretaries of defense who met with President Bush and Condoleezza Rice and Dick Cheney on Friday at the White House. What was the meeting about? What did you talk about?

ALBRIGHT: Well, what we talked about was basically private, but what is interesting is we were asked to come in to be briefed on the current situation in Iraq. And I must say that it was a much better meeting than the first one, because there was much more give-and-take. I told the president that I thought, in terms of Iraq, I still felt that we were on a split screen—there's their reality and then there's what one hears. I also made the suggestion that I just told you about on Iran. So I think it was a better meeting than the first one, where we basically were part of a photo op.

MADDOW: Why do you think he called a second meeting?

ALBRIGHT: Well, it's hard to tell exactly but I think that somebody must have said that it would be a good idea to consult with people. You know, the accumulated experience in that room actually goes into several hundred years, and I must tell you I felt very young. But I think it's a very interesting thing to do and useful, because these are people who ran their own departments at various times, and I just had the sense that there was a thinking on the part of some people in the White House that it would be a good idea.

MADDOW: It was just interesting, as a person who comments on the news every day, to have seen such a huge buildup to the first meeting and then the big photo op and then the revelation that he didn't actually let people speak their minds very much, and then this meeting, at least from the press perspective, just kind of came out of the blue.

ALBRIGHT: Well, I think it did for us too, I think a lot of people had to rearrange their schedules. You know, when you get called to come to the White House, no matter whether you agree with the president or not, you should be there. I appreciated the fact that we were not brought in there for a very peculiar family picture.

> "You know, when you get called to come to the White House, no matter whether you agree with the president or not, you should be there."

MADDOW: The most diverse family ever. Let me just ask you one other question. You have written in your book that the invasion of Iraq may be among the worst foreign-policy disasters in American history. If you were secretary of state right now, what would your advice be on the way out?

ALBRIGHT: Well, I think it is a disaster, mainly because of the repercussions for the whole of the Middle East and the fact that the country, at this stage, that has gained the most out of it is Iran. I think what needs to happen is, this year has to be used as a transition year. We can't just pick up and leave, but we do need to redeploy our troops, try to do more about securing the borders, and then, as I keep saying, and I feel so strongly about this, the regional countries have to be brought into this, that some kind of a contact group has to exist, because we cannot do this by ourselves. I'm minimally more hopeful with this new government, but I think we have to figure out how to move the Iraqis into running their own lives.

The very best in global industry... *working for you!*

COMPANY **Union Carbide Corporation**	SYMBOL Subsidiary of Dow Chemical Company	FOUNDED 1917

Here's a smart investment tip: Other multinational chemical companies may talk, talk, talk about safety, but only Union Carbide was bold enough to initiate a major disaster to see how people would react in a real-life crisis.

In the early hours of December 3, 1984, gas leaked from a tank of methyl isocyanate at a Union Carbide pesticide plant in Bhopal, India. Soon, around half-a-million unsuspecting residents were enveloped in a dense cloud of gas. A curious Union Carbide waited to see how would they respond. Interestingly, people awoke experiencing fits of coughing and found their lungs filling with fluid. During the first three days after the accident, between 7,000 and 10,000 people died, mainly from cardiac and respiratory arrest. This wealth of raw data led Union Carbide to reach an important scientific discovery: Poison gas leaks are dangerous.

To protect its good name, Union Carbide in 2001 became a subsidiary of the Dow Chemical Company, which has refused to accept any of Union Carbide's liabilities for the Bhopal experiment. And why should they? The benevolent Union Carbide has already paid each victim more than $500. Thanks, Union Carbide. You taught the business world that while everyone makes a mess, you don't always have to clean it up.

The Religious Right and the Political Wrong

Rev. Dr. C. Welton Gaddy

As a person who cares about religion and cares about democracy, I am offended by the gross amount of pious talk that finds no translation into political action—at least, no action that moves the nation any closer to true democracy. More and more, religion is being manipulated as a tool to advance political strategy. Increasingly, the voice of the Religious Right is taking precedence over all other voices, both religious and secular. Remember one thing: Not all people who talk a lot about religion are necessarily religious, and conversely, not all people who are religious necessarily talk a lot about religion.

DO AS THEY SAY NOT AS THEY DO

The fact is rhetorical flourishes about religion tell us little about the religious character of those who make them. Their actions are much more telling. So let me offer a few things to look for that may prove useful in unmasking politics posing as religion.

- Watch out for any movement or individual apparently more interested in condemning you than in establishing a relationship with you.
- Take a hard look at any movement or person dedicated to restricting rights rather than to extending rights.
- Beware of people more concerned with limiting freedom for the benefit of some than with guaranteeing freedom for the good of all.
- Look with suspicion at any initiative that attempts to rob an individual of the dignity and worth that belong to every human being.
- Think twice about people or movements that give financial breaks to the wealthy and allow an increase in the number of people living in poverty.

Regardless of words spoken, symbols cited, or texts quoted, efforts that claim the authority of religion often spring from interests in power and control, not religion or democracy. We must work hard to protect America's shared values and to return integrity to political processes. We must reclaim our freedom as we take back our nation. Nothing less than democracy itself is at stake.

INTERSECTION AWARDS

What is happening at the intersection of religion and politics is adversely affecting religion, spawning democracy-crippling divisions, and threatening the authority of the United States Constitution.

Every week on *State of Belief*, Reverend Dr. C. Welton Gaddy plays traffic cop at the intersection of religion and politics. He recognizes a person or a group that has jeopardized the integrity of religion and the vitality of democracy by ruthlessly ignoring the proper role of each—and causing a serious wreck. He also extends a "green light" award to recipients responsibly negotiating this dangerous intersection.

JUDICIAL ANOINTMENT Three ministers must have confused the meaning of the term "confirmation" when they decided to lend a helping hand to the Supreme Court confirmation hearings of Judge Samuel Alito. Entering the hearing room unnoticed, the intrepid holy men applied oil to all the seats and prayed for the thirteen committee members aloud. According to evangelical Christian leader Reverend Rob Schenck, "We did adequately apply oil to all the seats" to assure God's presence in the process. When guards prevented the ministers from re-entering the room the next day to continue their "consecration service," they stood outside the hearing room reading scriptures and repeating the Lord's Prayer. Before leaving, they used oil to mark one of the doors with a sign of the cross.

The last time I checked, the Supreme Court is charged with protecting the Constitution. That means guaranteeing freedom from religion as well as freedom for religion and keeping the institutions of government and the institutions of religion separate from each other.

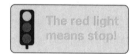

Source: *The Wall Street Journal*, January 5, 2006

CUP'A HATE, LIGHT AND SWEET Event organizers caused a kerfuffle when they asked a former Muslim to speak at an Idaho state prayer breakfast, overlooking (or maybe not) the fact that the speaker currently headed a ministry dedicated to converting Muslims to Christianity. Numerous religious leaders promised to boycott the event in protest of the negative implications toward Islam. The head of the group that invited the minister didn't help things when he said that Muslims want to kill all Jews and Christians. "They try to convert by the sword. Christians don't do that," he said. Hoo boy!

Folks, sponsoring a prayer breakfast to bring a community together around shared religious values is a great initiative. But a prayer breakfast that tears a community apart is a misnomer as well as a mistake.

Source: *Idaho Statesman*, February 14, 2006

PUPPET REGIME Evangelist Ken Ham is a self-appointed cheerleader of what he calls "creation evangelism." Translated, that means "stop the teaching of evolution." Ham has been traveling the country, training elementary-school students to challenge any teacher who mentions evolution or the Big Bang theory by audaciously asking the teacher, "Were you there?" In New Jersey, he used dinosaur puppets and silly cartoons to convince 2,300 elementary-school students that geology, paleontology, and evolutionary biology are bunk.

Hey, kids, what time is it? It's indoctrination time!

Source: *Los Angeles Times*, February 11, 2006

SECTARIAN SUBSIDY Looking after their own at the expense of the many, sectarian financial wizards in Maryland drafted an ingenious plan to help the state's Catholic schools stay in the black. The Maryland Catholic Conference got legislation in front of the state senate that would give tax breaks to companies that support a Catholic school education. A local TV news station reported that the bill would allow businesses "to take 75 percent of a tax credit and apply it toward scholarships or scholarship organizations." Now look, I certainly don't want anyone to be denied an education, and I don't want Catholic schools to be forced to close. But it is simply unconstitutional for the state to funnel taxpayer money into a religious institution. Never mind that the state has public schools to support!

Neither the American public nor the US Constitution sees public funding for private parochial schools as a good idea.

The red light means stop!

Source: **WBAL TV in Baltimore**

IT'S A SMALL WORLD, AFTER ALL A green light award goes to a positive development in public education—a world religions course in Modesto, California. The required ninth-grade course has been offered since 2000, and after its first six years, the First Amendment Center released a report finding that students in the class gained new respect for religious liberty and did not change their own religious convictions. Plus, the study found that overall respect for First Amendment freedoms including speech and assembly also increased among students. As I always say, freedom is religion's best friend.

The green light means go!

FAITH-BASED FUNNY BUSINESS Meanwhile in Wyoming, the state government funneled tens of thousands of dollars to a grant program administered by a private religious corporation. What's the so-called Department of Family Services doing giving money to a business that has funded churches, ministries, and antiabortion centers? Family Services gave at least $5,000 to the LifeChoice Pregnancy Center, which bills itself on its Web site as "an outreach ministry of Jesus Christ." (Now remember, it's we taxpayers who are footing the bill!) Wyoming's state constitution explicitly forbids giving state money to sectarian or religious groups, but the department's director tried to get around that rule by claiming that the state's money was mixed in with money from a federal grant for faith-based social services.

Folks, this is the long arm of President Bush's faith-based initiative in action—it's destroying the religious protections of the First Amendment across the country.

The red light means stop!

Source: **Associated Press, May 25, 2006**

THE CARDINAL OF COMPASSION A special "Green Light Award" goes to Cardinal Roger Mahony. Leader of the Roman Catholic Archdiocese of Los Angeles, Cardinal Mahony took offense at the government when it tried to tell the church whom it could serve. Namely that illegal immigrants should not receive the services of the church. Would an immigrant have to flash a green card to receive communion? So, the good cardinal instructed all 288 parishes in the Los Angeles diocese not to restrict their services to people in need, even if the bill becomes law. "The church is here to serve people," Mahony said. "We're not about to become immigration agents."

Go on doing what you're doing, Cardinal.

The green light means rock on!

Source: *Los Angeles Times*, March 1, 2006

Mr. Carter Talks to Washington

On December 1, 2005, former president and globe-trotting humanitarian Jimmy Carter mulled the state of values in our country with Al Franken.

AL FRANKEN: We are honored to be joined by President Jimmy Carter. Thank you, Mr. President, for joining us. [You have a] great new book, and it's a great topic, *Our Endangered Values*, and in it you write about how you are a man of faith, and how you have applied that faith in a way that is so admirable. I gave a speech at the Carter Center and I started it by responding to a Rush Limbaugh thing where he says, "Name one country where Jimmy Carter has helped people" [laughs], and then I checked off the forty countries where you've helped people. [Applause]

JIMMY CARTER: Al, I have a question, who is Rush Limbaugh?

FRANKEN: [Laughter] He is a guy who helps millions of people every day fool themselves.

CARTER: Oh, I see.

FRANKEN: In your book you address fundamentalism and you talk about religious values, and you make a distinction between that and fundamentalism.

CARTER: Yes.

FRANKEN: Talk about that.

> "Between Democrats and Republicans it's now an attitude of 'I am right and you are wrong and therefore we cannot cooperate.'"

CARTER: Well, this is my twentieth book and it's the first book I've ever written about political issues of the day, the rest of the books have been poetry and novels and things of that kind. But I have become so intensely concerned in the last five years about two major trends in our country and their merger that I decided finally to write this book. I describe fundamentalism as one of the root causes of the problem, but also one of the results. As I define it in my book on just one page, fundamentalists have always been men, the leaders, they always consider themselves to be superior and they feel an overwhelming inclination to dominate other people, particularly women. They subjugate women to men, and make them subservient to their husbands. They consider themselves to be uniquely related to God and endowed with insight that other human beings of an inferior nature don't have. Therefore they have to be 100 percent right and anyone who disagrees with them has got to be wrong and by extension inferior. It's impossible for them to ever admit that they have made a mistake. They consider it to be a violation of their principles to negotiate or mediate or compromise or even cooperate with people who differ from them. This is the case in both extreme Christianity and extreme Islam and other religions. But it also spills over into the political realms, and I think it's that fundamentalist inclination that has now permeated politics in Washington. And it has been one of the causes of dramatic changes in what used to be a harmonious and relatively cooperative attitude among Democrats and Republicans. Between Democrats and Republicans it's now an attitude of "I am right and you are wrong and therefore we cannot cooperate." In top circles in our country, you are either with us or against us and there is no way to reach out and form a cooperative team. So that is the essence of fundamentalism and unfortunately in the last five years or so, we have seen an increasing inclination for the ultra-right, and fundamentalists in religious circles, to combine their efforts and form alliances in politics. And this has broken down what I consider to be a historic and even religious characteristic of America. I happen to be a Christian, as you pointed out. Jesus taught, Render under Caesar the things that are Caesar's and unto God the things that are God's. Thomas Jefferson said we must build a wall between the church and state. Well, in the last few years that wall has been deliberately broken down, not secretly but ostentatiously and openly. These are things that have caused me concern and they've led to a series of other basic political changes in our country.

> "Thomas Jefferson said we must build a wall between the church and state. Well, in the last few years that wall has been deliberately broken down, not secretly but ostentatiously and openly."

FRANKEN: Talk to the distinction between the separation of church and state (which I'm a firm believer in) and the fact that religion and faith has informed political movements in very helpful ways, in the case of the abolitionists and in the case of Martin Luther King, who of course was a reverend.

CARTER: Well I consider myself to be a traditional evangelical Christian, and I realize that every person who goes into any realm of life, whether it be radio announcer or farmer or a submarine officer or a professor or whatever, takes into his daily life the basic elements of moral values and ethical principles that have been derived during his earlier years. Those are quite often inherited, sometimes they are taught by parents or family members or peer groups or others. Sometimes they're based on a particular religious faith, but whatever they are, they shape the basic inclinations of a person and it's almost impossible to imagine that a person wouldn't apply those principles if he or she is elected to public office. They usually include the most admirable elements of all religions, that is, a belief in justice, a belief in peace, a belief in service to others, the alleviation of suffering; those kind of things, obviously, are attributes of any human being. And you can exhibit those in a political office without letting one particular religion be exalted in politics, or without letting political elections be shaped by any particular religious group. The administration of or the implementation of your own religious or other ethical or moral values is natural for a human being in any realm of life. But to wield them so they influence people to the preference of a particular political party or particular religious faith, in a democracy, is what I deplore. [Applause]

FRANKEN: Talk about the way the wall has been broken down ostentatiously—are you talking about faith-based initiatives?

> "The administration of or the implementation of your own religious or other ethical or moral values is natural for a human being in any realm of life. But to wield them so they influence people to the preference of a particular political party or particular religious faith, in a democracy, is what I deplore."

CARTER: Well the faith-based initiative is one hell of an audit. In fact last year, as I describe in my book, about $2 billion of taxpayers' money was channeled into primarily Christian churches for the benefit of believers in the Christian faith. This is unprecedented in our country. As you know there was a big debate going on, primarily in Republican party circles, about whether those taxpayers' dollars should have to be distributed on a nondiscriminatory basis, that is, equally to Christians and non-Christians. And the decision was made that no, it is legal and proper under this administration to distribute them with the primary emphasis on fellow Christians. That kind of thing has never been done before in this nation, and it's one of several radical departures from previous historical policies that I describe in some length in the book.

FRANKEN: Mr. President, it occurred to me we should have played some Allman Brothers for ya, or something,

CARTER: [Chuckles] That's right. They raised me enough money to be elected president.

FRANKEN: Mr. President, as you say, *Our Endangered Values* is the first overtly political book that you've written of the twenty you've done. Let me ask you, on this issue of values, where have Democrats missed it? Or have they? I believe, listening to you, and then listening and thinking about the Bush administration and Ralph Reed and people like that, we should be able to win on values. [Applause]

CARTER: Well in the first place, we did win in the year 2000. And we shouldn't forget that. And secondly I think the 2004 election was highly skewed. The public opinion polls show that about 8 or 9 percent of Americans maintain that in the time of so-called war, they are inclined to support the incumbent president even if they disagree with his policies or his politics because he is the commander in chief. So I think the 2004 election was highly skewed by the fact that Americans were convinced that we were at war and our daily existence was threatened, and that we were being protected from the White House. And I think, that is an aberrational aspect that shaped the election in 2004. So it hasn't been a matter of values, it's been a matter of lack of ability to present our points of view accurately, and that's one of the reasons I wrote my book. I might add hastily though, that I don't consider *Our Endangered Values: America's Moral Crisis* to be a book about Democrats versus Republicans or liberals versus conservatives and so forth. What I consider to be of great concern to me is the radical changes that have been made in this administration compared to all previous administrations, and that would include George Bush Sr., Gerald Ford, Ronald Reagan, Dwight Eisenhower, and other Republican and Democratic presidents. These changes are of an unprecedented nature and have been made in some of what I consider to be our nation's basic moral values. One is peace. I happen to worship the Prince of Peace; I don't worship the Prince of Preemptive War. The president has announced that we have a new, unprecedented basic policy in our country of going to war with another country not just when our own security has been directly threatened, but if we don't like the leader of another country or we think that sometime in the near [or] distant future our country might be threatened. We have a right to bomb them, to launch missiles against them, to invade their country. That's a radical and very disturbing new basic moral value that's established as an American political policy.

> "I happen to worship the Prince of Peace;
> I don't worship the Prince of Preemptive War."

Another thing that concerns me very much is our almost total abandonment of being the nation that raises high the banner of human rights. We have abandoned the championship of human rights. It's inconceivable to me that we would now be arguing about whether America has the right to forgo all commitments to previous international agreements that we ourselves led in working out, to insist that our CIA and others, the military as well, has the right to torture prisoners who are helpless and held captive by us. As a matter of fact, as you know, the Second World War was permeated by horrible human rights violations, the most notable of which, of course, was Hitler's persecution of Jews in the Holocaust. These were helpless people who were tortured and executed when they were captives. And my own favorite uncle, Tom Gordy, was captured by the Japanese two weeks after Pearl Harbor, he was on the island of Guam, and he was tortured for four years. As a result of that the United States took the lead in going to Geneva and honing down in a very precise way a prohibition of torture of prisoners who were taken in a time of war. And now we have abandoned that.

Congratulations!

TOMMY NOE

for your service beyond the call of duty and steadfast dedication to the state of Ohio

AS DEMONSTRATED BY

your extraordinary community spirit, your work on behalf of the public trust, and your efforts to illegally influence the 2004 presidential election

YOU ARE HEREBY HONORED AS AIR AMERICA'S

CREEP of the WEEK

CREEP
of the
WEEK

LEFT COLLEGE TO PURSUE: Career as rare coin dealer

NUMBER OF NEW FELONY COUNTS NOE SET TO FACE IN COURT IN OCTOBER 2006: Fifty-three (including theft of more than $1 million in state money)

MOST INGENIOUS SCHEME SO FAR: Convinced Ohio Bureau of Workers' Compensation to invest in his high-risk rare coins fund. ($10 to $12 million in state assets is now missing.)

HOW NOE COPPED A PLEA IN A DIFFERENT CASE: By pleading "guilty" to charges of illegally funneling $45,000 to the 2004 Bush-Cheney reelection campaign.

WHAT HE ACTUALLY DID: Noe gave twenty-four people in Ohio $2,500 each for them to donate to the Bush-Cheney reelection committee. (The money individuals donate to a political candidate must be their own.)

WHAT FEDERAL PROSECUTORS HAVE CALLED NOE'S CRIME: The largest money-laundering scheme since the revision of federal campaign finance laws in 2002

WHAT ONE FEDERAL PROSECUTOR CALLED IT: "One of the most blatant and excessive criminal campaign finance schemes we have encountered"

WHAT HE GOT FROM THE ADMINISTRATION IN RETURN FOR HIS DONATIONS: Recognized as a "pioneer" by Bush-Cheney 2004, invited to Washington, DC, for inaugural festivities, and appointed to an influential committee at the US Mint.

WHY NOE SAYS HE PLED GUILTY TO THE CHARGES: "[To] spare my dear family and friends . . . further embarrassment."

WHERE NOE IS NOW: Out on $350,000 bail, living in Florida. (His sentencing is scheduled for September 2006.)

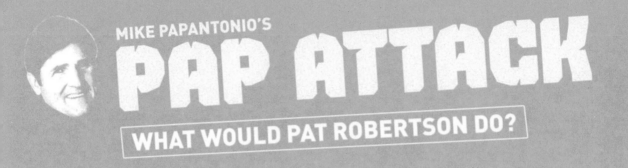

Karl Rove couldn't even wait for all the dead bodies in New Orleans to be counted before he started working out how to make the Katrina disaster into a platform for political paybacks.

He started by getting the Federal Emergency Management Agency (FEMA) to help raise money for Pat Robertson's 700 Club and its offshoot, Operation Blessing.

Now I have no reason to believe that ex-FEMA director (and intellectual giant) Michael Brown, a guy who was fired for incompetence from his previous job, was even aware of the jaded past of Operation Blessing.

In fact, it wouldn't be hard for me to believe that Brown, like Bush, doesn't read newspapers and didn't know that Pat Robertson is such a spooky lunatic that he had made the compassionate Christian plea to kill Venezuelan president Hugo Chávez just days before Chávez led the effort for international assistance in New Orleans. The truth is that the entire world understands that Pat Robertson is a dangerous *wingnut*, but Michael Brown, at the insistence of Karl Rove, pledged taxpayers' FEMA money to help bolster the Operation Blessing organization.

In 1990, Operation Blessing began to finance personal business ventures for Pat Robertson, and all those $20 love pledges that Robertson had been collecting for decades were ultimately, indirectly put to work to help Robertson start buying diamond mines in Zaire.

But in order to buy those diamond mines, Robertson had to be willing to make a devil's pact with Mobutu Sese Seko, who is best remembered for his many well-documented political murders in the former Zaire.

Robertson became close friends with Mobutu knowing full well that Mobutu had as much blood on his hands as Idi Amin did. In exchange for that friendship, Robertson was allowed to buy blood diamonds mined from the ground by Congo slaves at the direction of Mobutu.

But, hey, that's apparently fine with Robertson and his 700 Club executives—after all, what would Jesus do?

Then, in 1998 Robertson formed the offshore company Freedom Gold and sped off on his personal intercontinental jet to Liberia to cut a mining deal with Liberian dictator Charles Taylor. Taylor, you might remember, forced Liberia into a civil war, during which his dictatorial regime killed tens of thousands of Liberians, a charge for which he now sits awaiting trial for war crimes.

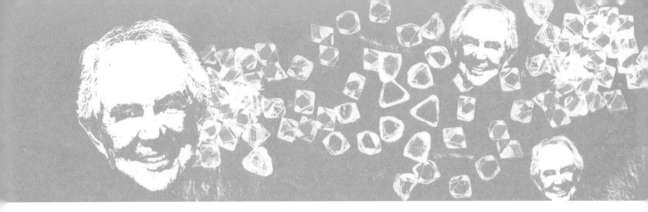

But Pat Robertson had a great friendship with Taylor. In fact, the friendship was so strong that Robertson gave this mass-murdering dictator a 10 percent partnership in his mining company.

The Bush presidency has been like a cash cow for Pat Robertson and his 700 Club. America's emerging evangelical right is, after all, the very heart of Rove's new Republican Party.

But Rove and Brown took this relationship to all new levels of ugliness when they filled the pockets of Robertson's personal cash machine known as Operation Blessing with FEMA money before the body count in New Orleans was even completed.

The Forgotten

Michael Stipe dropped by *The Majority Report* to talk about his efforts to help the people of New Orleans. It was February 10, 2006, almost a half year after Hurricane Katrina, and he had just released an EP, with the proceeds going directly to help an aid organization called Mercy Corps.

JANEANE GAROFALO: You've been working very hard with Katrina relief, but a lot of people have sort of forgotten about it.

MICHAEL STIPE: The fact is that five months later, I think a lot of people might think that there's been progress, that things are on the up-and-up, and people are slowly pulling their lives back together; I can tell you, having seen it firsthand, that's not the case.

GAROFALO: I was reading an article about the Florida families that were hit by severe hurricanes, I guess going on two years ago now, who are still in these little hovels that FEMA had set up for them in these terrible trailer parks. Isolated from everyone and everything, where the violence is escalating. You have families, a lot of unemployed families, and young people with absolutely nothing to do, no help, no anything. [They got] nothing that was promised to them from a socially responsive government, which this one is not. But as you may remember before the election, there was a photo op of George Bush with Jeb Bush handing out bottled water to the hurricane victims in Florida and then of course shortly after that, after the photos were taken, a lot of the people who were there just to show they were helping were pulled out of the communities.

SAM SEDER: Michael, tell us a little bit about the Mercy Corps and what they're doing.

STIPE: Mercy Corps is a well-known international aid organization that my band has worked with in the past. They go to disaster sites, and they do two things. They help with immediate aid and emergency aid in a situation like a tsunami or earthquake or in this case a hurricane. But then they also hook up community organizations with the people who live in the community that have been hit. In some cases, they bring direct money grants to them; in other cases, they help them, managerially, to reach a larger audience than they might have reached in the past. The difference between Mercy Corps and a lot of organizations that might go in and drop two tons of powdered milk and say our job is done here, is they go in and ask people what they need rather than telling them, and they listen, and then they respond very quickly. So they're doing great stuff in the Gulf region, and they're planning to be there for a while.

SEDER: Now what is it that people in New Orleans need and how are they getting in touch with the many people who are not in New Orleans anymore.

> "So many people have been displaced. The number that I've heard thrown around is a million and a half."

STIPE: So many people have been displaced. The number that I've heard thrown around is a million and a half. I know from living in Athens, Georgia, that our very small community of 100,000 people has a lot of evacuees. Atlanta has a huge number of people, and of course Texas and other parts of the south. A lot of people basically escaped and wherever they landed is where they are now. I think at Thanksgiving and at Christmas this past year, a lot of the media outlets found a good story or nice story and presented that, and it might have made people feel that things are okay and that people are okay down there, and that's really not the case. There might be a few exceptions, but I think that most of the people who were directly impacted by Katrina and then Rita, are still in pretty bad shape. You know in many cases they can't come back to New Orleans. There might be, from what I saw of the lower Ninth Ward, nothing left to come back to. It is as it was left. There are people's belongings [all around], their houses are three blocks away because they were pushed by the force of the water off their foundations, mashed into each other, and what trees are standing are dead from the water. It's really like Old Testament stuff.

> "Their houses are three blocks away because they were pushed by the force of the water off their foundations, mashed into each other, and what trees are standing are dead from the water. It's really like Old Testament stuff."

GAROFALO: We're inundated with stories and versions of stories that are the foundation myths that exist in our corporate media or in our society. But we rarely hear [about what you were saying about how] there is nothing to come back to. There are people that have been living their entire lives in refugee camps; internationally there's what's going on in Darfur; there are constantly situations that exist in our daily lives that we're never exposed to, that we don't get the information on, or we get little bits and pieces of it. It's very strange that you hear people who work in the news say we've got twenty-four hours to fill [and] that's why we're talking abut Aruba or James Frey and *A Million Little Pieces,* but that's not true. That's just lazy faux journalism.

STIPE: Well, it's entertainment, is what it is. They're probably very shrewd and very smart and have figured out that people don't want to see day after day what's going on in Darfur. Or it might come from a sense of helplessness. I mean maybe it's that life is hard enough and most people are struggling to get by in their own lives much less [want to] hear about horrible things that are happening in other places.

Record of Failure

On the Real hosts Chuck D and Gia'na Garel spoke with hip-hop legend DMC, formerly of Run-DMC, soon after Hurricane Katrina to talk about the disaster and how record companies have absented themselves from politics.

CHUCK D: Here we are in the land of bling-bling, place that invented the term, and all of a sudden Katrina comes about and really makes people think that there are other issues. All of a sudden there are cries for help and all of a sudden hip-hop decides to get a little serious.

DMC: Of course, I mean when you look at hip-hop, it gives a false illusion that everything is okay. When you look at the videos and hear the guys on records and hear the rappers they're like, "Everything is all good. I am putting my boys on and everything is all right, ya know what I am saying? I got money and everybody is eating, ya know what I am saying?" I sit there with my ten-year-old son and I say, "I don't know what they're sayin', because they're not sayin' nothing." When you look at hip-hoppers [like] Erik B & Rakim, they had the Rolls-Royces, they had the jewels, they had the custom-made suits. But everything outta Rakim's mouth was about life, not about how good he was living in the industry. He was talking about day-to-day, nine-to-five. Even if you go out to the club, when you get home in the morning, you wake up and you're dealing with the issues, you're dealing with economics, education, parents, preachers, teachers, police, religion. What bugged me out was when the hurricane happened, you really got to see how people are living. When you elect these politicians, they make all these promises to you in the beginning. But then, what do they do all year? This is not supposed to happen, and even if this happens—this is supposed to be America. Like Chuck said, we got the bling, we got millionaires, billionaires, zillionaires, trillionaires—a catastrophe like that happens in America, we are supposed to be able to fix it in a matter of seconds. I thought this was the place to be—we have everything, but maybe we don't.

> "When the hurricane happened, you really got to see how people are living."

CHUCK: Also New Orleans has been very good to all of us. A wealth of New Orleans music has influenced rock 'n' roll, rap 'n' roll, and everything. And for the first time you had the whole world watching. I was just over in Paris and London, and people there were surprised to find out that New Orleans was a black city.

DMC: Really? Shocking.

CHUCK: When [Public Enemy] would go to New Orleans and play stadiums and arenas—you had an 85 percent black audience in there.

DMC: And people got nervous. People were like, "Wow. Where did all those black people come from?" That is the illusion that they get. A lot of people was getting mad at Bush for various reasons, but what bugged me out was exactly what Kanye [West] said, [that George Bush doesn't care about black people]. I was thinking if New Orleans wasn't that black, Bush might have landed that plane and walked through that day, but he surveyed it first. He was really not working this. When that catastrophe happened, it showed that these people that are put in the places of power are really not doing their jobs. It was like a rock covering a bunch of ants and bugs. When you lift that rock up, you see all those bugs.

CHUCK: Run-DMC was the first group to come along with endorsement deals and be able to still hold a path. Kanye West says, "Bush doesn't care about black people." Two days ago Pepsi dropped his sponsorship. You can't do this because a person has a right to make a statement. Where is the outcry from the people, where is the support?

DMC: People was asking me, "What did you think about Kanye West's statements?"

GIA'NA GAREL: What did you think about that?

"When that catastrophe happened, it showed that these people that are put in the places of power are really not doing their job."

DMC: I said, "This is America. He has the right to say anything and everything that he feels he needs to say." And people, the real people, the people with the power should have supported him or at least said, "Okay, let's use this statement as a wake-up call. Let's really find out. Do these people really care about the poor or the blacks or the not-well-offs?"

CHUCK: What's up with the execs in the music business? Sometimes we can't blame artists. They got to get developed. But there should be record company presidents [who] at least say, "We want our artists, if they are going to sell to the people, to be about the people."

DMC: You can blame it on the artists, but also at the same time—it is the executives making all the money off the artists. They say money is power and communication is power. The executives should be guiding the artists, or at least encouraging them to do something and say something and be real. A lot of executives at the record companies just get outta the way and say, "It ain't us, it's them." Hold up, you all are making all this money off us. I have a rap where I say, "Our clothing, our music—hip-hop dictates what people wear, what they drive, how they walk, and how they talk. More powerful than any politician, preacher, or parent."

Straight Talk from the Sundance Kid

At the Take Back America Conference in Washington, DC, in June 2006, Robert Redford, a longtime environmental activist, spoke with Rachel Maddow about global warming and the grassroots efforts to do something about it.

RACHEL MADDOW: I've interviewed a lot of famous people in my radio career, politicians and musicians and artists and authors and actors, and you by far are eliciting the most hysteria from my friends and family. I wonder if you're hoping that the kind of fervor you inspire in people—and you really do—can be turned to your advantage in ending our dependence on foreign oil.

ROBERT REDFORD: Well, I mean, that's very flattering. Not to be falsely humble, but I don't know how I might translate to the public in terms of fervor. I would hope that there's a fervor about the issue. And I think one is building because I think finally after all these years, you're seeing something coming together that actually should have come together through leadership but it hasn't. There's never been a greater lack of leadership on an issue than there is now with this administration. So what's happening is, the best of America, which is a cross-section of grassroots groups . . . When you take labor and you take the environmental groups and you take religious leaders and you take military leaders and pull them all together around one issue, saying with one voice, "This is important, this has to be dealt with, we have to get off our dependence on oil, it's hurting our economy, it's hurting our national security, it's hurting our environment," in lieu of the voice that should have been coming from the top, you've got a pretty great thing. And that's why I'm here, in support of that.

> "There's never been a greater lack of leadership on an issue than there is now with this administration."

MADDOW: Does that make it a more sustainable movement, to not have a single charismatic leader identified with it? If it is a more grassroots, bottom-up-type movement, does that make it stronger?

REDFORD: I think so. I think there's nothing better, there's nothing more positively American, than grassroots movements. Because it really does represent the voice of America at large, rather than narrow voices that are coming from the top that are tied to special interests, as this administration has been.

MADDOW: Do you believe that global warming, that the issue of oil dependence, the links between our national security and our energy security—do you feel like those issues are ever going to be tough-guy American macho issues? I feel like stuff has to be a tough-guy issue in order to really cross over and really persuade people in the political field.

"There used to be a phrase 'Speak softly but carry a big stick'; now it's 'Speak loudly and carry a big stick.'"

REDFORD: Well, I think our culture has really gotten more into this whole tough-guy thing. I mean, there used to be a phrase "Speak softly but carry a big stick"; now it's "Speak loudly and carry a big stick." But however it's done, I think what's important is to tell the truth, which we just haven't gotten for a long time. I mean, my god, we're in a political environment where lying is almost a political asset rather than a shame. When it gets to that point, it's pretty hard to get the truth out. So I think when you take this group [of grass-roots organizations] and it has the coalition it does, you're going to have the truth coming out. I think that's what the people want. It's what they deserve, and I think that's what they're going to get. They haven't been getting it from their leadership, that's for sure.

THIS IS WORKING VERY WELL FOR THEM
A Timeline of the Hurricane Katrina Disaster Explaining How It Hugely Inconvenienced President Bush

If the federal nonresponse to Hurricane Katrina was not perfectly emblematic of the Bush administration's contempt for government, it would just be sad. Instead, it's a case study in the right-wing principles of small government. When something goes wrong on the domestic front—hey, s**t happens. The faith-based groups will clean up the mess. In the words of the bipartisan congressional committee assigned to investigate the catastrophe, "If 9/11 was a failure of imagination, then Katrina was a failure of initiative. It was a failure of leadership."

CAST OF CHARACTERS
George W. Bush, president
Michael Chertoff, Homeland Security secretary
John Wood, Chertoff's top deputy
Michael Brown, Federal Emergency Management Agency (FEMA) director
Marty Bahamonde, FEMA regional director
Max Mayfield, director of the National Hurricane Center
Haley Barbour, Mississippi governor
Kathleen Blanco, Louisiana governor
Ray Nagin, New Orleans mayor

All times listed are CDT.

Friday, August 26

After Hurricane Katrina strikes Florida, leaving eleven dead and a million without power, the National Hurricane Center predicts Katrina will become a Category 4 hurricane. Governor Kathleen Blanco declares a state of emergency in Louisiana.

Saturday, August 27

Governor Haley Barbour declares a state of emergency in Mississippi.

5am
Katrina upgraded to Category 3 hurricane. New Orleans Mayor Ray Nagin declares a state of emergency. Residents urged to evacuate. Traffic backs up for miles. More than 100,000 disadvantaged, elderly, and disabled people without cars do not leave at all.

"We want you to take this a little more seriously and start moving—right now, as a matter of fact." — *Mayor Nagin*

> "It's not like this was a surprise. We had in the advisories that the levee could be topped," Mayfield said.

Sunday, August 28

2am
Katrina upgraded to Category 4 hurricane.

7am
Katrina upgraded to Category 5 hurricane.

9:30am
Mayor Nagin issues first-ever mandatory evacuation of New Orleans, saying "We're facing the storm most of us have feared. This is going to be an unprecedented event."

Afternoon
President Bush, on vacation at his ranch in Crawford, Texas, is briefed via video conference by Max Mayfield, director of the National Hurricane Center. Also included on the conference are Michael Chertoff, Michael Brown, Governor Blanco, and other officials. Mayfield warns them of the potential disaster the storm could bring, including a storm surge capable of overtopping levees in New Orleans and winds strong enough to blow out windows of high-rise buildings. "We were briefing them way before landfall . . . It's not like this was a surprise," Dr. Mayfield said. "We had in the advisories that the levee could be topped."

4pm
National Weather Service issues a special hurricane warning that states, in the event of a Category 4 or 5 hit, "Most of the area will be uninhabitable for weeks, perhaps longer . . . At least one-half of well-constructed homes will have roof and wall failure. All gabled roofs will fail, leaving those homes severely damaged or destroyed . . . Power outages will last for weeks . . . Water shortages will make human suffering incredible by modern standards."

Late pm
Reports of water toppling over levees begin to come in. As many as 30,000 evacuees flee to the Superdome, where there is little more than thirty-six hours' worth of food.

Governor Blanco sends a letter to President Bush requesting aid. However, this request does not include the most immediate and necessary presence of thousands of National Guard to aid in search-and-rescue operations and maintain order. With almost 40 percent of Louisiana's National Guard on active duty in Iraq, the governor is left with only 4,000 members. Other governors, including New Mexico's Bill Richardson, offer to send troops.

On Sunday, Governor Blanco accepts Governor Richardson's offer of his state militia but doesn't make the formal request for approval to Washington's National Guard bureau until Tuesday. Washington then takes another two days to move.

Louisiana National Guard requests 700 buses from Federal Emergency Management Agency (FEMA) for evacuations. FEMA sends 100.

> "If you look at my lovely FEMA attire you'll really vomit," Brown e-mailed his staff.

Monday, August 29

7am
Katrina makes landfall as a Category 4 hurricane.

8am
"I've gotten reports this morning that there is already water coming over some of the levee systems. In the lower Ninth Ward, we've had one of our pumping stations stop operating, so we will have significant flooding, it is just a matter of how much." —*Mayor Nagin, to reporters*

8:51am
"If you look at my lovely FEMA attire you'll really vomit. I am a (sic) fashion god." —*Michael Brown, e-mail to staffers "Re: New Orleans update"*

11:13am
White House circulates an internal memo about levee breach that states "flooding is significant throughout the region and a levee in New Orleans has reportedly been breached, sending 6–8 feet of water throughout the ninth ward area of the city."

Morning
"This is a Category 5 hurricane, very similar to Hurricane Andrew in the maximum intensity, but there's a big big difference. This hurricane is much larger than Andrew ever was. I also want to make absolutely clear to everyone that the greatest potential for large loss of lives is still in the coastal areas from the storm surge." —*Max Mayfield*

President Bush flies to Arizona and shares birthday cake with Senator John McCain who is turning 69.

11am
In a memo to Chertoff, Brown describes Katrina as "this near catastrophic event" but otherwise omits any severe or urgent descriptions.

Late morning
Levee breaches.

11am
President Bush visits an Arizona resort to promote Medicare drug benefit.

8pm
Governor Blanco again requests help from Bush, pleading, "Mr. President, we need your help. We need everything you've got."

10:30pm – Midnight
Contrary to White House and FEMA's initial claims, news of the collapsed levee findings reach John Wood, Chertoff's top deputy, the White House, and the Homeland Security Operations Center. The administration fails to act on the report, and buses are not sent to help evacuate the city until Tuesday, when the flooding reaches the Superdome.

Tuesday, August 30

11:04am
The president gives a 35-minute speech defending his Iraq policies at the naval base in Coronado, California. The White House announces that the president is cutting his five-week August vacation short (by a day) to oversee the federal response effort for Hurricane Katrina. Afterward Bush clowns around with country singer Mark Willis's guitar.

(continued)

Midday

"It was midday Tuesday that I became aware of the fact that there was no possibility of plugging the gap and that essentially the lake was going to start to drain into the city."—*Michael Chertoff*

(The Bush administration had first learned of the levee breach on Monday morning, August 29th.)

"The looting is out of control. The French quarter has been attacked . . . We're using exhausted, scarce police to control looting when they should be used for search and rescue."—*New Orleans Council-woman Jackie Clarkson*

Evening

Conditions deteriorate further at the Superdome. One person jumps from a roof, committing suicide. The dome is closed to new evacuees. People begin to congregate at the nearby convention center. There are few or no supplies there. TV news show badly dehydrated and traumatized victims sitting next to rapidly decomposing bodies. FEMA had planned to have 360,000 ready-to-eat meals delivered to the city and fifteen trucks of water in advance of the storm. But only 40,000 meals and five trucks of water had arrived.

The USS Bataan, a 844-foot ship with hospital facilities, including six operating rooms and beds for 600 patients, sits offshore virtually unused.

Bush returns to Crawford for final night of vacation.

Wednesday, August 31

11:20am

FEMA staff tell Brown that people are dying at the Superdome. Later, Brown's press secretary e-mails the FEMA people on-site, that during his visit, Brown needs more time scheduled to eat at a restaurant, saying, "he needs much more that (sic) 20 or 30 minutes. We now have traffic to encounter to go to and from a location of his choise (sic), followed by wait service from the restaurant staff, eating, etc. thank you."

12:20pm
"Sir, I know that you know the situation is past critical. Here are some things you might not know. Hotels are kicking people out, thousands gathering in the streets with no food or water. Hundreds still being rescued from homes. The dying patients at the DMAT tent being medivac (sic). Estimates are many will die within hours . . ." —*FEMA staffer to Michael Brown in e-mail*

12:24pm
"Thanks for update. Anything specific I need to do or tweak?" —*Michael Brown, in e-mail back to staffer*

Early pm
National Guard troops arrive in Louisiana, Mississippi, Alabama, and Florida two days after they are requested.

4pm
President Bush, back at the White House, says FEMA has moved twenty-five search-and-rescue teams into the area. As for those stranded at the Superdome, "buses are on the way to take those people from New Orleans to Houston," the president promised. The *New York Times* noted "nothing about the president's demeanor . . .—which seemed casual to the point of carelessness—suggested that he understood the depth of the current crisis."

"Please roll up the sleeves of your shirt . . . all shirts. Even the President rolled his sleeves to just below the elbow . . . In this crisis and on TV you just need to look more hardworking . . ." a FEMA staffer e-mailed Brown.

8pm
"I must say, this storm is much much bigger than anyone expected." —*Michael Brown*

the federal government—today," Brown says to Ted Koppel. Koppel responds, "Don't you guys watch television? Don't you guys listen to the radio? Our reporters have been reporting on it for more than just today."

Thursday, September 1

Morning
"I don't think anybody anticipated the breach of the levees." —*President Bush to Diane Sawyer on* Good Morning America

"This is a national emergency. This is a national disgrace. FEMA has been here three days, yet there is no command and control. We can send massive amounts of aid to tsunami victims, but we can't bail out the city of New Orleans." —*Terry Ebbert, New Orleans homeland security director on* Fox News

2pm
"This is a desperate SOS. Right now we are out of resources at the convention center and don't anticipate enough buses. We need buses. Currently the convention center is unsanitary and unsafe, and we're running out of supplies." —*Mayor Nagin, in public plea for help*

"I've had no reports of unrest. If the connotation of the word *unrest* means that people are beginning to riot, or you know, they're banging on walls and screaming and hollering or burning tires or whatever. I've had no reports of that." —*Michael Brown*

"We just learned of the convention center—we being

Friday, September 2

President Bush makes his first visit to the disaster area and stops at Mobile, Alabama; Biloxi, Mississippi; and Louisiana. He is given a DVD of the week's newscasts to review on Air Force One because staffers thought Bush "needed to see the horrific reports coming out of New Orleans."

10:30am
"Brownie, you're doing a heck of a job." —*President Bush, at Alabama press conference*

"Now tell me the truth boys, is this kind of fun?" Tom DeLay asked.

The delivery of three tons of food to refugees is delayed because air traffic is halted for President Bush's visit.

Noon
Congress approves first $10.5 billion for immediate rescue-and-relief efforts. States as far away as Utah, West Virginia, Wyoming, and Michigan offer to accept refugees, who fill shelters in neighboring states. More than fifty nations pledge assistance.

Saturday, September 3

"Touring this critical site yesterday with the president, I saw what I believed to be a real and significant effort to get a handle on a major cause of this catastrophe. Flying over this critical spot again this morning, less than 24 hours later, it became apparent that yesterday we witnessed a hastily prepared stage set for a presidential photo opportunity; and the desperately needed resources we saw were this morning reduced to a single, lonely piece of equipment." —*Senator Mary Landrieu, Democrat from Louisiana*

9am
President Bush attempts to blame state and local officials by saying "the magnitude of responding to a crisis over a disaster area that is larger than

---

the size of Great Britain has created tremendous problems that have strained state and local capabilities. The result is that many of our citizens simply are not getting the help they need."

Sunday, September 4

10:17am
"Please roll up the sleeves of your shirt . . . all shirts. Even the President rolled his sleeves to just below the elbow.
   "In this crisis and on TV you just need to look more hardworking . . . ROLL UP THE SLEEVES!" —*FEMA staffer to Michael Brown via e-mail*

Monday, September 5

"What I'm hearing which is sort of scary is that they all want to stay in Texas. Everybody is so overwhelmed by the hospitality. And so many of the people in the arena here, you know, were underprivileged anyway so this [chuckles]—this is working very well for them." —*Former First Lady Barbara Bush, referring to evacuees at the Houston Astrodome*

Friday, September 9

"Now tell me the truth boys, is this kind of fun?" —*Former House Majority Leader Tom Delay, speaking to three evacuees at the Houston Astrodome*

Homeland Security Secretary Michael Chertoff recalls Brown to Washington, DC.

Monday, September 12

In Washington, DC, Brown announces his resignation from FEMA. The White House replaces him with R. David Paulison, a top agency official with disaster-recovery experience.

THEY SAID WHAT??!?!!

During a House debate distinguished by its staggering series of idiotic or mendacious remarks, Congressman Henry Hyde attempted to provide a moral argument against the use of embryonic stem cells in medical research. His assertion that embryos were not just potential human beings but were already actual human beings was followed by a rather disturbing declaration.

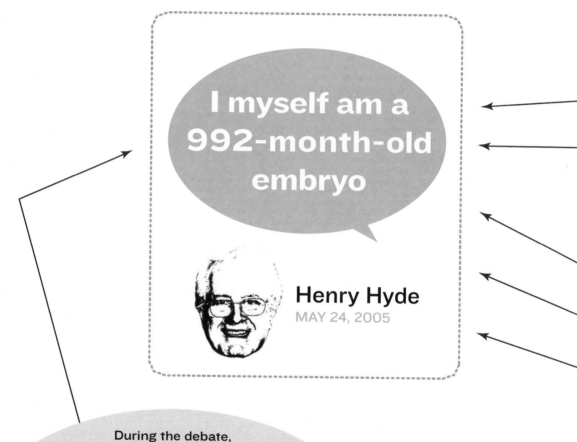

During the debate, House Republican leaders repeatedly sought to argue that embryonic stem-cell research could be replaced by research on adult and umbilical cord stem cells. Unfortunately, this position directly contradicted the official opinion of the National Institutes of Health—but hey, who cares about facts when you can just grandstand and spout fire and brimstone.

We've heard the expression "you're only as old as you feel," but don't you think you're carrying this a bit too far?

At least now we know why you described your extramarital affair when you were in your forties as a "youthful indiscretion." (Historical note: This youthful indiscretion was revealed by Salon.com when, as House manager for the impeachment of Bill Clinton, Hyde daily sought to tar and feather the president for his own youthful indiscretion, one that unfortunately occurred in the Oval Office.)

Uh, sir, if we may say so, the idea of you as a giant, 200-pound embryo is really creeping us out.

Actually, Hank, not to get technical on you, but an embryo is an embryo from the moment of fertilization through the first eight weeks of gestation. Then it becomes a fetus—and if it's aborted, it won't be paid for with Medicaid funds, thanks to the Hyde Amendment. Of course, we understand that science has no place in as distinguished a deliberative body as the US Congress. However, those of us in the reality-based community would like to point out that (1) no, you're not an embryo; (2) you haven't been one for more than a thousand months; and (3) we might forgive the misstatement—even find humor in it—if there weren't so many lives at stake. By standing in the way of stem-cell research, you have said very clearly that the United States no longer deserves to lead the world in scientific research and might as well throw in the towel on diseases like Parkinson's and Alzheimer's.

Didn't they have science class back when you were only, say, a 90-month-old embryo?

Congratulations!

RICK SANTORUM

for your extraordinary achievement

IN THE FIELDS OF

influence peddling, funneling GOP toadies into influential K Street jobs, securing loans from campaign contributors that regular voters can't get, and spending PAC money on Starbucks coffee

YOU ARE HEREBY HONORED AS AIR AMERICA'S

CREEP
of the
WEEK

CREEP
of the
WEEK

CLASSIC SANTORUM: In an April 2003 interview, Senator Santorum told a reporter from the AP: "In every society, the definition of marriage has not ever to my knowledge included homosexuality. That's not to pick on homosexuality. It's not, you know, man on child, man on dog, or whatever the case may be." *See? Classic.*

CLASSIC SANTORUM, PART II: Senator Santorum was chosen by the Republican Party to draft legislation that will tighten restrictions on lobbyists. And yet, according to the Federal Election Commission, Santorum has raised the most money of any senator from lobbyists for his 2006 reelection bid. *In Webster's dictionary, this is known as "irony." In Yiddish, it's called "chutzpah." And in French, it's known as "bulls**t."*

EYE ON THE PRIZE: According to Senator Santorum, "defending marriage" is the "ultimate homeland security." *Right! Because what terrorists hate most about America is our . . . weddings.*

SANTORUM MAKES A STAND: In a February 2006 op-ed piece for the *Philadelphia Inquirer*, Senator Santorum wrote: "If our ports are not protected, then, truthfully, neither are we." Strong words! And yet, on six separate occasions since 2003, Senator Santorum voted NO on measures that would allocate more money to fund US port security.

Eleven years ago, seven CEOs from America's tobacco industry stood up in front of Congress, raised their right hand, and began lying like convicts caught red-handed at a murder scene. Fortunately their own files, which they had mistakenly believed had been destroyed, bore witness to their atrocities.

The files showed that they had bribed congressmen and government regulators to keep quiet about the fact that, for decades, the tobacco industry's in-house scientists had been telling those CEOs that there was zero doubt in their minds that tobacco was killing millions of Americans by way of cancer, heart disease, emphysema, and about a half-dozen other fatal diseases. And it became clear that they were aware these dangers as early as the 1960s.

Those CEOs also kept secret the fact that there was a specific plan for targeting teenagers as young as fourteen years of age to hopelessly addict those children to tobacco products.

Memos and documents show that they knew kids were at their most impressionable between the ages of twelve and fifteen. They strategized that if they could hook them early, statistically, they could keep them for at least the next twenty-five years or until they died of cancer, whichever came first.

It is painfully difficult to read the in-house papers and the scientific data that these companies had in their possession for decades, while half a million people a year were dying from using their product.

The memos are almost surreal in their callousness. They demonstrate a near-psychopathic indifference toward human life, an arrogance that is almost unimaginable.

These apparently morally and spiritually bankrupt elitist white guys also cost American taxpayers more than $20 billion a year in health-care costs for smokers who could not quit no matter how hard they tried.

In other words, those seven CEOs who lied before Congress and never went to jail made profits on a par with Bush's Saudi oil princes and then you, as a taxpayer, got the bill for the medical mess left behind.

Bill Clinton sued those tobacco criminals for $130 billion to repay back the federal government. Then Attorney General John Ashcroft, in the dark of night, secretly reduced that $130 billion claim to a $10 billion claim—as a payback to contributors who had given Republicans more than $40 million in the last decade.

Here's where it really gets even uglier.

Karl Rove was the most senior political advisor and public relations consultant for tobacco giant Philip Morris from 1991 to 1997. Rove received hundreds of thousands of dollars in fees and then with President Bush, pushed tort reform in an effort to protect the tobacco industry from lawsuits.

Just when you believed that this Bush bunch couldn't possibly look any filthier than they do after their love affairs with Enron, Halliburton, Saudi Arabian oil princes, and a war based on lies, we learn that another of their longtime corporate lovers is the tobacco industry, a business they want to shower with a $120 billion political favor.

Keep it up, George. You won't be in office forever.

When the Lunatics Are in Charge of the Asylum

On June 15, 2006, Randi Rhodes played a clip from *The Daily Show,* which featured excerpts of a Bush news conference the day before during which the president had behaved in what can only be described as a disturbingly silly manner. Calling on a reporter named Roger, he joked, "Roger, Roger." He commented that another reporter had asked a "pretty good question for a substitute guy." And then he asked a reporter for the *Los Angeles Times,* a man who has a degenerative eye condition that has left him legally blind, and who must wear sunglasses, if he was going to ask his question while wearing his sunglasses. That might have been understandable if he hadn't made such an issue of it, clowning around and making the reporter, Peter Wallsten, the butt of several jokes. In fairness, the president later apologized to Wallsten, but the episode was disconcerting nonetheless; so disconcerting to Randi, in fact, that she called on Dr. Justin Frank, author of *Bush on the Couch: Inside the Mind of the President,* for an explanation.

RANDI RHODES: So why does the president act like a clown when dignity is called for? Does his entire staff show up in a tiny car? I mean this is the leader of the free world and I'm embarrassed, I'm embarrassed by this guy. So, what is wrong with the president?

DR. JUSTIN FRANK: Well, I think what is wrong with the president is that he feels extremely pleased with himself. I remember that he was like this in the second debate with Kerry; at one moment he answered a question right, and he was prancing around like it was an exam or a test, forgetting that he was president. And he slides very quickly into a kind of grandiose state that is bordering on being manic. So what happens is, when you're manic and very happy, you make puns, like he did with Roger Roger, you feel like you're invincible, you can have that swagger that he had in that particular press conference yesterday. It was like Mission Accomplished Redux. It was exactly the same thing that we've seen before with him, which is that when he's feeling good, everything is good, the whole world is good, and he can make fun of anybody he wants, and he doesn't really care about anything. And I think it is embarrassing, and I think there's discomfort with a president who's not only disrespectful, like you say, and who's immature, like you say, but also with a president who's actually out of control. And when he's really excited like that, he feels he can do whatever he wants. He's very hypomanic. And the people who are manic, and I've known many in my practice over the years, especially when they don't have their lithium on board, they really can be extremely funny for about two minutes, and then they become tiresome, and after you listen to them for a little while, they're not funny at all. But in his case, because he's the president and this is a serious matter, and they've just announced today that we've reached the 2,500 mark for US dead in Iraq, this is a serious matter in every way possible, and yet he can't contain himself. I watched the whole press conference, and after I knew I was going to be on your show, I actually went to whitehouse.gov and watched the whole thing again. And I was struck by how professional he was when he was reading his script. It was when he was off-script that he seemed to kind of come unglued and get a little bit manic, and then he would catch himself and be okay again.

"I think there's discomfort with a president who's not only disrespectful, like you say, and who's immature, like you say, but also with a president who's actually out of control."

RHODES: We've got, like, a manic fratboy in charge of the country.

FRANK: Exactly.

RHODES: It's so frightening to me because this is a time when you really need a strong resolve, a strong president; he chose this war, he inserted our kids into this war, and they won't change the strategy; all they'll do is make politics around the policy. And you watch Bush yesterday and you just expect that's he's going to grab one of the reporters in the corridor and give him a wedgie instead of showing the world how we're going to solve this horrible problem of opening up the gates of hell over there. And he's always doing this, making these verbal gaffes; it's like his mother, who said about the Katrina victims, "Oh, well, I think it's working out very well for them." Do they have some sort of a blunder gene?

FRANK: Well, this is not a blunder. This is much worse than that. This is an example of a person who says he puts the safety of America first, and who says he cares about Americans first, but what he doesn't say is that he puts the safety of himself first. One reporter actually asked that, "How come you only gave them a five-minute notice [when you visited Iraq]?" And he responded by saying "People want me to take care of myself, and Iraq is dangerous blah blah blah—"

RHODES: Yeah, "I'm a high-value target."

FRANK: That's right, "I'm a target." But what is clear is that for a person who was reeling in the polls and having a terrible time of it, to then go and have this moment of grandiose experience with the soldiers and with the premier of Iraq, it's like it tipped him over into a manic state. So that he comes back in a very kind of manic, grandiose state. And what comes out when you're manic is that you are indifferent in the way that his mother was indifferent to the Katrina victims, but it's much more frightening because I think that he's completely out of touch with his own grandiosity. And the press tried to talk about it a bit, but basically they are enabling him; they're in a chronic state of enabling an alcoholic because they are afraid to confront him, not only because they won't be invited back, but I think they're afraid to confront him because there's another part, and it applies to lots of us, that we don't want a president who's going to just collapse right in front of us. And I think people are afraid that if they confront him too much, he'll have a temper tantrum. Because when you confront a manic in a very clear, direct way, confront them in a steady, stable way, they really lose control and become enraged. And I think that people are afraid of that, partly because they want to save face for America, and partly because they're afraid for their own jobs, and partly because everybody depends on him being presidential.

> "This is an example of a person who says he puts the safety of America first and who says he cares about Americans first, but what he doesn't say is that he puts the safety of himself first."

RHODES: Wow. What did you make of, when he was in Iraq and he did the little visit with the troops who work inside the embassy, and he started to cry—did you see that?

FRANK: I didn't see it on TV, but I heard about it. He said he was very moved by being in there. But that's ugh, I just don't buy it. I mean, I think if there's any crying, it would be tears of joy and relief that he's still in charge and still president. His main goal has to do with staying in control. But when I watched the whole press conference, those were really moments where he was in a kind of manic, out-of-control state, but the rest of the time I thought he was hanging in there. What he does when he's very manic and when he's grandiose is, he repeats certain phrases over and over again, progrowth, democracy—

RHODES: Terrorists.

FRANK: Terrorists, all those things and this new term "together forward," operation together forward. I think that every time he has one moment of good news, he is ecstatic, and you see that in little kids and [as] you were saying with frat boys. They get an A on a test after they had an all-night drunk, and then they think, "Oh my God, this is just great, I'm on top of the world."

RHODES: So we've got a president whose policies, not his personality, but his policies are all about torture and killing and occupation of sovereign nations—

FRANK: Exactly!

RHODES: So, he behaves like Al Bundy during press conferences, but he's Ted Bundy when he formulates his policies.

FRANK: Yes. Exactly. I think that's a great image. Because what happens is, when he is forming policy, a lot of it is based on contempt. And one of the hallmarks of a person who is manic is the manic triad, or the three parts of a manic defense. One is called control, where you're in control of everything; two is contempt, where nobody really matters except you; and then there is triumph, where you feel like you are triumphant over everything and you can do whatever you want. And he shows all three of those things—control, contempt and triumph—in a way that you really see in untreated people in hospitals or occasionally when people are just sliding into a manic state.

RHODES: So, wait a minute, what I don't understand though is, if he is indeed manic, and he needs lithium, let's say, why don't they just give it to him?

FRANK: They will. I would think they give him things.

RHODES: You think that they are—

FRANK: A lot of times he seems a little bit drugged when he's on TV, and a little bit sedated. Some of the times I've seen him, he looks really sedated. I don't know what they give him, but they must give him something.

> "Some of the times I've seen him, he looks really sedated. I don't know what they give him, but they must give him something."

RHODES: I need sanity when I'm looking at this insane man.

FRANK: He is insane and the problem is that he makes everybody else, everybody watching him, start feeling these things ourselves because we wonder why nobody's saying anything and why the press doesn't say anything.

RHODES: Well, that's a good explanation—they just don't want to sacrifice American security by showing that the president's a lunatic.

FRANK: I think so. I really think so.

AIR AMERICA RADIO PSYCHO-POLITICAL PERSONALITY PROFILE EXAMINATION

Air America Radio hires only the most dedicated and passionate progressives. To ensure that its staff is made of the right stuff, AAR examines urine samples for traces of Lexapro, Paxil, Zoloft and other antidepressants (high-strung people tend to be more productive) and asks applicants to submit to a series of psychological tests. The famous Air America Radio written examination is designed to reveal latent political sympathies. Considered 37 percent effective at identifying hidden conservative traits in candidates, this test has been adopted as an industry standard by liberal media companies.

You never know who the person sitting next to you is capable of voting for until it's too late.

> **PART I: Pick the statement that best describes what you would do in each of the following circumstances.**

1. When someone gives me the finger on the highway, I . . .

   ○ Honk my horn, roll down my window, and make sure the offender sees the gun rack attached to my rear window.

   ○ Hate myself.

2. When a new family moves in next door, I . . .

   ○ Bake them a casserole and use the opportunity to peek inside their house.

   ○ Go through their garbage to make sure they recycle.

3. When a senior citizen stops me on the street at night and says he thinks he dropped his keys in the gutter, I . . .

   ○ Don't think twice and scour the area until we find them, even if it will make me late for a date that I set up on Nerve.com.

   ○ Keep walking. You never know where the perverts are.

4. If I were to notice a strange polyp underneath my arm in the mirror one morning, I would . . .

   ○ Immediately call my family doctor. The medical establishment works for me, even though I feel bad for the people who can't afford health care.

   ○ Immediately scour my home for chemicals or additives that may have caused this.

5. If my country were to launch a preemptive military strike against a tin-pot dictator, my reaction would be . . .

○ He got what's coming to him. Even if I would personally never volunteer to serve in the armed forces, I believe that you stand by the decisions of the Commander-in-Chief, especially in a time of war.

○ Panic.

> **PART II: Rate the following statements on a scale of I to IO in terms of their accuracy, I being a flat-out lie and IO being irrefutably true.**

_____ If you can't read an election ballot in English, sorry, *amigo*, you don't get to vote.

_____ I will be a millionaire one day even though I am washing dishes now. That's the American way.

_____ I would like television even more if there were more FCC regulations and fines for indecent programming.

_____ Public schools offer our children weird socialization.

_____ The most misunderstood character on *Hogan's Heroes* was Colonel Klink.

_____ I like Fox News, but wish they were more opinionated in their reporting. I don't just want facts… I also need to know how to interpret them.

_____ Yoga is a self-indulgent practice for rich people who are only concerned about their own pleasure and satisfaction.

_____ There should be an asterisk next to Barry Bonds' name in the record books.

_____ The Watergate scandal is an example of everything that's wrong in today's world—a power-crazy president destroying the Constitution.

_____ The Watergate scandal is an example of everything that's wrong in today's world—a liberal media that doesn't know its rightful place.

_____ Life begins at conception and ends at birth.

_____ This country would be a lot better off if businesses were allowed to regulate themselves.

_____ As the world's richest and most powerful nation, it is the United States' obligation to show less fortunate countries how to manage their internal affairs.

(continued)

PART 3: Multiple Choice

I. If I won the lottery, I would . . .

- ○ Give it all to survivors of the genocide in Darfur.
- ○ Buy a small arsenal and store it in my basement. Just in case.
- ○ Finance a series of assassinations and "black" operations to destabilize the mullahs' regime in Iran.
- ○ Invest heavily in stem-cell research in order to clone myself.

2. At public schools, students should learn . . .

- ○ At their own pace, always remembering that it is the joy of learning that matters, not the grades.
- ○ Intelligent Design, sexual abstinence, and the Bible.
- ○ That the world is controlled by a small cabal of wealthy Jews and their lackeys, the US government.
- ○ That God loves them no matter what.

3. The fundamental role of government is to . . .

- ○ Provide for the needy and protect every individual's rights.
- ○ Deliver the mail and that's about it.
- ○ Fight them over there so we don't have to fight them over here.
- ○ Clear out needless regulations that can only stunt the private accumulation of wealth.

4. Immigrants who sneak into America should . . .

- ○ Be given work, but only at depressed, illegally low wages.
- ○ Be given basic care, shelter, and a chance to earn a living with dignity.
- ○ Be applauded for their ingenuity at evading the border patrol.
- ○ Be given their own sitcom on Fox.

5. The biggest problem facing America today is . . .

- ○ A $7 trillion deficit.
- ○ Global warming.
- ○ Flag burning.
- ○ Gay marriage.

6. Digging for oil in the Arctic National Wildlife Refuge would mean . . .

- ○ The United States could reduce its dependence on foreign oil, at least for a minute or two.
- ○ Destroying thousands of acres of pristine coastal plains.
- ○ Jobs for thousands of Americans.
- ○ America might have to change its name someday to "The United States of ExxonMobil."

7. America needs to support Israel's right to exist because . . .

○ It is the only stable democracy in the Middle East

○ If we don't, the terrorists win.

○ Israel is a strategic ally in a dangerous part of the world . . . whose military is uniquely qualified to do our taxes.

○ Streisand calls the shots. And we do what she says.

8. *The New York Times* . . .

○ Was a decent newspaper when Judith Miller was working the "Weapons of Mass Destruction" story but has since lost all credibility.

○ Is a cushy haven for "major league a-holes" who are in love with their own opinions.

○ Is a cover operation for French intelligence.

○ Is decent entertainment, on par with *Friends* reruns but not as good as a new episode of *CSI*.

9. People who drive Hummers are . . .

○ Making global warming worse.

○ Supporting the jobs of US autoworkers.

○ Compensating for having a small penis.

○ Making it easy for the rest of us to spot the jerks on the highway.

10. When I see a transient on the street, I . . .

○ Think to myself, "There but for the grace of God, go I."

○ Wonder what happened in his life that made him so lazy.

○ Buy him a one-way bus ticket to Berkeley. If those hippies love the idea of a welfare state so much, they can deal with the problem.

○ Feel glad that my community's local faith-based initiative will soon show this unfortunate soul the way to a more righteous path.

11. The latest problems in the Middle East are . . .

○ Caused by the Zionist entity that subjects every living Arab to unbearable shame and suffering through the simple fact of its existence.

○ Is of no concern to me. Let them blow each other up.

○ Is a sign of the beginning of the apocalypse. Bring it on!

○ A hiccup on the way to a free Middle East. Nobody ever said change was easy!

12. If I was a software billionaire and had three adult children, I would . . .

○ Divide my estate equally among the three without regard for their abilities or career or lifestyle choices.

○ Set up a foundation in my name to fund cancer research. I don't believe in inherited wealth.

○ Give to each of my children according to his or her needs.

○ Leave it all to the one child who seems most likely to expand the business empire. Survival of the fittest, sweetheart!

Liberal Lexicon

A FIELD GUIDE TO THE LANGUAGE OF THE NORTH AMERICAN LIBERAL

CAMPAIGN FINANCE REFORM What everyone in Congress says they want . . . until they're up for reelection. See "Never gonna happen."

COMPASSIONATE CONSERVATIVE A person who reluctantly concedes that a lethal injection must be accompanied by a Coors Light.

FUNDAMENTALIST Someone who accepts the texts of sacred religious works as the literal word of God—for example, one who practices the commandment "Thou shalt not kill" by blowing up an abortion clinic.

GAY MARRIAGE A government-sanctioned lifetime-contract of misery, disappointment and frustration conservatives are battling to keep from homosexuals.

GUN CONTROL Two words that make Second Amendment advocates want to shoot free speech supporters.

HUMAN RIGHTS An endangered and archaic principle occasionally cited by the Bush administration to justify interventions in sovereign powers; usually cited patronizingly in conversation with Russian and Chinese leaders. Does not apply to gay U.S. citizens or to residents of the detainment camp at Guantanamo Bay, Cuba.

ILLEGAL IMMIGRANT Someone who sneaks into America in search of freedom and opportunity and discovers he would have had better access to health care... if only he had stayed at home.

INTELLIGENT DESIGN A creation theory that makes allowances for the divine intervention of God . . . but not for logic, science or fact.

THE LIBERAL MEDIA The source of all America's problems, due to stubborn insistence on reporting bad news about Iraq, Iran, North Korea, New Orleans, global warming, and other crises.

LOBBYING The answer 62 percent of congressmen give to the question, "Where do you see yourself in four years?"

MANDATE A delusional state in newly elected presidents, characterized by mania, grandiosity, and aggression. Frequently a compensation response for victories won by abnormally small or artificially enhanced margins. Cited as false justification for controversial legislation presented within first 100 days in office (e.g., Bush's "tax cuts for the rich" and Thomas Jefferson's proposal to ban Whigs from marrying).

MASSACHUSETTS LIBERAL Honorific applied to statesmen who have devoted their careers to bettering the prospects of all Americans; believed to originate in historical associations with Massachusetts as a center of patriotic valor. See formative events (the Stamp Act Congress, the First Continental Congress) and acts of civil disobedience (the Boston Massacre of 1770 and the Boston Tea Party of 1774). See also John Hancock, John Adams, and Sam Adams.

NATION BUILDING What George W. Bush insisted in 1999 he wouldn't do if elected president. Too bad he was talking about the United States.

NEOCONSERVATIVISM A discredited political ideology that thrives in certain hermetically sealed environments, like late-twentieth-century Washington, DC, think tanks and journals financed by a small group of industrial barons. Noted for belief that United States will reshape world by using force to win friends at gunpoint.

NONPARTISAN A mythical creature. Much like the chupacabra, Big Foot, and Republicans who will admit being friends of Jack Abramoff.

PRO-LIFE A word that fits more easily on an abortion clinic protest sign than: "Force women to carry to term babies they may not have planned for, may not want, or may not be able to take care of properly or that have been conceived as the result of incest or rape."

SPEAKING FEES On a politician's tax return, it's what bribes are referred to as.

STRAIGHT TALK EXPRESS The name of John McCain's 2000 campaign bus, named for his pledge to tell voters what he really thought about controversial issues and people, including the Reverend Jerry Falwell, whom he called "an agent of intolerance." Six years later, the same bus was *not* used to deliver McCain to Falwell's Liberty University, where he gave a commencement speech and appeared to begin the process of pandering to the fundamentalist voters he will need in 2008.

TALKING POINTS Carefully scripted disinformation widely distributed among conservative operatives and media lackeys so that politically motivated lies remain consistent and their true origins obscure. Through repetition and vehemence, talking points appear credible to lazy reporters and many citizens who obtain information via conservative-controlled media.

TAX-AND-SPEND What conservatives charge liberals do to America's wealthy to support America's poor. What liberals charge conservatives do to America's poor to fund the war in Iraq.

VALUES VOTER A member of the electorate said to vote in accordance with his or her moral values; plausible only if said values are wholly and entirely defined as anti-abortion, anti-gay rights and anti-separation of church and state.

VAST RIGHT-WING CONSPIRACY The extensive Republican cabal of shadowy millionaires and puppet masters who facilitate a steady stream of vitriol against all Democrats, particularly those perceived as electable, via the funding of right-wing pundits, radio hosts, analysts, and other opinion influencers.

Media Mind Game
Mark Riley

I had an epiphany about ten years ago when I was invited to a White House picnic for the press corps. I was there for about twenty minutes when it hit me that all these people (liberals and conservatives alike)—all the members of the press, all the politicians, all the lobbyists—are interrelated and they all depend on each other. To most of the country the term "inside the Beltway" is a kind of euphemism, but I saw it in action that day.

In Washington no one really has permanent friends or enemies because everyone is so interdependent. The politicians are dependent on the press for good coverage and the press is dependent on the politicians for access. If they can't get access, they've got nothing to report. And that's the danger of the corporatization of media. When I first started working in radio, for example, news wasn't a profit center. News was something you did because your license said you were required to operate in the public interest. Little by little, that's changed. The biggest impetus to making media "go corporate" was the Telecommunications Act of 1996. That allowed the consolidation of broadcast outlets that didn't exist before. The effect has been to make the need for access even more pronounced because there is more pressure to perform and make money. The object before was to fulfill an obligation that those stations and outlets felt they had to their listeners and viewers. The object now is the bottom line.

THE WHITE HOUSE PRESS CORPS'S VELVET ROPE

One of the great examples of the importance of access is the true story of Jeff Gannon. This guy managed to get a White House press pass through murky executive office ties and was therefore empowered to write stories that sounded authoritative for a conservative blog. I don't care if he was gay, straight, a prostitute or not, the only reason people cared was because he got access. And I think the real story is, Why did none of the members of the White House press corps say anything? I mean, they are a very tight group, but nobody said, "Who is this guy?" The reason was that it's like Studio 54—once you are in the door, nobody questions why you are there because "you're one of us."

The problem is, if you're not "one of us," you might lose a story to someone else and in the corporate-controlled media, if you lose the story you might lose your job. And in the big rush to get the story by having the most connections, you lose some reporting skills.

Don't get me wrong. There are still good reporters out there breaking news that might be harmful to their relationships in DC. But in the corporate media world, if it comes down to doing your job or maintaining access, access always wins.

So as reporters hustle to maintain their access the danger exists that they will lose their objectivity and become nothing more than an echo chamber or squawk box for the people they are covering. They are afraid that if they don't sound like a press release they will end up out of the loop.

LEAKY LIKE A FOX

The Bush administration played a similar game with the Valerie Plame leak. When they outed her as a CIA operative in retaliation for her husband, Joe Wilson, publicly disagreeing with the administration over Iraq, it was more then just petty revenge. These guys had a political objective: to make anyone who thought about crossing the administration about the run-up to the war in Iraq scared to death to open their yap. Remember, the people they leaked the information to were not inconsequential reporters. I may not always agree with Judith Miller and I may not think she is the best writer or reporter, but she wrote for the *New York Times*—she was not inconsequential, and neither is *Time*'s Matt Cooper. And what did these guys—Cheney or Libby or whomever—use to get them to take the bait? You guessed it, the carrot of access.

> "It's called the big lie. It's tell the lie, go for the strength! If your opponent is strong because he's been brave and morally righteous, then attack him on that level."
> —Jane Fonda
> on *The Al Franken Show*

What reporter is not going to be thrilled to get a call from one of these guys saying, "Hey, come have lunch with me at such and such a hotel?" So they go and they sit and they talk and they talk about a million things so the reporter doesn't know what the agenda is until later.

They also do it this way because it gives them a great defense later if they are accused of leaking.

"We talked about a lot of things," they say.

And that gives them plausible deniability and the ability to go even further, like, "I don't remember what exactly we talked about, there were so many topics."

Or "I thought the reporter told me about Valerie Plame."

I have to admit it's clever, but after a while it's transparent. It's the old saying, fool me once, shame on you; fool me twice, shame on me. The players in this little game aren't dolts. They know when they're being courted, and they know when they're being suborned.

THE INFOTAINMENT CULTURE

When I was growing up there were four TV channels. Now there are more than 400 plus a whole bunch of audio channels. What opinion makers understand is that the never-ending news cycle has changed the entire nature of both journalism and politics. The line between journalism and opinion has been thoroughly, thoroughly blurred and it's not going to get any better. When a majority of kids get their news from Jon Stewart (and I like Jon Stewart) and consider his show a news show, the lines have been blurred for them.

When you have Rush Limbaugh calling himself America's most trusted anchorman, the lines have been blurred. Anchorman? He's not an anchorman, but that's okay because most people don't know. They may know that he took some drugs that he shouldn't have, but they don't mind him being called an anchorman when in fact he is just a blowhard with an opinion—like me.

It's this blurring of the lines that makes it easier for people in the Bush administration to suborn legitimate journalists because all the magazines and newspapers and news channels are competing with one another, and they all want scoops that will sell.

You can be doing the greatest news broadcast in the Western world, full of great journalism from great reporters in far-flung parts of the globe, but if you lose money you're done. And you can be doing a b.s. newscast full of bias and full of improper advocacy, but if you are number one or number two in your time slot, you're going to stay on the air. That's because the way people perceive the original mandate that allowed the TV and radio stations to exist has changed.

THEY SAID WHAT??!?!!

In a Senate hearing, Senator Ted Stevens, Republican from Alaska, expressed his opposition to "net neutrality" legislation that aimed to protect consumers from rapacious fees for Internet service. The question remains why he felt qualified to speak on the subject. Oh, right, you don't need to be qualified to govern. Our bad.

What happens to your own personal Internet? . . . I just the other day got—an Internet was sent by my staff at 10 o'clock in the morning on Friday and I just got it yesterday.

The Internet is not something you just dump something on. It's not a truck. It's a series of tubes. And if you don't understand, those tubes can be filled and if they are filled, when you put your message in, it gets in line and it's going to be delayed by anyone that puts into that tube enormous amounts of material, enormous amounts of material.

Senator Ted Stevens
WEDNESDAY, JUNE 28, 2006

The scary thing is that Senator Stevens chairs the Senate Committee on Commerce, Science, and Transportation. That means he is a key decider about the future of the Internet. Cool!

Right, so all you knuckleheads out there stuffing your messages into tubes, knock it off. You're clogging Ted Stevens' own personal Internet.

Maybe, Senator, if you'd put your e-mails on that bridge to nowhere you demanded the taxpayers build in Alaska, they'd get to you faster.

No disrespect, but we thought that by now you would have asked for $200 million in pork to build an information superhighway in Alaska.

An historical aside: Senator Stevens has been a resolute supporter of drilling the Arctic National Wildlife Refuge and is the man behind Alaska's famous bridge to nowhere, a proposed $223 million project that would connect a city with 8,000 residents to an island with 50. When Congress contemplated diverting money for his bridge to help with relief for victims of Hurricane Katrina, Stevens had a conniption and threatened to quit his job as senator.

Thanks for clearing that up. Next time we need tech support, we're just going to call you. Could you explain to us how digital video-on-demand works?

Hey, Ted, can we use your personal Internet tubes to maybe e-mail some oil drilling equipment to Alaska? That way, as soon as we get the green light to drill in the Arctic National Wildlife Refuge, we'll be all set.

COMPASSIONATE NEPOTISM

When It Comes to the Republican Party, No Child Is Left Behind

Whether it's finding a cushy job in private industry for an underachieving son or helping a daughter explore the rewards of government service, Republicans are truly the Family Values folks. Never let inherited wealth or an innate sense of entitlement keep you down. If you've been looking for an incentive to work for a living, take heart in these success stories.

I Think I Can: Thirteen Success Stories o

Janet REHNQUIST*
*Daughter of Justice William Rehnquist

The odds were against her, but little Janet wouldn't let privilege stand in her way. Appointed Inspector General of the Health and Human Services Department in August 2001, she showed respect for her roots when she delayed an audit of Florida's pension fund as a favor to Jeb Bush, another victim of privilege. Three words for Janet: *Resolute, responsible, related.*

Eugene SCALIA*
*Son of US Supreme Court Justice Antonin Scalia

Help name the new president? The least we can do is take care of your son! While the Senate was away on recess, Geno Scalia was made Solicitor of the Dept. of Labor, even though he had crusaded against several worker-safety regulations. Now he's back in the bosom of DC law firm Gibson, Dunn, and Crutcher, who argued Bush v. Gore.

Michael FLEISCHER*
*Brother to former White House Press Secretary Ari Fleischer

What kind of qualifications does it take to get a big, important job rebuilding Iraq? As a New Jersey businessman, Mikey seemed destined for a dark, tragic life of ease before being appointed Deputy Director of Private Sector Development for the Coalition Provisional Authority in 2003. Mikey on Iraq: "The only paradigm they know is cronyism."

Philip PERRY*
*Vice President Dick Cheney's son-in-law

Even with the handicap of being married to Elizabeth Cheney, Philip refused to give up his dream of becoming General Counsel of t Department of Homeland Security. His previous posts Acting Associate Attorney General at the Department o Justice and general counsel to White House Office of Management and Budget shows how far he had to clim

Elizabeth CHENEY
*Daughter of Vice Presiden Dick Cheney

Probably the most heartwarming story on this page, Elizabeth was a little-known daughter of a current VP when, out of nowhere, she was picked by Condi Rice to be Principal Deputy Assistant Secretary of State for Near Eastern Affairs and Coordinator for Broader Middle East and North Africa Initiatives. An inspiration to all VP daughters.

Michael POWELL
*Former Secretary of Stat Colin Powell's son

Originally appointed to the FCC b Clinton, Michael was given the lea of the agency by Bush in January He resigned to set up "Camp Cron a nonprofit facility that helps directionless youth of influential politicians find a path to an even better life.

Thanks, sis!

Compassionate Nepotism

Deborah DANIELS*

*Former Budget Director Mitchell E. Daniels Jr.'s sister

Nominated for Assistant Attorney General in March 2001, Deborah never questioned her ability to rise to the top, despite the fact she was only a mere White House Budget Director's sister when others were the vice president's daughters. For girls like Deborah, failure is not an option. She just sold the rights to her heroic life story to Paramount, with Kirk Cameron attached to play her supportive brother, Mitchell.

Mark McCLELLAN*

*Former White House Secretary Scott McClellan's brother

Mark has come a *long way* from when he worked in his family's neighborhood stonewalling business. He has served on the President's Council of Economic Advisers, was commissioner of Food and Drugs and is now administrator for the Centers of Medicare & Medicaid Services. How did he get all of these gigs? We asked him, but Mark humbly insists he *"can't comment on an ongoing investigation."* His brother would be proud.

Bruce MEHLMAN*

*Brother of Republican National Committee chair and Bush's 2004 campaign manager, Ken Mehlman

When he wanted to become Assistant Secretary of Commerce for Technology Policy, Bruce knew the odds were stacked heavily in his favor. But that didn't stop him. A got-given, if not a go-getter, Bruce has a bright future ahead of him.

J. Strom THURMOND*

*Son of Republican Senator Strom Thurmond of SC

Despite being the white spawn of the famous segregator (as opposed to a secret black one), J. Strom still managed to to find success in a world that hates rich whites.

David BUNNING*

*Son of Sen. Jim Bunning, R-KY

The American Bar Association rated Bunning unqualified for the bench, but Bush nominated him to be Federal Judge for the Eastern District of Kentucky anyway. An inspirational TV film, *A Bench Too Far*, again starring Kirk Cameron, chronicled Bunning's battle to succeed despite his insurmountable connections.

Julie MYERS*

*Wife of the chief of staff of Homeland Security, niece of former Joint Chiefs of Staff chairman General Richard Myers

No experience? No problem! Another recess appointment, Julie—the girl with zero law enforcement know-how, is ICE, ICE baby in charge of US Immigration and Customs Enforcement.

Julie, you're doing a heck of a job!

George Herbert WALKER III*

*First cousin of the first George Bush

George Herbert Walker III faced many trying moments attempting to fit his entire name on job applications (a little-known problem for wealthy, connected individuals). He says it made him stronger.

I remember deciding to study news editing at the University of Florida back in 1975. One big factor in that decision was that at that time, I had huge respect for the profession of journalism and the people practicing it. I was inspired by great journalists like Upton Sinclair, who took monumental risks with his career by actually doing his job and demanding answers from government and from corporate America when those institutions engaged in a level of corruption that threatened to undermine the foundations of our democracy.

I also admired journalists like Edward R. Murrow, who, among his many other efforts, elbowed and pushed his way through the gauntlet of corporate media suits in order to expose and embarrass the dangerous, maniacal Republican senator Joe McCarthy, who would have trashed democracy for good had it not been for Murrow's astounding courage.

I recently introduced the *Washington Post*'s Bob Woodward to a crowd of about 500 people who had come to hear him talk about the role American journalists should play in preserving American democracy.

Halfway into Woodward's speech, I began to feel ashamed and embarrassed that I had been the one to introduce this onetime icon of investigative journalism.

The words coming out of his mouth were words I would expect from Judith Miller, Tim Russert, Wolf Blitzer, or Brian Williams.

It was painful to watch this man, whom I had once held in such high regard, shame himself by becoming an apologist for George Bush and Dick Cheney's disastrous administration.

In a period of about forty-five minutes, Woodward told us:

1) The invasion of Iraq was not based on intentional lies. Instead, he told the crowd with a straight face, his friend Dick Cheney actually believed Saddam Hussein was a military threat. And when he was put on the spot and reminded that Secretary of Defense Donald Rumsfeld, Cheney, and Rice, just a year before they invaded Iraq, had made public statements that Saddam was absolutely no threat, he moved with an almost weasel-like segue into the issue of:

2) Treason gate: If you listened carefully, you could actually hear our Cheney apologist leading you to believe that this whole nasty leak business was not as serious as it was being made out to be. That, golly, all that

name-dropping about CIA operative Valerie Plame was nothing more than normal chatter in the journalism business. I suppose he had to take that position since the facts that are now unfolding make it clear that Bob Woodward may be a bigger part of the scandal than he would like to be.

Woodward has not been a real journalist since about 1972, when he did his last great work picking a fight with a corrupt, dangerous American presidency.

Since the time of that important victory for investigative journalism, Woodward has been cozying up to the powerful and influential in exchange for access, in exchange for sources, in exchange for being one of the anointed insiders who only gets information when he plays the part of an organ grinder's trained monkey.

Woodward today would be as much of an embarrassment to Sinclair and Murrow as he was to me when I heard him tell that crowd that there was no war profiteering taking place in Iraq. Or when he tried to compare this buffoon president of his to President Harry Truman.

The scene was damn near as surreal as watching the reptile man exchange wedding vows with the bearded fat woman at a carnival freak show.

But these vows were between Woodward and Cheney. This was a marriage between unlimited, unfettered access for Woodward and whitewashed historical revisionism for Dick Cheney.

After all the smoke clears, Bob Woodward will still sell books that brag about how he is at the very top of the food chain when it comes to journalists' access to this disastrous president and his administration.

And it's doubtful that Woodward will ever feel much shame or regret as he cashes all those royalty checks, because the man I saw that day was too far gone.

But that position of honor and esteem that you once held, Mr. Woodward, where your talent and tenacity could have been compared with real investigative journalists like Upton Sinclair and Ed Murrow, well, I'm afraid you sold that position for a handful of royalty checks and access to a president who is just as much an embarrassment to most Americans as you are to the profession of journalism.

Just the Facts Please, Ed

On June 24, 2005, *The Al Franken Show* saw hosts Franken and Katherine Lanpher and guest Joe Conason confront author Edward Klein on factual errors, distortions, and the misleading claims made in his attack book about Senator Hillary Rodham Clinton, *The Truth about Hillary.*

AL FRANKEN: Thank you, Ed, for joining us.

EDWARD KLEIN: Thank you for having me, Al.

FRANKEN: Okay, would you call this book your best work?

KLEIN: I think this is the best book I've written, yes.

FRANKEN: Oh, good. Now I think I found a mistake.

KLEIN: Congratulations.

FRANKEN: Yeah, now do you have the book?

KLEIN: In front of me? No.

FRANKEN: Okay, but you wrote it, so you know the book.

KLEIN: I think so.

FRANKEN: Yeah. Okay, and on page 172—

KLEIN: Yes.

FRANKEN: This is a thing about [Senator Daniel Patrick] Pat Moynihan [Democrat from New York] not being able to say [Clinton's] name [during a press conference to announce her candidacy for the New York seat in the US Senate, from which Moynihan was retiring]. Now let me quote what you wrote: "'God, I almost forgot,' he said, with a mischievous grin." That's talking about Pat Moynihan, the late senator from New York whose seat Hillary took. "'I'm here to say that I hope she will go all the way, I mean to go all the way with her. I think she's going to win. I think it's going to be wonderful for New York.' For Moynihan, apparently, it was easier to say 'she' than 'Hillary.'" Now did you leave anything out there, in between the two sentences you quoted?

KLEIN: Are you reading from my book?

FRANKEN: Yes.

KLEIN: What's the title of my book? I don't think you mentioned it.

FRANKEN: *The Truth about Hillary.* Well, I did, I actually did mention it in the lead-in.

KLEIN: Well, in any case, let me answer your question. Pat addressed—as Joe Conason, who's sitting there with you can, I'm sure, attest—Pat addressed the assembled press and mentioned Hillary's name three times.

FRANKEN: Now did you leave anything out in between the two sentences that you quoted?

KLEIN: Not that I'm aware of.

FRANKEN: Well, you did. And what you said after you quote the two sentences from Moynihan was—

KLEIN: Were there ellipses between the two sentences?

FRANKEN: No.

KLEIN: No. No. So in other words, there's something that is missing.

FRANKEN: Yeah.

JOE CONASON: Al, why don't you read what Senator Moynihan really said as opposed to what's in Mr. Klein's book.

FRANKEN: Well, this is what Moynihan said, and this is how he got into it. He said, "Now I have the great pleasure to welcome Mrs. Clinton to the farm and turn over the microphone to our candidate. Before you do, before I do . . . Oh, my god, I almost forgot. Yesterday Hillary Clinton established an exploratory committee as regards to her candidacy for the Senate, United States Senate from New York, a seat which I will vacate in a year and a half." And then you pick up with "I'm here to say, I hope she will go all the way. I mean to go all the way with her. I think she's going to win. I think she's going to be wonderful for New York." So you leave out—

KLEIN: I left out an ellipsis.

CONASON: You did not.

FRANKEN: You didn't leave out an ellipsis. You deliberately left out the—

KLEIN: There's no—

CONASON: I know you don't have the book in front of you. How much would you like to bet there's no ellipsis on that page?

FRANKEN: No, he's saying that's what he left out.

KLEIN: That's what I'm saying, Joe.

CONASON: No, there's no ellipsis.

FRANKEN: No, he's saying he left it out.

KLEIN: I should have put in an ellipsis.

CONASON: Oh. And why would you have cut out the two references to her name and put in an ellipsis? That would have been equally dishonest.

FRANKEN: You know why? Because this is what I think, Ed, and you may take issue with this. I think you deliberately left it out because it would have hurt the sentence where you say, "For Moynihan it was easier to say 'she' than 'Hillary.'" I think that's why you left out the sentence that says "Hillary."

KLEIN: Well, I—

FRANKEN: Really, honestly now, could you address that?

KLEIN: I'd be happy to.

FRANKEN: Yeah.

KLEIN: First of all, I didn't know that you were a mind reader, that [you know] why I did something.

CONASON: Oh, you're not in a good position to say that—

KLEIN: No? Why not?

CONASON: —after writing this. Because you've read her mind over and over again, and I doubt you've ever met her.

KLEIN: Oh, really?

CONASON: Oh, there's quite a bit about what's in her mind in this book that you could have no possible way of knowing.

KLEIN: Well, let's start with the Moynihan—

CONASON: But answer this. If you had put in an ellipsis, wouldn't the purpose of that have been to deceive?

KLEIN: No, absolutely not. Joe, this is ridiculous. You know, we [both] know very well that the Moynihans had no use for Hillary.

CONASON: I happen not to agree with that.

KLEIN: You don't agree with that?

CONASON: But why—if that were true—why would you need to deceive the readers into thinking he hadn't mentioned her name?

FRANKEN: That's true, you know, usually when you have a good case, you don't have to deceive people.

CONASON: I mean, I'm not able to read Senator Moynihan's mind. He's gone. I know he had disagreements—

KLEIN: You didn't have to read his mind.

CONASON: —I know he had disagreements. But certainly if he really disliked her so much, why would you need to deceive the readers about what he actually said that day? Did you not look it up?

KLEIN: My intention in this book was not to deceive anybody.

CONASON: Why did you do that, then?

KLEIN: Well, I didn't do it intentionally, and if I left out some words, I'm sorry. That certainly was not my intention, and we know that when Pat finally came to do the endorsement, he didn't use her name.

CONASON: What?

FRANKEN: What? This is the endorsement!

CONASON: This is the endorsement. There's video, there's audio, it's on a transcript.

FRANKEN: Oh, come on, Ed! You can do better than that.

CONASON: He used her name. He used her name twice and you left it out.

FRANKEN: Just, just admit it that you did this, you left it out so you could make your point, which is "for Moynihan, apparently, it was easier to say 'she' than 'Hillary.'"

CONASON: I don't understand how you could write the sentence "It was easier to say 'she' than 'Hillary'" if you read the transcript where he mentioned her name twice.

FRANKEN: Three times. Anyway, Ed, we want to give you a chance to kind of respond, because you might get the feeling it's three against one, but I've got to tell you, Katherine just loves the book.

KLEIN: Well, that's good to know. Let me ask you a question, Joe.

CONASON: Sure.

KLEIN: I'm sorry. Al.

FRANKEN: Yeah?

KLEIN: Let me ask you a question.

FRANKEN: Sure.

KLEIN: When you asked me on this program and spoke to my publisher—

FRANKEN: Yes.

KLEIN: —did you tell them that Joe Conason was gonna be on?

FRANKEN: Yes!

KLEIN: You did? Well, nobody told me.

FRANKEN: Well, your publisher should have told you, because I couldn't have emphasized it more. The publisher's name, again, is Adrian—

KLEIN: Zackheim.

FRANKEN: Zackheim. No, no, no. I discussed that at great length.

KLEIN: Good. Well, he didn't discuss it with me, but in any case, in the interest of full disclosure, don't you think you should tell your audience where Joe has stood on this book—what he's done up to now?

CONASON: We talked about that last week.

KLEIN: Okay.

FRANKEN: We really did.

KLEIN: Fine. Fine.

FRANKEN: And, you know, he's not alone. There are critics of the book like John Podhoretz, and he's a conservative. He writes, "This is one of the most sordid volumes I've ever waded through. Thirty pages into it, I wanted to take a shower. Sixty pages into it I wanted to be decontaminated. And 200 pages into it, I wanted someone to drive stakes through my eyes so I wouldn't have to suffer through another word." Now this is a conservative.

CONASON: Yeah, I've gotten more positive mail from conservatives about my column about this book in the Observer than I have from right-wingers in a long time.

FRANKEN: But I'm sorry that Adrian didn't tell you, because you should have known that, but that's really your publisher's fault.

KLEIN: Okay.

FRANKEN: Okay?

KATHERINE LANPHER: [Let's] get back to the question of just how conscious you were of putting deception in the book.

KLEIN: I don't believe there is deception in the book—and if I've left out an ellipsis, I'm sorry. I certainly didn't intend to.

FRANKEN: Okay, let's talk about the FBI files that you talk about, which was called "Filegate." And you call it the "Purloined FBI Files," and you write about it on page thirty-nine.

KLEIN: [Affirming] Mm-hmm.

FRANKEN: And later, in a *Salon* interview, you said, "Like Nixon, Hillary has used FBI files against her enemies."

KLEIN: [Affirming] Mm-hmm.

FRANKEN: Now, you know that she was absolved of this by the Office of Independent Counsel.

KLEIN: Well, she may—

FRANKEN: I mean, shouldn't you have written about that? Shouldn't you have given that information to your readers?

KLEIN: It's still my belief and contention that Craig Livingstone was responsible for taking those files, and that he was operating under direct orders from Hillary.

CONASON: Do you know whose files those were? I mean, did you ever look at the names of the people whose files they were?

KLEIN: They were a lot of Republican activists—

CONASON: They were not, actually. Name one Republican activist whose file was taken. One.

KLEIN: I couldn't do that 'cause I—

CONASON: You couldn't! 'Cause you haven't looked at the names! Did you ever look at the names?

KLEIN: No, I haven't.

CONASON: Okay. You've never looked at the names, but you know they're a lot of Republican activists. How would you know that if you've never looked at the names?

KLEIN: I've read it in the *New York Times* and other publications.

CONASON: Oh, no, you didn't. You did not. Because the people whose names were on that list were former White House employees. Most of them were people like gardeners and janitors and people like that. I've looked at every name on that list.

KLEIN: Former White House employees in the previous Republican administration.

CONASON: Oh, no. James Carville's name was on that list! Why was his name on the list?

KLEIN: Many Republican officials [were] on that list, as well.

CONASON: There were?

KLEIN: Are you saying there weren't?

CONASON: No, I'm saying there were no Republican activists of any note on that list. If you look through that list, it's hundreds of names of people that you had never heard of and that the Republican Party had no significant connection to.

KLEIN: Okay—

CONASON: And the fact is that those names were taken by mistake, which is what the Office of Independent Counsel determined, and that Mrs. Clinton never used them for any purpose. And you know what, Ed? If you'd done any reporting, you would know that, but you didn't even look at the list.

KLEIN: No, I haven't seen the list. I—

CONASON: You didn't bother to look at the list!

KLEIN: Well, I didn't look at the list because I wasn't doing a book, Joe, on the list. That was one paragraph in a 300-page book, and it was a summary of what the charges were against her.

FRANKEN: But you've been going on interviews saying, "Like Nixon, Hillary has used FBI files against her enemies." Now, that's a very serious charge.

KLEIN: How about the, how about the, the, um, Internal Revenue Service—

CONASON: Don't change the subject, Ed.

FRANKEN: Oh, wait a minute. I asked you—

KLEIN: Why can't we talk about various organs of the government?

FRANKEN: Because I want you to answer one question at a time. "Like Nixon, Hillary has used FBI files against her enemies." I think that's a very, very serious charge. Would you characterize that as a serious charge?

KLEIN: I certainly would.

FRANKEN: Yeah.

KLEIN: And I would say that there are many publications that have said the exact same thing.

CONASON: Name one that has any—

KLEIN: The *New York Times*, for one.

FRANKEN: Said that, no, it never—

KLEIN: The *Washington Post*, for two.

FRANKEN: Baloney!

CONASON: The *New York Times*? You mean William Safire wrote that? Is that who you're talking about? 'Cause he had no evidence for it either.

KLEIN: Well, you think Safire's a congenital liar.

CONASON: I do. I've said it many times in print.

KLEIN: [Laughs]

CONASON: He said a lot of things about Hillary Clinton that were totally wrong. He predicted she would be indicted and said that he would "eat crow" if she wasn't. And she wasn't.

FRANKEN: And he did eat the crow, and I saw it. Okay. Let's turn to page 188 and Suha Arafat and that hug and Hillary's step-grandfather. Would you like to correct the record on that?

KLEIN: Yeah, one should have gone before the other, and that was a mistake.

FRANKEN: Okay, now what was the significance of that mistake, do you think?

KLEIN: Well, I think that Hillary was trying to position herself with the Jewish voters in New York. I think we can all agree on that.

CONASON: Unlike every other politician.

KLEIN: But she had a particular problem, which was that she was perceived by many Jewish voters, I think Mr. Conason even would admit to this, as not being sufficiently pro-Israeli.

FRANKEN: Well, but what you do is you try to draw a cause and effect.

KLEIN: I've said that that was, in fact, a chronological mistake. She discovered her grandfather, great-grandfather or grandfather, step-grandfather, had been partly Jewish, and then she went to the Middle East. That's true.

FRANKEN: Let me read you what you wrote. "At the end of Mrs. Arafat's speech, Hillary applauded enthusiastically, then gave Suha Arafat a big hug and kiss."

KLEIN: Is that true? Is that true, Joe?

FRANKEN: Let me read the thing and, and then you can respond. "The photo of the two women kissing, which played around the world, sowed serious doubts about Hillary in the mind of many Jewish voters. When Hillary realized that she had gotten herself in a jam with Jewish voters, she suddenly turned up a long-lost Jewish step-grandfather—an announcement that was dismissed by many."

CONASON: This is such sloppy work.

LANPHER: Hang on! I want Ed Klein to respond.

FRANKEN: What I'm saying is, Ed, the chronology there is there for a reason. You're saying that she suddenly discovered this because of the hug.

KLEIN: Yeah, well—this is a chronological mistake in the book, and I've admitted to it.

FRANKEN: Okay.

CONASON: Okay.

FRANKEN: Okay. How about the, ah, LAX thing? The haircut that supposedly held up traffic at LAX.

KLEIN: [Affirming] Mm-hmmm.

FRANKEN: Now you know that that's not true, right?

KLEIN: No, I don't know that's not true.

CONASON: Again because you didn't do any reporting. That story was debunked at the time that it came out twelve years ago. I mean, it's just astonishing to me.

KLEIN: What?

CONASON: How little work was put into this book in terms of trying to establish whether any of this stuff that you've written here is true!

KLEIN: So you're saying, Joe, that the president did not hold up traffic—

CONASON: Yeah.

KLEIN: —at LAX?

CONASON: Not only would I say that, but that's the established fact that's been reported after that story came out in the *St. Louis Post-Dispatch*. The FAA made it very clear that not one flight was held up as a result of that.

KLEIN: Well, Joe—

CONASON: And that was established a long time ago.

KLEIN: You and I are reading different newspapers, I think.

CONASON: No, it's not a matter of reading different newspapers; it's a matter of what the Federal Aviation Administration said about this incident. It was debunked at the time.

FRANKEN: Do you want to hear what the *St. Louis Post-Dispatch* said?

KLEIN: Well, if you'd like to read it—it's your show.

FRANKEN: Okay. The story was that planes were kept circling as President Bill Clinton had his hair clipped on Air Force One at Los Angeles Airport. This was 1993, not last month. "The haircut by Beverly Hills stylist Christophe became such a metaphor for perceived White House arrogance that the president himself felt compelled to apologize for reported flight delays. But the reports were wrong. According to FAA (Federal Aviation Administration) records obtained through the Freedom of Information Act, the haircut May 18th caused no significant delays of regular scheduled passenger flights, no circling planes, no traffic jams on runways. Commuter airlines that fly routes routinely confirmed that they had no record of delays," etc., etc., etc.

CONASON: What's peculiar to me is, you don't seem to care whether you get these things right or not.

KLEIN: What's peculiar to me, Mr. Conason, is that you're still stuck back in 1993 instead of 2005.

CONASON: No, you were writing about something that happened in 1993.

KLEIN: Yeah, but this book is about whether Hillary Clinton is qualified by virtue of her character to be president of the United States.

LANPHER: Well, let me ask you a question, Edward Klein, and that is, When you have so many errors accumulating, why should we take your interpretation seriously?

KLEIN: But I dispute that there are so many errors accumulating.

CONASON: Well, let's ask about another one. There's a woman you name in this book named Nancy Pietrafesa—

KLEIN: [Affirming] Mm-hmmm.

CONASON: Who you say was rumored to be Hillary's lesbian lover.

KLEIN: [Affirming] Mm-hmmm. That's true.

CONASON: Well, I don't know if it's true or not.

FRANKEN: That's true, that she was rumored?

KLEIN: There were rumors, yes.

CONASON: Yeah, those are great journalistic standards. But you misspell her name throughout the book, did you know that?

KLEIN: Well, do you know that three other authors have also misspelled her name?

CONASON: Yes, I figured that must have been because that's where you got it from.

KLEIN: Yeah, well, I certainly didn't get it from the other two who spelt it differently than I did. But her name appears in Gail Sheehy's book on Hillary.

CONASON: Is that where you got it?

KLEIN: It appears in Roger Morris's book.

CONASON: Right. Is that where you got it?

KLEIN: And it also appears in David Maraniss's book.

CONASON: So you're a terrible reporter, but a good stenographer.

KLEIN: All three of these writers spelt her name in three different ways. I'm sorry that I misspelled [her name]—that I used an *e* instead of an *a*.

CONASON: Well, let me ask you something. Did you try to find her so you could ask her about this rumor?

KLEIN: Of course I did!

CONASON: You did.

KLEIN: Of course!

FRANKEN: And you had trouble? Because the *New York Post* didn't seem to have trouble.

CONASON: Did you try with all the different spellings?

KLEIN: No. I, I—

CONASON: I guess not!

KLEIN: I tried to reach her, and in fact left messages for her.

CONASON: Really? Where?

KLEIN: Where she lives!

CONASON: Which is?

KLEIN: Listen, Joe, I don't have her address in front of me.

CONASON: You have no idea where she lives, and you're lying right now.

KLEIN: I'm not lying, Joe.

CONASON: Yeah, you are.

FRANKEN: I want to go back to something—Melanie Vermeer.

CONASON: Verveer.

KLEIN: Verveer.

FRANKEN: Yeah.

CONASON: Who is Melanie Verveer?

KLEIN: She was her chief of staff for a while.

CONASON: There is no person named Melanie Verveer. There's Melanne Verveer, who you refer to as "mannish looking," which she's not. But her name is Melanne, *m-e-l-a-n-n-e*. Now, since you don't know the first name of her chief of staff, why should anybody think that you know anything at all about Hillary Clinton?

FRANKEN: Well, I want to go to—

LANPHER: Please, let him respond!

KLEIN: I don't think the question is worth my responding.

CONASON: Because you don't know, right?

KLEIN: No.

CONASON: You didn't know her real name.

KLEIN: She was referred to as "Melanie" to me many, many times.

CONASON: [Laughs] By who?

LANPHER: Really?

KLEIN: I think that's how—

CONASON: No one calls her "Melanie."

KLEIN: Well, I think that's how a lot of people referred to her.

CONASON: Nobody calls her that.

FRANKEN: Now I know Melanne. I know her husband, and I have to take offense on calling her mannish, 'cause I know Melanne, and I think she's a good-lookin' woman. And let's say, Ed, someone referred to your wife in a book as "simian," say. Would you—by the way, I doubt your wife is simian looking. I'm sure that she's very beautiful, because you're a very manly looking man. You're very heterosexual looking, I must say. In the back of the book you look like you're in really good shape.

CONASON: I have this feeling that he's never seen Melanne Verveer, whose name he doesn't know. Have you ever seen her?

KLEIN: Ah, no, I have not.

CONASON: But she's mannish-looking to you? Even though you've never seen her?

KLEIN: She has been described to me that way, yes.

CONASON: Who described her to you that way?

KLEIN: Several people who knew her.

FRANKEN: Who knew her as "Melanie"?

KLEIN: Yes, and who called her "Melanie" to me.

CONASON: Well, maybe they knew someone else. This could all just be another case of terrible reporting or mistaken identity.

FRANKEN: There is a Melanie who used to be a male and is a professional tennis player.

CONASON: You know, Ed, you've been a reporter for a long time, or at least purporting to be a journalist. Isn't it true that the first thing you learn when you're starting to be a journalist is to spell the names right?

KLEIN: It's such a silly comment, Joe, that it's beneath—

CONASON: You got a lot of them wrong.

KLEIN: I got some of them wrong, but I, I'm sure you've misspelled names in your career.

CONASON: I try to correct them.

KLEIN: Well, I will try to correct these in my second edition, and third and fourth edition.

FRANKEN: Okay, let's go to your motivation. You said to *Salon*, "Isn't it Dr. Johnson who said that any writer who doesn't write for money is a fool? What I do for a living is write popular nonfiction, and the more popular it is, the more books sell, and the more money I make." Now, I write books too, and I just gotta tell you that that's not my motivation.

KLEIN: No, you're a political analyst. I'm not.

FRANKEN: Oh. Okay.

KLEIN: You're a political person. I'm a biographer.

FRANKEN: [Affirming] Mm-hmmm.

KLEIN: There's a difference.

FRANKEN: And do you think that maybe some of these conservatives who are reacting to the book, like Peggy Noonan and John Podhoretz and others, are reacting because it feels like you're just cashing out here?

KLEIN: No. I don't think that's the reason. If you'll let me, I'll answer that.

FRANKEN: Yeah, go ahead, go ahead.

KLEIN: I think there's a great deal of confusion on the part of the conservatives [about] how to deal with Hillary. They don't know whether to deal with her directly and in a forcible manner, because the last time they tried that with the Clintons during the whole Whitewater and impeachment imbroglio, they were criticized for going overboard and for being too extreme. And they felt they were burned by that experience. So they have recently been cozying up to her and debating how they're going to handle her. And I think this book, which I've written, is a book that could be written about a man. In other words, it takes Hillary Clinton seriously, and it treats her as I would have treated a male subject of a biography. And there's a great deal of concern on the part of conservatives that this is gonna turn her into a victim and make her stronger than ever. So that's the fundamental reason there's been this split among conservatives about this book.

FRANKEN: Well, Ed, I will say that John Podhoretz's headline on his thing was "Smear for Profit." So I think that he actually does believe that you did this for money. And actually you do say that that's why you write books. But I want to thank you for joining us, and I know that this couldn't have been fun, because it really was us ganging up on you, so I really appreciate it.

KLEIN: You're welcome.

Redemption Song

On *Politically Direct* in late July 2005, David Bender chatted with David Crosby and Graham Nash about music, politics, and political music.

DAVID BENDER: We love this country. So, let me start off with a threshold question. You've been doing this now for a very long time, you've been making music, and you've been out there making change. Is there a moment now where you're getting discouraged, where it feels like it's not paying off, it's not worth it anymore?

DAVID CROSBY: Sometimes. I balance it with having the knowledge that I felt like that in the middle of the Nixon era, too, when I was confronted with this war that kept going on forever, no matter what we did, and the country was even more polarized, if anything, than it is now, or at least as polarized as it is now. I sometimes thought then that I just couldn't take it anymore and that it was all headed so wrong and there were such venal, ignorant, shortsighted people running things that it would make me nuts.

BENDER: Don't they look good now though? Don't the Nixon boys look—

CROSBY: No, they just look more inept than these criminals. They're both a set of bad guys but they were less practiced at it than they are now. The kleptocracy, as I like to call it, now, are extremely good at covering their tracks and spinning and lying and doing their dirty deeds in the dark. They're very much better at it, particularly in avoiding media scrutiny.

BENDER: Graham, between the Nixon era and now, you became a citizen. Any regrets?

GRAHAM NASH: Not at all. This is still an incredible country, this is still the best country I've ever found to live in. No, I don't regret it at all. And thank God for the pendulum, because it will swing back, it will swing back and bite them in the ass.

> "I sometimes thought then that I just couldn't take it anymore. There were such venal, ignorant, shortsighted people running things that it would make me nuts."

BENDER: The two of you've just been in Europe, I think twice in the last year. What's the perception now of this country?

NASH: Well one of the things that you really realize is that we're so USA-centric here. We think that the entire universe revolves around New York City. And it doesn't. When you go over to Europe, they're thinking about what's happening in Barcelona, what's happening in Paris, what's happening in Madrid. They're thinking about their own world. They very rarely think about America, and when they do, they think we're stupid.

CROSBY: Yeah, we do have a very insular way of looking at stuff, very isolated, and they don't. If they're friendly, they look at you and go, "What were you thinking? How'd you get that chimpanzee in the White House?"

BENDER: Twice.

CROSBY: "What, what, what are you thinking?" And, then we tell them, we did *everything* we could, everything we could think of, everything that our friends could think of, to fight it, and they give us this sort of pitying look and a pat on the back.

> "The kleptocracy, as I like to call it, now, are extremely good at covering their tracks and spinning and lying and doing their dirty deeds in the dark."

BENDER: But that goes back to my original question. We've done everything we could.

NASH: No, we haven't.

CROSBY: No, we did everything we could *then*, we haven't done everything we could do.

BENDER: I've been doing this since Robert Kennedy's campaign, but the truth is, I've never seen a situation [with] all branches of government controlled by the Republicans. This president is getting everything he wants. He's about to get his first Supreme Court appointment. Aren't we seeing a sea change that was different than anything we saw in the Nixon and Reagan days?

NASH: Yeah, it's like David said before, they've been practicing for thirty-five years, since Nixon. They've been practicing this. And between the first George Bush and the second George Bush, the neocons have gotten a really strong hold on this country.

BENDER: In the late '60s and '70s, we took to the streets. We marched, we actually made a difference by drawing attention to an unjust war. There doesn't seem to be anything like that now; are people numb to it?

CROSBY: Well, you're dealing with a different media. At that point, the three main networks were all independent, they were owned by themselves; now all the networks, every major media outlet except this one, is owned by a major international corporation who makes money off of war.

BENDER: So, Graham, what gives you optimism?

NASH: Looking at my kids.

CROSBY: Me, too.

NASH: What can you do? I look at their faces, and you just have to keep fighting. You have to keep telling them what's going wrong. My kids are pretty aware, and even they start to get a little discouraged. We have to pull each other back on track, because it's not all futile, it's just a phase that we're going through, and I don't want to be overly simplistic but it will pass.

BENDER: David, you have a new song "They Want It All"—who wants it all?

> ## "We have to pull each other back on track, because it's not all futile, it's just a phase that we're going through, and I don't want to be overly simplistic but it will pass."

CROSBY: It's about corporate greed. It came about because I was watching a woman who had worked for Enron, who had been working there for forty years, or something like that, and she'd been saving up and had this vision, as did thousands of people, of "I'll finally get to the day when I can quit and I can have a little period of my life when I get to do what I want and I'll be safe and secure and I won't be out on the street." And then it was gone. They stole it. And here is Ken Lay, running the company, claming he knows nothing about it, which is an obvious lie, and the reason he wasn't getting prosecuted and nothing was getting done was that Ken Lay was the president's buddy.

BENDER: "Kenny boy."

CROSBY: Kenny boy. The president did his campaign in Ken Lay's plane. And he was the single largest contributor on record to George Bush's campaign, and why weren't they getting prosecuted? Gosh, I can't think why. And it seemed such a classic and egregious example of wrongness, you know, and of corruption, it really pissed me off.

BENDER: I've seen you guys do it in concert; it always gets an amazing response. People are looking for some outlet to say, "We've had enough of this."

CROSBY: Well, they don't like it. They don't like the government being for sale. They really don't.

NASH: I can sense looking out at audiences and playing to them, that there's a sea change coming, I can really feel it. It looks pretty bleak right now, but I'm beginning to hear talk of impeachment, I'm beginning to hear talk of unraveling this incredible knot that these people have constructed around themselves.

BENDER: The numbers are bearing you out.

CROSBY: Yeah, didn't he just lose another four points or something?

BENDER: He's down to the low forties and it's touching thirty plus.

CROSBY: Well, you know, that's what happened in the Vietnam time, too. After a certain while, even the farmer in Iowa doesn't want his kid to go to war. And Americans are not dumb, you know, most of them are able to tell they're being lied to.

BENDER: Does it feel different when you're touring in red states than blue states?

CROSBY: Not really. We pull the kind of audience that are fairly aware in any state.

BENDER: Graham, what do you think?

NASH: I agree with David. The people that come to see us, it's almost like preaching to the choir because they believe in what we've stood for all our lives.

BENDER: But you're also getting young people.

NASH: Absolutely, we were watching a ten-year-old kid singing the words to several of the songs, one of them being "Don't Dig Here," which is amazing.

> "I can sense looking out at audiences and playing to them that there's a sea change coming; I can really feel it."

BENDER: Before I let you guys go, politically, who do you like? Who's out there on the horizon?

NASH: Barack Obama.

BENDER: Barack Obama, senator from Illinois.

CROSBY: He was very impressive. The guy's got a real brain, and he does seem to have some cojones; he's a pretty brave guy. I've been dealing for a long time with the one Republican I have any respect for, and that is John McCain. And I do have respect for him because he did try to fight the good fight on campaign financing reform. But I don't think there's very many new people coming up into politics that are worth a damn because you know, politics isn't worth a damn as it's practiced in this country.

Quick Profits, Dead Patients

Mike Papantonio

I remember telling my wife, Terri, that in 2004, I would be spending more time cohosting *Ring of Fire* than I would trying cases as a products liability lawyer. It appeared to me that she was fine with that because I think she believed that taking a break from trying cases against some of America's most corrupt corporations would soften some of my cynical edges, at least for a while. In the back of her mind, I'm sure she was hoping I would be hosting one of those warm and fuzzy feel-good shows where deserving families get the keys to a new home or where really obese people get paid a million dollars to lose a couple of hundred pounds. Frankly, I'd probably enjoy hosting a show like that.

The truth is, the kinds of stories Bobby Kennedy and I cover on *Ring of Fire* cannot possibly be packaged with happy endings. If we do our job, most of our stories are simply a reflection of the new Dark Age that has been visited on America since the day "The Shrub" and his Republican Congress rolled into town. And few stories better exemplify this new darkness than the tale of pharmaceutical companies.

NOT NECESSARILY THE NEWS

The pharmaceutical giant Merck is actually better than most of the major networks at producing television news stories. In fact, Merck, just like most of the other pharmaceutical giants, feeds the major television networks what has become known in the industry as *fake news* in the form of prepackaged video news releases, referred to as *VNRs*. What the big pharmaceutical companies really love about the VNRs they create is that they really don't have to tell the whole story about any of the killer dangers that are usually attached to the normal use of some of their biggest moneymaking medicine.

The typical pharmaceutical VNR usually surfaces for the first time during the launch period of a new blockbuster drug that is supposed to help drug-dependent Americans sleep better, not be so sad, not be so angry, lose weight, or make aches and pains disappear. But we usually can expect the next rounds of VNRs to surface after the drug begins to kill and cripple those same consumers by the dozens.

For example, three years ago when Merck finally had to admit that their blockbuster anti-inflammatory drug, Vioxx (rofecoxib), could kill users by way of a brain hemorrhage, a blood clot, or a heart attack, the VNR that Merck released was damn near black humor.

It was a prepackaged puff piece that explained how a three-year study showed that Vioxx was gentle on the stomach. But what that sales-pitch VNR failed to mention was that that same three-year study concluded that Vioxx was almost five times as likely to kill consumers by way of a heart attack than Vioxx's competitors.

Merck intentionally left out any mention of the many ways Vioxx could kill a patient who probably was only trying to make a few aches and pains disappear.

And since news journalism is dead or dying within most of America's television outlets, that Vioxx video news release played to millions of Americans as if it were actually a news story that had been researched, written, and produced by the news department of the television stations where it aired.

It is, after all, a lot to expect for a conglomerate TV organization to actually ask tough questions of a pharmaceutical advertiser that ponies up millions of dollars every year for feel-good advertising about their drug de jour.

American consumers have little or no chance of actually knowing what to expect from the pills they pop into their mouths these days because the overwhelming majority of the time, the real facts—the real dangers—are hidden from them. Not by mistake, not by simple innocent oversight, but by design.

A PRESCRIPTION FOR TROUBLE

Part of the problem is that most doctors who prescribe Big Pharma's high-profit witches' brews truly believe they are safe because, just like consumers, those doctors can't imagine that the medicine business would operate in any way but safely and responsibly. Focus group after focus group has pretty much shown that Americans want to believe that Big Pharma would never put profits ahead of safety.

In spite of those beliefs held by doctors and their patients, history shows that consumers have more than a few reasons to be scared as hell of a drug industry that has lost its moral compass.

The reasons consumers should be terrified are not complicated. The analysis begins exactly where you would expect. It begins at the top with the drug industry's new short-term CEO mentality. Two decades ago, it was typical for most CEOs of huge drug companies to have a long-term mentality in the way they shepherded the growth of their companies.

Steady, predictable sustainability was the growth model that was typically in place. A frenzied rush to the market with a risky, unproven, and poorly tested potential blockbuster drug simply was not the way the drug industry used to do business. Old-school CEOs created an environment that built their companies the old-fashioned way, with caution and with a sensible desire to prove safety in clinical trials before a drug was pitched to doctors.

Today, there exists a siege approach, a short-term, quick-profit, bigger-bottom-line mentality that CEOs buy into because their multimillion-dollar compensation packages depend on quick success and a lot of it.

CEOs are forced to justify their private jets and posh vacation homes paid for by stockholders. And worse yet, unless every 10-K that a drug company CEO signs his name to shows an increase in line with Wall Street expectations, he is branded as a pathetic underperformer. That's not to say he gets paid any less— it's really more of a dent to his ego. He still is going to be paid by a ratio of 500 to 1 compared to the company's more expendable, disposable worker.

WHEN THE WATCHDOG'S AWAY . . .

But then, you might ask yourself, isn't the FDA still going to be there to oversee the reckless abuses that are such a routine part of the new quick-profit mentality of drug company CEOs?

Well …no, not exactly, because George Bush has successfully created an agency running food and drug oversight that is just as dysfunctional as everything else "The Shrub" has touched.

We used to be able to say that our biggest problem was that the big drug makers could manipulate the FDA because the drug industry has more money, more scientists and researchers, and more political influence than the FDA. But ever since "The Shrub" moved to Washington, the threat is a little more direct because Bush, by way of Karl Rove, immediately began paying back the drug industry for that $60 million they delivered to Republican political candidates over the last six years.

So, today we have a Bush-restructured FDA that is mostly made up of doctors, scientists, and researchers who have direct financial relationships with the world's biggest drug companies. The more those drug companies make, the more money those doctors, scientists, and researchers make. In fact, Bush's very first appointment to the FDA was a man by the name of Daniel Troy, who built his unimpressive career as a lawyer defending Pfizer every time that drug monster killed a few hundred consumers.

Troy was the architect of an FDA policy paper that attempted to give complete immunity to any drug manufacturer who was sued by a consumer or his or her estate who was killed or crippled by a defective drug, as long as the FDA had given that company permission to sell that drug. The obvious problem there is that in this corporate-dominated climate, hardly any drug fails to get FDA approval because money, power, and politics always deliver for Big Pharma.

So, the bad news for consumers is that if they believe that Bush's new FDA is watching their back, they are pretty much delusional.

Bush has deconstructed the FDA the same way he has deconstructed virtually every governmental entity that used to give a damn about the health, safety, and welfare of American consumers, and that has been a huge profit bonanza for the drug industry.

DOCTORING THE FACTS

But again, how about the doctor who prescribes that drug that their patient saw on some slick VNR? It's unlikely that the patient understands that the drug was probably rushed to market in a frenzy by a bottom-line-driven CEO. The patient has no way of knowing how inadequate clinical testing really was. And that patient has no understanding about just what a corporate lapdog the FDA has become. But surely that doctor who has been to four years of college and five years of medical school will know if that new wonder drug will help a patient sleep better or lose weight without killing them in the process.

Well . . . not exactly because most of the time when a pharmaceutical company has something to hide about the dangers of a drug, they are as good at hiding it from doctors as they are from patients.

A perfect example of how drug companies keep the truth from doctors is Merck's best-selling painkiller. A review of the court records that have been uncovered in the Vioxx litigation show a very specific, well-engineered plan to keep doctors completely in the dark about how ridiculously dangerous that product could be for users. In order for the typical prescribing doctor to have discovered the hidden dangers of Vioxx, she would have needed special training as an epidemiologist or, in the alternative, she would have needed direct access to all the terrifying clinical data that was squirreled away in the file cabinets at Merck. Most of the scariest evidence about the dangers of Vioxx never even surfaced until Merck was sued. How could a doctor possibly know something that was specifically hidden from her by the manufacturer? But it's important to understand that the Merck cover-up is not unique.

The truth about Redux (dexfenfluramine) and Pondimin (fenfluramine) was so well hidden that most doctors could have never figured it out, no matter how diligent and focused they were. These were drugs that killed and crippled people wanting to lose a little weight. Just like Vioxx, they weren't drugs that were going to save anyone's life. The cover-up in that drugs-gone-crazy story was put together in such a way that neither doctors nor patients could have possibly known that these drugs would shut down and destroy heart valves that keep blood properly flowing through the human body.

Here were weight-reduction drugs that never actually worked to sustain weight loss, but they represented cash bonanzas for their manufacturers. But more important, all the time consumers were popping these Madison Avenue–driven "wonder drugs," the in-house scientists and marketers had a secret. Their secret was that they knew exactly the physiological mechanics of how these drugs caused human heart valves to become useless, diseased tissue that would kill and cripple consumers. In the end, hundreds of consumers died agonizing deaths and a few CEOs pocketed millions in bonuses for ignoring the obvious.

And there is, of course, the story about Rezulin (troglitazone). The sales spin on Rezulin was that it would improve the lives of diabetics. The part of the story that Pfizer failed to mention was that Rezulin would turn the human liver into useless mush. All their in-house data told them that. In fact, the data were so clear that dozens of countries around the world prohibited the sale of Rezulin to their consumers. But Pfizer convinced our FDA that although the drug could not be sold in countries like Jamaica, Chile, and Croatia, it was still good enough for Americans. The Rezulin story is an elegant cover-up by Pfizer in which doctors who believed they were appropriately treating their patients for diabetes were actually slowly killing those patients. It was death by liver failure that killed dozens of patients in that high-stakes game of hiding the truth from prescribing doctors.

Just as the story goes with most of these blockbuster drugs, Rezulin was not a necessary drug at all. There were alternatives that did not kill patients. But dozens of patients died in that big-profit-drug story. Pfizer Incorporated made about a billion dollars, and Lodewijk J.R. de Vink cashed in on more than $150 million worth of stock options after serving as CEO for only two years.

Mainstream media with very few exceptions barely understood the story well enough to do any intelligent reporting on this drug tragedy, but then again, that has become the norm in investigative reporting.

No one at the FDA lost their job for an almost criminal level of incompetence. No one went to jail. And the lawyers who uncovered the hideous scheme by Pfizer were accused of being selfish ambulance chasers who interfered with the future development of lifesaving drugs because they had the audacity to initiate a lawsuit against a drug manufacturer that was ruthlessly exploiting both consumers and doctors.

So, like most of our stories, this one does not have one of those endings where the folks at *Extreme Makeover Home Edition* make us all feel good when they hand a deserving family the keys to a new home. No, this is a story where, in the end, patients are either dead or crippled. There is no happy ending where drug-industry executives and the FDA's willing participants go to jail for what is, most of the time, manslaughter at the very least. Instead, CEOs get to keep their multiple millions of dollars in blood money, and they will no doubt share some of it with unprincipled, piggish, probably Republican politicians looking to fatten up their war chests for the next political race.

Who's to Plame?

On July 15, 2005, the ranking Democrat on the House Judiciary Committee, John Conyers, called in to *The Randi Rhodes Show* to talk about a letter he sent to the president, demanding answers in the Valerie Plame affair.

RANDI RHODES: I want you to explain to people what this letter that was signed by 91 members of Congress asked of the president.

JOHN CONYERS: Dear Mr. President, we urge you to require that Karl Rove either come forward immediately to explain his role in the Valerie Plame matter or to resign from your administration. One or the other.

RHODES: You know yesterday in the Senate, the Democrats brought a bill to the floor, saying that you can't do this [leak a CIA operative's name] and if you do, you have to give up your security clearance. And they voted right along party lines—the Republicans said no, even if you out a CIA operative, you shouldn't have to give up your security clearance. What is wrong with this party?

CONYERS: What we have to do is really urge and persuade the American people to put an end to all of this revisionist examination of the truth that's going on here. That is allowing people to say anything they want, to backtrack, to repudiate the obvious facts. I mean it's not just with Rove. But it's with the president [too].

"We want the American people to know now. They've got to wake up, they've got to demand that the truth be told, and they've got to take action where the truth is not told."

RHODES: And every time somebody lies and gets caught, somebody else has to be smeared. I don't know that that's illegal, but I will tell you that it's disgraceful, and that there is absolutely no honor in it. There's no character, there's no integrity in this White House, and the fact that they lied to the American people about issues of nuclear weapons, aluminum tubes, uranium, and yellow cake . . .

CONYERS: Weapons of mass destruction.

RHODES: Weapons of mass destruction, stockpiles of sarin gas, and unmanned aerial vehicles that can get here and spray us. It's institutional corruption. It's all about money and oil.

CONYERS: Exactly.

RHODES: This is big stuff. It's huge. This is not a little thing anymore. Every single person who returned to the administration from either being a secretary of defense previously or from being a CEO of Halliburton previously or [from] being somebody who was involved in Iran-Contra [which was the] same thing, selling TOW missiles to Iran, laundering the money thru Saudi Arabia, and then funding an illegal war. It's the same players, it's the same killers, it's the same death-squad leaders; let's not mince words here. And we have a president who obviously lied to the American people about any number of issues to do with weapons of mass destruction.

CONYERS: And as we can see now, the media is now slowly coming around, but did it take a Randi Rhodes and John Conyers to alert them to what they could read and perceive themselves?

RHODES: Congressman, I'm going to tell you something—they ignore you at their own peril, and here's why. The Downing Street minutes should have gotten attention, they should have been looked at for the benefit of the people who have sent their sons and daughters into harm's way in an ill-conceived, ill-planned, and lied-about war. These are good hard-working Americans who are patriotic, who obviously joined the service because after September 11, they believed their country needed to have people come to its defense. I know, I wanted to rejoin. I was in the Air Force.

> "We're going to the poorhouse hat in hand domestically because of these failed policies that have been kept hidden and rationalized."

CONYERS: You were already in once?

RHODES: Yeah, I was in, but I wanted to go back and they said you're too old, but honestly, I have never seen such a misuse of real patriotism by a president who is just looking to exploit resources for his own benefit.

CONYERS: And you know there's no reason for us to wait for historians a decade from now to [find] this out when no one will care except a handful of people that are specialists. We want the American people to know now. They've got to wake up, they've got to demand that the truth be told, and they've got to take action where the truth is not told, especially when it endangers not just the nation, but our citizens, our military. And it's stripping our treasury of its resources. We're going to the poorhouse hat in hand domestically because of these failed policies that have been kept hidden and rationalized. We've been misled for three solid years.

The View from Big Sky Country

In June 2005, David Bender spoke with Montana governor Brian Schweitzer on *Politcally Direct* about his time in the Middle East and why some politicians love to divide us.

DAVID BENDER: You spent seven years in Saudi Arabia. What was that experience like?

BRIAN SCHWEITZER: It was from about 1980 to 1987. And, of course it was the most closed society in the world. It probably still is. But it's opened a fair bit since. Back then you couldn't go to Saudi Arabia as a tourist. You were either there as a development engineer or you were there as a diplomat. I, unlike almost every other American who worked there, didn't work for one of the big oil companies or one of the big construction companies. I started by working for a Swedish engineering company that had the contract to build what became the world's largest dairy farm. They had all the sophisticated engineering background to milk the cows and to process the milk, but they'd never been involved in desert irrigation and, of course, that was my specialty. I was young. I was only, I guess, twenty-four years old.

BENDER: You and your wife traveled there?

SCHWEITZER: Yes, actually we met in college. She was studying botany. I was getting my master's degree in soil science. And about a year and half after I was in Saudi, she came over.

BENDER: Did you see in that experience—I mean, seven years, you're learning a lot about the culture—did you have a sense of how Americans are treated now—as [the] enemy or as someone not welcomed on Saudi soil?

SCHWEITZER: Oh, no. When I was there they actually treated Americans better than they treated anyone else, including other Muslims from Sudan or Egypt or from other places. They treated Americans better than they treated Europeans.

BENDER: Was that mainly from the royal family and not a policy that was felt all the way down the line? I mean, there's clearly a division within Saudi Arabia.

SCHWEITZER: Well, the royal family, at that time, had a much stronger hold on the country than they have today. But the Wahhabis were present even then. Many of us think of the Shiite as being the most fundamentalist part of Islam, but the Wahhabi sect of the Sunnis, in Saudi Arabia, [is] the most fundamentalist of all the Islamic people.

BENDER: And that's where bin Laden came from?

SCHWEITZER: He is a Wahhabi. It's been, oh, shall we say, an uneasy alliance between the royal family and the Wahhabis. The royal family, as you know, became so wealthy because they own all the subsurface rights to Saudi Arabia. They own all the oil. And to placate the Wahhabis, they've given them a great deal of money over the years. But in many cases, the Wahhabis, they have an agenda that is 180 degrees from the leaders in the royal family. Now it's become a problem. And I don't know that the royal family can put the genie back in the bottle.

BENDER: Have you seen *Fahrenheit 9/11*?

SCHWEITZER: I have not seen *Fahrenheit 9/11*.

BENDER: But you understand that he [Michael Moore] posits that it's the Saudi connection with the Bush family that has been responsible for a lot of our policy decisions and that has, over the years, inhibited our ability to be flexible in the Middle East. Do you hold with that at all?

"Many of us think of the Shiite as being the most fundamentalist part of Islam, but the Wahhabi sect of the Sunnis, in Saudi Arabia, [is] the most fundamentalist of all the Islamic people."

SCHWEITZER: Well, I just think that there is a lot of hypocrisy in our relationship with the Middle East, full stop. Let's think about this. Right now we're in Iraq, and I think the official reason, at least this month, is that we're there to create a democratic republic. Well, that's interesting because our main allies in the area are all functional monarchies: Kuwait, Saudi Arabia, Jordan. Now what do you think our allies in the region think when we say we are going to create democratic republics in the Islamic world, and that that will make the world a better place? What kind of message are we sending to the folks who consider themselves to be our allies? I think there is a wink and handshake going on. But of course, I am the governor of Montana and I am obviously not sitting in the meetings that we're having in Washington, DC.

BENDER: But a lot of us first read about you when you said that you felt that the National Guard troops that should be available this summer in Montana are off in Iraq. When you announced that you were requesting that the White House look at that, what was the response that you got from the Bush administration?

SCHWEITZER: Well, we were dismissed. Frankly, they just said no. I'm a businessman, as you know. I've never been elected to anything before this job as governor of Montana. A good business, and I believe a good government, is one that has a good sense of planning. And as I looked at what some of the critical problems might be in a state like Montana, one of them was wildfires. Wildfires aren't like your garage burning down. They are predictable. When you have a series of dry years in a row, everything is set up for a big fire season. As early as February I had been listening very strongly to the folks in Washington, DC, telling us governors that we are ultimately responsible for our own homeland security. "Don't come whining to Washington, DC. You need to have a portfolio of protection. You need to plan for anything that might happen in your states." So I looked at our assets, and I saw that we have in Montana twelve Black Hawk helicopters in the National Guard. At that time ten were in Iraq, now we have nine of them in Iraq. So we have three out of twelve. Each of them hauls 660 gallons of water. We have three CH-47`s, those are Chinook helicopters, they'll haul 2,000 gallons, but we didn't have flight crews to get them into the air. If you are in the business of flying or maintaining helicopters or airplanes, you're likely to have people working for you that have been in the military. People that have been in the active service in the military, very often, end up being in the National Guards back in their home states. How about our police force, our sheriff departments? A lot of them are in Iraq. How about, for example, Montana's own Department of Natural [Resources and Conservation]? We have some Huey helicopters, those will haul 360 gallons of water, but many of our pilots and people who maintain them are also members of the National Guard and, you guessed it, in Iraq. In 2000, we had 1,900 guardsmen and -women on our fire lines in Montana. Today we have 1,200 available.

"I think that some of the problem is all these media consultants and pollsters. They have politicians scared of their own shadow."

BENDER: A lot of people have talked about this administration's planning for what happened in Iraq as being faulty and lacking any vision. The same thing is happening, in your view, in our homeland?

SCHWEITZER: A dozen years ago, if you looked at America's military, it was a ten-to-one ratio of active to guards and reserve. In other words, for every guardsman and reserve person, there were ten active soldiers. Today it is two to one. So I think they're trying to run a military on the cheap. They're saying we will, at any time we choose, grab the guardsmen from the states. But every governor is the commander in chief of their own National Guard. So I think the bare minimum is that we should ask governors, "What do you anticipate being your problems and when would you have them?" A state like Montana, it would be July and August for the wildfires, states like Mississippi, Alabama, Louisiana, and Florida, it would be during the hurricane season. Every state has their own certain situation. Why not rotate guardsmen and -women based on what might be happening back home? That just makes good common sense and that's the way you'd run a business. And I don't know that these folks know how to run a business.

BENDER: You've developed a reputation, in a short period of time, as a plain speaker. You've talked about admiring Harry Truman, John Kennedy, people who spoke their minds and also spoke from the heart. Do you think that there is substance in style? We've been hearing a lot about the Democrats' message not getting out. Is that a part of the problem?

SCHWEITZER: Oh, I think that some of the problem is all these media consultants and pollsters, and all the rest of it. They have politicians scared of their own shadow. If you believe in something, just say it. If you have an idea, just say it. Politics ought to be a marketplace for ideas, and unfortunately, what we have are politicians who get talking points from pollsters and media consultants. And by definition, these folks will never be leaders. They are followers. So just don't listen to those characters. If you're getting your talking points from your own party, which by definition is just trying to embarrass the other side, you're probably not going to have a very crisp message.

> "If you're getting your talking points from your own party,
> which by definition is just trying to embarrass the other side,
> you're not going to have a very crisp message.'"

BENDER: Let me ask you about something Howard Dean said about the Republican Party largely being a white, Christian party. Following up on that statement, people have discovered that, yes indeed, 82 percent of Republicans are white Christians. But 57 percent of Democrats are white Christians. Now I know you have a strong religious background, you went to a Catholic school, and you come from a religious upbringing. How do you talk straight about that without seeming to bring bias into it?

SCHWEITZER: Well, what I think is interesting is the amount of hypocrisy that seems to be coming from those who comingled religion with government. I listen to people who talk about pro-choice, pro-life, all the rest of this stuff. And when people come to me and say, "Governor, I'm pro-life, are you?" I say, "Hmm, let me ask you a couple questions, because I'm a Catholic and we view pro-life as not just a single issue. First, let me ask you, what do you think of the death penalty?" and they say, "I'm for it." So then I say to them, "What do you think of preemptive war?" "Well, I'm for it." Finally I say, "What do you think of abortion?" "Well, I'm against it." "Hmm, well I think you only get one out of three."

BENDER: It's not a passing grade.

SCHWEITZER: It's not a passing grade. Do you remember who the first evangelical president of the United States was?

BENDER: A Democrat, Jimmy Carter.

SCHWEITZER: Right. But sometime after that it was determined that evangelicals shall be Republicans. Well, evangelicals are Christians. They believe in the teachings of Jesus, and the teachings of Jesus talked about how we shall clothe the poor and feed them, talked about how we shall take care of the children, talked about how we shall treat each other with respect. And they, I think, firmly believe all those things. But they've partnered with a group of people who don't believe in prenatal care, postnatal care, don't believe in kindergarten education, and aren't particularly prepared to invest in public education. So it's an uncomfortable alliance that they've got. There are many people who are pro-life who have decided that they will cast their lot with the Republicans, because I believe the evangelicals fully expect them to appoint Supreme Court justices who would repeal *Roe v. Wade*.

BENDER: They've said that. It's not even a question.

SCHWEITZER: All right, so what are the consequences? If the president chooses Supreme Court justices and the numbers on the Supreme Court are enough to repeal *Roe v. Wade*, Republicans will lose every election from the courthouse to the White House and back. Many Republicans know that. So, I think that many evangelicals will reassess their positions, and they'll say, "Well, some Democrats are pro-choice, some are pro-life. But all Democrats, or most Democrats, believe in the teachings of Jesus, which is we shall take care of the poor and the disadvantaged."

BENDER: When people come to you and say, "Governor, what's your position on civil unions or gay marriage," what do you say?

SCHWEITZER: I say I don't support them. I represent Montana, and the folks of Montana have overwhelmingly said (in fact we had a referendum that made it an issue) that we will not have gay marriages in Montana. Most of the folks in Montana think that marriage is something that has been built in part, for procreation. That being said, we should not be separating people based on their sexual preference. We ought not use this as code words for being against people who are gay and lesbian. I think it's abundantly obvious that gay and lesbian people are very productive parts of our society, great scientists, great in the arts, great community leaders, and have got moral values that would put some of these people who are thumping their chests all the time talking about moral values to shame. And I just don't believe that this society ought to be dividing itself over people's sexual preference. But this divisive rhetoric goes on, on both sides. And this is what is unfortunate in politics in America today. People raise money on divisive rhetoric, both on the left and on the right. And when there's controversy in government these single-interest groups are out raising money like bank robbers. When the Bush administration says they would like to drill in ANWR [the Arctic National Wildlife Refuge], "Giddyap," says the environmental community, "we can raise a lot of money on that." When the Republicans are talking about reversing *Roe v. Wade*, "Giddyap," they say over on the left, "we can raise a lot of money on that."

BENDER: Sure.

SCHWEITZER: And the same thing goes on when Democrats start pushing an agenda. So you see, it's the special interests on both sides of these issues that have made a huge industry out of divisive politics. And they try to drive politicians to say divisive things, to be involved in divisive issues, because that helps them raise money. The system kind of smells.

The very best in global industry... *working for you!*

COMPANY Fannie Mae   **SYMBOL** FNM   **FOUNDED** 1968

Looking for a high-risk investment that has the risk underwritten by the American taxpayer? Meet Fannie Mae. The government created Fannie Mae to buy home mortgages and trade them on the market. It's supposed to increase home ownership. What it does is let us gamble with other people's mortgages. Invest in Fannie Mae and you'll be doing something about the crushing consumer debt in this country. You'll be getting rich off of it.

Here's the best part: Fannie Mae has a $2.25 billion line of credit with the US Treasury. Simply put, all bailouts will be paid for by taxpayers. So investors get a free ride while taxpayers pay for a piece of Fannie they never even see. Now that's free enterprise. Make it work for you with Fannie Mae.

Congratulations!

DONALD RUMSFELD

for your unceasing labors

ON BEHALF OF

*the religious fanatics
in charge of Iran*

YOU ARE HEREBY HONORED AS AIR AMERICA'S

CREEP
of the
WEEK

BEST SECRETARY OF DEFENSE, EVER: **Many media outlets called for Rumsfeld's resignation following the revelation of prisoner abuse at Abu Ghraib, including the magazine *The Economist*, which wrote: "Time for him to go: George Bush is a fool for keeping Donald Rumsfeld in his job."**

GREAT NEWS: **In April 2006, six retired US military generals called for Rumsfeld's resignation over his mishandling of the war in Iraq.**

A COMPLIMENT FROM (RET.) MARINE CORPS GENERAL ANTHONY ZINNI: **"Rumsfeld has committed acts of gross negligence and incompetence."** *Okay, an unflattering compliment.*

A COMPLIMENT FROM (RET.) ARMY MAJOR GENERAL JOHN BATISTE: **"My own decision to speak out goes back to watching firsthand the arrogant and contemptuous attitude of Rumsfeld as he ignored the advice of military experts during preparations for war, and then living with the impact of those strategic blunders as a division commander in Iraq."**

BUT BUSH SAW IT DIFFERENTLY: **"I hear the voices, and I read the front page, and I know the speculation. But I'm the decider and I decide what's best. And what's best is for Don Rumsfeld to remain as the secretary of defense."**

STILL, IF THINGS GO SOUTH: **Before joining Bush's cabinet in 2002, Donald Rumsfeld was chairman of the board of directors of Gilead Sciences, the company that makes Tamiflu—the drug the National Institute of Allergies and Infectious Disease is pushing as the number-one drug to treat avian flu. So, as the government scares people about the coming pandemic, the secretary of defense stands to make millions. His holdings in Gilead are estimated to be worth between $5 and $25 million.**

CAN'T TEACH AN OLD DOG: **As CEO of GD Searle in 1983, Donald Rumsfeld is alleged to have used his influence with the Reagan administration to have the FDA approve the artificial sweetener aspartame, which is sold under the brand name, NutraSweet. At the time, scientific tests strongly indicated that the sweetener caused brain tumors.**

THEY SAID WHAT??!?!!

We're used to lies and outrageous misstatements from Karl Rove, known to some as Turd Blossom. But this particular one may have been a personal best. Speaking to Conservative Party of New York State more than two years after President Bush had declared the end of major combat operations in Iraq, Rove seemed mighty defensive about . . . *something*. (Hmm, methinks the lady doth protest too much?)

In fact, only one of 535 members of Congress voted against authorizing military action in Afghanistan.

> Conservatives saw the savagery of 9/II in the attacks and prepared for war; liberals saw the savagery of the 9/II attacks and wanted to prepare indictments and offer therapy and understanding for our attackers.

Karl Rove
JUNE 22, 2005

And you saw 9/II and instantly recognized the endless political potential in keeping Americans scared.

Speaking of therapy and understanding for our attackers, any word on when you all are going to round up Osama bin Laden, dead or alive? (The tough talk makes us hot.)

Funny thing about that particular steaming pile of lies, Karl—the president went out of his way to thank members of both parties as he signed the USA Patriot Act in October 2001, just weeks after the attacks. He said both parties were united in their resolve to fight terrorism. For some reason he didn't mention anything about "therapy" or "understanding" the enemy.

And furthermore, Democrats in the House and Senate gave the Bush administration every single thing the White House asked for to launch a war in Iraq, even when it was your bogus connection between Saddam and Osama.

Yeah, yeah, we know. All your bad ideas in 2005 tanked—social security "reform," the Harriet Myers nomination, flag burning amendments, and of course, all that unpleasantry over your telling Robert Novak about Valerie Plame. This 9/11 thing is your political binky, your pacifier, the way you try to get your mojo back. We get it. But do you really expect people to keep falling for the same old b.s. again and again?

When it comes to thinking about how so-called conservatives "prepared for war," we'd like to quote 9/11 widow and family advocate Kristin Breitweiser, writing in Huffingtonpost.com: "Did your preparations include: sound intelligence to warrant your actions; a reasonable entry and exit strategy coupled with a coherent plan to carry out that strategy; the proper training and equipment for the troops you were sending in to fight your war? Did you follow the advice of experts such as General Shinseki who correctly advised you about the troop levels needed to actually succeed in Iraq? No, you didn't."

"In New York, where everyone unified after 9/11, the last thing we need is somebody who seeks to divide us for political purposes." —Senator Charles E. Schumer, Democrat of New York

The Western Pacific island of Saipan is an American Commonwealth of the Mariana Islands. For tourists from the outside looking in, it truly looks like a storybook island paradise. But to parts of corporate America like Wal-Mart and Abercrombie and Fitch, it is just another place on the globe where workers can be horrendously exploited in horrible sweatshop conditions completely below the radar screen. And best of all, they can still put "Made in America" on the label.

Naturally, when segments of corporate America want to exploit or abuse workers anywhere on the globe, they call on the Republican leadership—people like Senator Bill Frist, Senator Rick Santorum, or Dick Cheney—all predictable, reliable bottom-feeders. But for the special dirty deed of protecting their evil sweatshops in Saipan, they went to real corruption pros. They went directly to Tom DeLay and Jack Abramoff.

Liz Claiborne, Brooks Brothers, and Old Navy wanted to be certain that they could forever run sweatshops in Saipan. And those companies had every reason to know that these were not just typical sweatshops. These were sweatshops that were mostly made up of female Chinese teenagers who cleared about 90¢ an hour during their fourteen- to fifteen-hour workdays. They were basically held prisoner in work barracks surrounded with barbed wire—barracks without toilets, without showers, barracks where many of the teenage Chinese workers ended up being forced into prostitution servicing businessmen looking for a few more great capitalist opportunities in that Saipan island paradise.

Before the new brand of Republican corporatists elbowed their way into Washington like brownshirts taking control of the German Reichstag, the Clinton administration was calling for protection of these Saipan slaves, and people like Representative George Miller were demanding that US environmental and labor laws be enforced there. This would have spelled disaster for the greed mongers of the Saipan clothing concerns, so their undisputed leader, the mogul Willie Tan, called on Mr. Fix-It himself, Jack Abramoff. He was immediately on board, going so far as to call legislation to regulate the island's garment factories "immoral laws designed to destroy the economic lives of a people." He went on to compare them to the Nuremberg Laws restricting the lives of German Jews under the Nazis.

There was a lot of clothing industry lobby money to spread around, so Abramoff put together a Congressional fact-finding junket for DeLay and some of his friends, including the who's who of real twisted right-wing Republican opinion leaders. After a week of luxury hotels and bodysurfing, the junket team, those same frauds who are so quick to hide behind Christ and the American flag to disguise their putrid character, came back and told George Miller that Democratic legislation that would have closed down those hellholes, disgusting symbols of capitalism gone bad, would

never see the light of day. And in fact, here is a quote that accurately sums up the way that the Republican leadership embraced what they saw in Saipan: "You are a shining light for what is happening in the Republican Party. You represent everything that is good about what we're trying to do in America in leading the world in the free market system."

That quote came from Tom DeLay as he toasted the American corporate leadership in Saipan.

And in another quote from that dinner, DeLay let everyone know whom they could thank for his support.

"When one of my closest and dearest friends, Jack Abramoff, your most able representative in Washington, DC, invited me to the islands, I wanted to see firsthand the free market success . . . Even though I have been here for only 24 hours, I have witnessed the economic success . . . [but] you are up against the forces of big labor and the radical left. Dick Armey and I made a promise to defend the island's present system. Stand firm. Resist evil. Remember that all truth and blessings emanate from our Creator."

Those words have become symbolic of just how much *filth* and moral squalor George Bush and his Republican Congress have spread around since they moved to Washington in 2001.

The truth is that, in the end, Air America can report stories, Rachel Maddow can pick the details apart, Al Franken can make you laugh, Randi Rhodes, Mike Malloy, and others can make their calls to arms. But once we leave those stories at your doorstep, it's up to you to help do something about them. In the election cycle of 2006, you have your chance—get involved. Because as long as these new Republicans occupy our nation's capital, tragedies like Saipan will continue to linger right at our doorstep.

Conservatives Hate Old People and Want Them to Die

Sam Seder

I'd like to beg the reader's forgiveness. I know it was somewhat irresponsible for me to entitle this essay "Conservatives Hate Old People and Want Them to Die." It may be more accurate to state "Republicans Hate Old People and Want Them to Die." After all, it's not the Conservative Party that has controlled the levers of our government for the past six years and expressed such disdain for old people through the legislative process. However, I actually think the truth is that conservatives really, really hate old people and desperately want them to die and so do Republicans. Yes, *hate* is a strong word, but what better term applies when an administration, a party, an ideology has demonstrated seething contempt for the well-being of the vast majority of Americans and an even larger plurality of the rest of the human race? Put simply, they hate humanity. Okay, maybe they're just chronically paranoid and deeply suspicious of humans, but it feels like hate to me.

Anyway, truth be told, I realize that you might find it debatable that conservatives hate old people and want them to die. Let's examine, shall we?

WHEN THEY'RE SIXTY-FOUR

Let's start with Social Security. Now it is true that Social Security provides a safety net for orphans and people who become disabled, but its primary function is to ensure that senior citizens spend their golden years not having to eat cat food or sleep on the streets. It literally keeps two-thirds of our seniors out of poverty. Conservatives hate Social Security. They've hated it since 1935, the year President Franklin Delano Roosevelt signed it into law. They hated it so much that their vehement opposition was included in the Republican platform for that election cycle. They thought it would never work. They got that wrong; it has been the single most successful government program, maybe in the history of man. They still hate it.

Remember when Al Gore talked about a lockbox? Remember when nobody had a clue what he was talking about but everybody thought it was fun to make fun of Al Gore for saying *lockbox*? Turns out the joke was on us, particularly those of us getting old. Al Gore wanted to put a lock on the box of money known as the Social Security Trust Fund. This is a box of money to which everybody who gets a paycheck contributes about 6 percent, which is matched by their employer. That money earns interest and pays out Social Security benefits to older Americans who, back in the day, contributed money to pay for their older Americans. It's a rainy-day fund that has extra money in it for times when there are more old folks than young folks paying into the system. It works pretty well and should be full of cash for at least thirty-five years if absolutely nothing is done to add to it. Even then, Social Security will work almost as well with just the money younger workers will be putting into it. But Al Gore never got to put that lock on that box. And George Bush and the Republicans opened it up and started taking money from that box and leaving IOUs. They used the money to offset the cost of their tax cuts to the mega-rich who usually make their money from capital gains, not paychecks. Then the Republicans turned around and said, "Social Security is broken—all that's left in the trust fund are IOUs. Let's scrap it and privatize the whole thing, that way it will artificially inflate the stock market, put huge fees in the pockets of our Wall Street buddies, and we won't have to pay off the money we took from working people to pay for tax breaks for millionaires." They didn't say that last part. They're not that honest.

But they hate Social Security. They hate it because it shows people just how good government can be, and if there is anything a conservative hates more than old people, it's good government. So, let's review. Old people love Social Security because it ensures that no matter what risks they take or problems they have in life, they won't have to eat cat food when they retire. Conservatives hate Social Security, ipso Coulter facto, conservatives hate old people. But wait, there's more . . .

To compound-fracture the financial injury, while senior citizens literally worry themselves sick over their vanishing retirement funds, they're also forced to decipher the Republican prescription drug plan.

CONSERVATIVE DRUG DEALS

The Republicans wrote and passed the huge disaster called Medicare Part D. It is a new prescription plan for Medicare and Medicaid recipients, most of whom are old people, who happen to be sick or need medication. The title of this essay is not "Conservatives Love the Pharmaceutical Industry," but it could have been. The prescription Part D plan was written by two Republicans, one who worked for the Bush admin-istration and one who was a congressman. While writing the bill, both of these guys were literally interview-ing for their next jobs as lobbyists for the pharmaceutical industry. They got the jobs and, based on the work they did before getting them, their new bosses probably let them take real long vacations. The prescription Part D plan, while a shitty deal for seniors, is a great deal for the pharma industry. They get $180 billion worth of profits primarily because the bill does not allow Medicare and Medicaid to negotiate a volume discount for its patients.

Conservatives supposedly love the free market, but apparently, not as much as they hate seniors.

Old folks on the prescription Part D plan have had trouble getting their medications and, in some cases, have had to pay thousands of dollars more a year for them. The more skeptical of you out there might say, "Well, just because they lined their pockets on the backs of old people doesn't mean Republicans hate old people. It just means that enriching themselves is more important than taking care of old people." To you I say, "Touché." But there's more . . .

THE COLD SHOULDER

This past winter wasn't that cold, what with the Republican-funded global warming and all. We were lucky, or more specifically, old people without a lot of money were lucky, because the conservative hatred of old people never allows for old and sick people to receive subsidies to pay their home heating-oil bills. In fact, if it weren't for a guy conservatives hate, Venezuelan president Hugo Chávez, lots of old people may have died this past winter by freezing to death. You see, Republicans defeated multiple attempts by Democrats in the House and in the Senate to pass low-income home heating-oil assistance legislation. Conservatives didn't want any government money wasted on helping the old and infirm stay warm over the winter. They had too many capital gains tax cuts, abstinence-only programs, and highway deals that helped increase the value of their personal real estate holdings (Hi, Speaker of the House Hastert!) to fund. So, the president of Venezuela had to provide low-cost heating oil for seniors and poor people in six Northeastern states through the Venezuelan-owned Citgo Petroleum. That's right, Venezuelans are watching the same "CARE"-type commercials on their TVs as we are, except their ads explain how elderly Americans will freeze to death unless Venezuelans help—conservative Republicans in the US Congress hate old people enough to let them choose food over warmth during the winter. It's bad enough conservatives hate old people, but do they have to make this country a third-world charity case because of it?

BANKRUPTCY BLUES

Then there's the bankruptcy bill. Now, to be fair (which I always am), in passing the bankruptcy bill, conservatives showed their love of the credit-card industry and corporations (both of which include people who will be old someday) and expressed hatred not solely for older Americans, but really for all Americans. As you may not know, more than 50 percent of the people who file for bankruptcy do so because of medical bills, those of their own or their loved ones. Of the remaining 50 percent, almost half are dealing with the loss of a job or divorce. So it's not like anywhere near the majority of people who file for bankruptcy are doing so because they bought too many boats or developed too many money-losing Atlantic City casinos. Even so, the Republicans passed a bankruptcy bill written by and for the credit-card industry (at least they have the good manners to swell Republican campaign coffers). The bill essentially makes any individual who declares bankruptcy an indentured servant of predatory financial institutions. But wait, you say, that doesn't mean Republicans hate old people. It just means that they hate all Americans—at least those who can't contribute huge sums of money to their campaigns! Well yes, dear Reader, you have triumphed again. However, you have forgotten to take into account the amendments to the bankruptcy bill sponsored by Democrats that Republicans shot down.

That's right, for every draconian, corporate-sponsored Republican piece of legislation, there's always a Democratic amendment trying to chip away at the greed and theocratic essence inherent in most Republican lawmaking. In this instance, there were tons. People struck by natural disaster should have wider bankruptcy options. Republicans not only say "F that," but Republican congressman James Sensenbrenner told Katrina victims to "get over it" and just become homeless slaves to their creditors. The Republicans shot down amendments that would have exempted US military forces fighting in the Republican debacle in Iraq. They shot down amendments that would have helped ill people and children. And finally, they shot down amendments that would have allowed elderly people to protect up to $120,000 of equity in their homes from creditors so that they wouldn't get thrown out on the street. Not only that, just to make old people feel bad, the Republicans allowed multimillionaires to retain full equity in their homes if they had enough money to set up expensive financial instruments to do so. To be fair, I'm sure some of those elite millionaires are old, but that's not why the Republicans like them.

Finally, there's Grover Norquist, Jack Abromoff's slush-fund king, who sits as a philosopher king in the inner circle of power with other great minds like Karl "with a K" Rove, Donald "I have enabled more war crimes than you can spell" Rumsfeld, and "Deadeye" Dick Cheney. Norquist told a Spanish newspaper how conservatives and Republicans are counting the days until the elder generation dies off because those people can remember the New Deal. The last thing this administration needs is citizens who can recall a government that actually served the people rather than kowtowed to the private interest. After all, how can you rewrite history when there are still folks walking around who lived it and know better?

Look, I don't know that I've convinced you that conservatives and Republicans hate old people. I think it's pretty clear that if you're not a corporation or a millionaire and you are getting older, then they hate you and want you to die already. Or, at the least, they couldn't give a shit about you. Which may not be hatred but feels an awful lot like it!

The very best in global industry... *working for you!*

COMPANY **Monsanto Company**   SYMBOL **MON**   FOUNDED 1901

If you want to know where the smart investor puts his money, then you need look no further than Monsanto, the leading producer of agricultural and chemical-related products. Founded more than one hundred years ago in a patriotic quest to fulfill America's need for saccharin, Monsanto continues its tradition of bettering the lives of millions of fortunate consumers.

From New York to Singapore, people use countless gallons of Monsanto's Roundup in a never-ending battle against the menace of weeds. Skin disorders and spontaneous abortions are a small price to pay for the pristine fairways at Augusta National. But that's only the beginning. Our $4 billion-a-year drug unit makes the hottest painkiller on the market: Celebrex. Who knows what medical miracle our labs will come up with next. A pill to help with the resulting gastrointestinal hemorrhages, perhaps? Only time will tell.

But enough about the consumers. Sure, they're a necessary asset, but Monsanto's main concern is with its stockholders. That's why we rush all our genetically modified crops to market before the biological risks are fully understood. It's all part of this company's fine tradition of investor responsibility.

Monsanto, making billions the biochemical way.

Think Globally, Vote Locally

Chuck D

Voting in the United States in this millennium reminds me of that Temptations hit "Ball of Confusion." It's easy to look at voting as the powerless activity of an earlier century. In a nation very weak in geography skills, world history, and knowledge of diversity, we Americans have been programmed to look at the electoral process as a symbol of freedom rather than an enforcement of selection. The truth is that the electorate process has become as formulaic as a cash register at Mickey D's—just hit the colorful icons for your next Prez.

We are in a time where freedoms need to be thoroughly re-explained, and not necessarily in a "Dwight D. Ike / Norman Rockwellian from another era" type of way. It's sliding the "m" in "the masses" one space over to the left to truly show how the "powers that be" look at real people.

As if explaining the importance of the vote to the general society isn't hard enough, to those under thirty years of age, the meaning is connected to another time, another state of mind, and a different soundtrack. With so much hypocrisy and catfighting floating to the top of American politics, apathy seems to be endorsed, supported, and backed by the culture bandits of big business.

Efforts to reach the youth that were jump-started in the 1990s, programs such as Rock the Vote, Choose or Lose, and Rap the Vote, had the air sucked out of their optimism by the blatant evidence of cheating during the 2000 election. So now what?

Historical perspective must be ingrained into the structural psyche of both the youth and young adults of America. This is a country where it seems that the over-forty demographic doesn't consider eighteen- to thirty-year-olds as being equals, thus trickery and games are played. Within the radiation of a TV-movie nation, whippings of mass distraction are inflicted on today's youth. The young adult–oriented mass-media outlets, such as Viacom, are seemingly extending teenage years to twenty-nine, while the young get fed candy and sleep.

Only about 34 percent of all Americans have passports; a damn shame for a so-called international western country. Along with these mental global limitations, cultural expansion has created a worldwide introduction to misinformation that has further turned away the youth of America from believing in the voting process and other things red, white, and blue.

How do I myself encourage the new urban lifescape of America to believe in the voting process? Well, first off, I don't sugarcoat anything, and I begin by comparing some other governments to the one here in the

USA. I don't say that one is better than the other, or whether someone would prefer to live in France, Cuba, or Ghana, but I encourage people to learn about these political and electoral structures and the involvement their people have in their government and then compare them to ours. Then I move on to speak of the direct sacrifice that black people and women have made especially in the context of a historical perspective and how we need to remember, honor, and respect what they did so that we could have the power that we have today.

Although recent programs like Vote or Die in 2004 were gallant efforts to motivate the youth, the marketing scheme behind it ultimately proved the program was only temporary. It evolved from celebrities, who by participating had their careers propelled. And it was found that not everything in life that's supposed to "stick" can be based on advertising alone. There were unanswered questions on the day after election day. Many folks were further disillusioned on the liberal side, the democratic side, the black community side, and most important the youth side. Deflated.

I joined the ranks of Air America Radio in spring of 2004 to participate in a new, growing momentum of diverse understanding that I wanted to live on past election night '04. I learned so much that year from my cohosts, Lizz Winstead and Rachel Maddow on *Unfiltered*. The yearning and the demand for diversity exploded on that show. Learning from the comedic wit of Lizz, I reduced my conversation about the need to vote down to a quick sound bite, telling people that voting was as essential as washing your ass in the morning. It's just something you're supposed to do in the morning as an adult. Don't look for results and applause just because you carried out your responsibility. Thus you cannot complain if something stinks, especially if *you* did not wash. Voting ain't something you're just supposed to do and don't look for props either just because you did it. In learning from Rachel Maddow, I explained to folks that learning about your local and closest surroundings here in America can bring forth a more direct effect in the voting process. Learn the local score. This means congresspersons, school boards, sheriffs, and judges. At the very least, pay attention to it as much as folks follow their everyday ESPN statistics and sports pages. You'll find that in many cases, those same names on the ballot can give you opportunity or lock you up. As a people, we need to be privy to all these basic details before we have anything presidential coming up out of our mouths.

So with this in mind, I'm still chopping down the tricknology that governments use today to sweep the people into impulsively doing, without thinking. The best Americans are the ones who are truly citizens of the world. The voting process echoes the tone of realization that this is the only earth we have. A tone that should be about protecting this natural planet, beyond any language barrier, waters, and the so-called governmental borders. A tone that should never be below this world but most certainly not above it.

Truly to all in the best efforts in peace.

The Sound of Freedom

Gia'na Garel

The most significant aspect of a box of completed ballots is the synchronicity involving like-minded people. Whether the votes vary to the left or to the right, it's the process of speaking up that bespeaks freedom— the state of mind that encourages individuals within a society to yay or nay and give their opinion. An act that in an autocratic society would be unheard of.

When some form of intervention occurs and alters the authenticity of those collected voices, what will follow such deception is silence. In the distrustful quietness of a society offering no opinion, where neither yea or nay is being heard, lies the seed for a dictator. Trust has to be earned and reaffirmed for these Americans to keep themselves free from the silent ignorance of an out-of-control leadership.

Many Americans secretly like having their systems structured and issues involving more mundane matters to be attended to by supposedly well-appointed reps. When it flows well, it's forgotten about until there is a problem. It's like deferring the best basic bodily functions to your spleen or your liver because they run fine without your input. You don't intervene until there is a problem and why should you bother if up until that point all is running well? Many of us, more than we care to admit, cast a ballot and defer every govern-mental matter, and thus all the power, to our elected parties; and then we ignore them until something breaks. Seldom are we part of the preventive process after we vote.

Whether or not we trust the process of the final vote, it is the act itself that signifies freedom and that's good. Unfortunately, the chorus of sentiment must be continuously echoed as we will hardly be offering up much voice as we yell from within the clenched fist of said dictator. Every time we are asked to speak up, we are asked to trust the process to be an extension of freedom. At least, that's the idea.

ARE YOU PARANOID?

This test has been designed by Air America Radio to weed out the crazies. Please circle Likely to Be True or Not Likely to Be True after each of the following hypothetical situations.

QUESTION 1 The leader of a powerful democracy sends his emissary—a war hero himself—to appear before representatives from around the world to make a frightening allegation: The leader of a rogue nation has been secretly building the components of a deadly bomb that could destroy the world. Armed with irrefutable intelligence, aerial photographs, and ground-level first-hand accounts, the emissary's presentation is captivating . . . except for one minor detail. Everything he says was entirely fabricated in order to justify the toppling of an unfriendly regime that controlled a precious natural resource.

LIKELY TO BE TRUE   NOT LIKELY TO BE TRUE

QUESTION 2 During the 1950s and 1960s, the intelligence arm of a popularly elected, democratically run, and constitutionally based government used to routinely tap the phone calls of individuals it deemed suspicious, dangerous, or a threat to national security. Even people the government "just didn't like" had their private conversations monitored. Thankfully, when the unconstitutional eavesdropping program was made public by the media, it was shut down forever.

LIKELY TO BE TRUE   NOT LIKELY TO BE TRUE

QUESTION 3 The leader of a democratic nation orders his subordinates to leak the name of a classified secret agent as retribution against her husband for not toeing the party line.

LIKELY TO BE TRUE   NOT LIKELY TO BE TRUE

QUESTION 4 In a complicated double-reverse psych-out, a candidate for a democratic country's highest office leaks—through a surreptitious cadre of supporters—to the media a document that when first made public actually damages said candidate's reputation. However, upon closer scrutiny, the document turns out to be false, thus lending credence to the popular misconception that there is a media conspiracy to undermine the candidate's reputation.

LIKELY TO BE TRUE   NOT LIKELY TO BE TRUE

QUESTION 5 A nation is at war and 2,500 of its soldiers have already died. As the conflict rages on, the country's body of elected officials dedicates hundreds of hours to debating and voting on a constitutional amendment that would prevent gays from marrying.

LIKELY TO BE TRUE   NOT LIKELY TO BE TRUE

QUESTION 6 Before launching an invasion of a foreign country, the war leaders give a billion-dollar no-bid contract to their former employers and friends to rebuild the far-away nation that was about to be destroyed.

LIKELY TO BE TRUE   **NOT LIKELY TO BE TRUE**

QUESTION 7 The leaders of a country founded upon the notion that all men are created equal and endowed with certain inalienable rights actively and secretly circumvent those long-standing ideals during wartime. This nation's prisoners-of-war are not treated according to decades-old, internationally sanctioned standards of decency—but are accused of crimes, beaten, and held without oversight or the possibility of appeal.

LIKELY TO BE TRUE   **NOT LIKELY TO BE TRUE**

QUESTION 8 The leader of a nation, up for reelection—with no combat experience of his own—is able to successfully smear his war hero opponent by alleging that he wasn't so brave and, worse, that he had committed horrible war-time atrocities.

LIKELY TO BE TRUE   **NOT LIKELY TO BE TRUE**

QUESTION 9 A team of clandestine operatives of a political candidate (again, one with no combat experience) smear his surging opponent through a whisper campaign, creating rumors that during the time this opponent was a prisoner of war (30 years previously), he had been disloyal to his country. And that during this same period, he fathered a child of mixed race, out of wedlock.

LIKELY TO BE TRUE   **NOT LIKELY TO BE TRUE**

If you answered Likely to Be True to questions I or 3–9, or if you answered Not Likely to Be True to question 2, then you might be suffering from paranoid delusions. Please do yourself and those around you a favor and immediately seek psychiatric counselling.

What I Want in My Next President

Rachel Maddow

I want the next president of the United States to be a lot like George W. Bush. Not a warmongering, power-drunk imbecile who prides himself on not reading—not that way. I want a George W. Bush–model presidency because I want a president who was not chosen for his supposed electability.

There's nothing in George W. Bush's pre-Rove background to suggest anything in his future that's more presidential than being a president's son. Come on, no one scours the ranks of DUI male cheerleaders when they're looking for "electable." But the conservative movement wasn't looking for electable when they lit upon George W. Bush—they were looking for a standard-bearer, and they knew they could create the electability, the backstory, the myth, and the machine to put him in office.

I want the next president of the United States to be a progressive standard-bearer. (I'm not sticky on terminology—*progressive* is fine with me, or *democratic* or *liberal*, or *not-flying-monkey-death-cult-wingnutty* is fine, too.) I just don't want to waste time searching for some perfectly electable savior candidate.

A MATTER OF STANDARDS

There's no trouble coming up with the standard I want to be borne by the next president—progressives know what our values are:

- Protecting the Constitution and the rule of law
- Protecting personal freedom and privacy from government intrusion
- Government that is freaking competent
- Government that isn't for sale
- American leadership among nations—through being right, not just through our might
- Respecting our military enough to use it only in cases of last resort
- Fair rules for businesses to protect competition, investors, workers, and consumers
- Financial responsibility
- Economic fairness
- Nondiscrimination
- Sticking up for the underdog, for the little guy
- A chance at the American dream for this generation and those that follow us

These majoritarian values need their own DUI cheerleader president: an imperfect, human, personable standard-bearer. A politician who knows how to articulate solid progressive values in a way that connects with people. Not a sock puppet without a brain of its own—after all, progressive values require a competent government and that means a competent leader. But if the progressive movement grew candidates for the Democrats the way the conservatives grow theirs for the Republicans, there'd be a heck of a lot more to look forward to in the next presidency, wouldn't there?

That said, this whole shebang only makes sense if Democrats and progressives start running campaigns that aggressively promote progressive values instead of some candidate's idealized personal biography. If you think there's any chance of that, fire Bob Shrum again and call me in the morning.

CHALLENGES FOR THE NEXT PRESIDENT

Here are the two big flaming bags of poop the next president will find on the front stoop of the White House on Inauguration Day 2009: the war on terrah and the unitary executive. (I prefer to think of the unitary executive as the *unitard* executive, which implies both unstylishness and retardation, but I've been advised against it by focus groups convened by Bob Shrum.) The next president needs a plan for extricating us from both of these flaming poop sacks—they're both designed to outlive the presidency of George W. Bush and to steer American politics in Republicans' favor long after he's started cashing his presidential pension checks at whatever bar is closest to his mom's place in Kennebunkport.

First, the war on terrah, terror, whatever. It used to be the war on terrorism. Then briefly it was the global struggle against violent extremism. On August 6, 2004, Bush actually said it ought to be called "the struggle against ideological extremists who do not believe in free societies who happen to use terror as a weapon to try to shake the conscience of the free world." Now it's the war on terror. Snappy, I know. But think about that actual phrase for a second: a "war on terror." In other words, waging war against the feeling of being scared. Which is even more ridiculous, arguably, than the original war on terrorism, which was war against a tactic used by bad guys of all stripes. If this seems like a rather vague parameter for war, it's because it's designed to be. Scared feelings will never be banished from the earth by US smart bombs, nor will terrorism, nor will global violent extremism or whatever it was Bush was talking about that weird day in August. The war on terror is designed to be vague enough to persist indefinitely—it's a permanent war, even if it's kind of a fake one.

If you want to avenge 9/11 and prevent the next one, if you want to take apart al Qaeda and hasten the downfall of theocratic tyrannies that mint new fundamentalist, violent, anti-Western crusaders, then hey, I'm all with you. But that kind of an agenda calls for police actions, prosecutions, trials, convictions, plea agreements, specific targeted strikes on terrorist training facilities, international cooperation, diplomacy, building support for moderate forces in the Islamic world, and disavowing tyrants like the Bush family pals running Saudi Arabia (which minted fifteen of the nineteen 9/11 hijackers). The Bush war on terror isn't doing much of any of those things, and certainly it's doing none of them well.

The next president is going to have to define real threats to the country and distinguish them from the politically advantageous herrings Bush/Cheney have been reddening since 9/11. The next president will have to be willing to talk about the boondoggles and distractions and opportunism thus far in the so-called war on terror, to dismantle the ridiculous Department of Homeland Security, to reestablish the distinction between the military and the intelligence services, to rebuild international relationships, and to slap the chemical companies and Big Oil into compliance with policies that make this country safer. In other words, the next president is going to have to annul the fake war on terror and actually work on real national security instead.

That's going to require a whole bunch of new slogans, a full-throated pro-national-security democratic chorus of support, and a plan for getting troops out of Iraq as soon as possible.

As long as we're in Iraq, the fake war on terror is permanent. Why did we really invade in the first place? It clearly wasn't the threat posed by WMD, or Saddam's fake nuclear program, or to stop corruption in the oil-for-food program, or to avenge the Kurds, or to create a Jeffersonian beacon of democracy, or to pave paradise and put up a parking lot, or whatever their other retroactive justifications have evolved into by the time you read this. The point is and has always been to build permanent military bases and a huge Vatican City–style embassy complex there, and to control Iraq's resources as best we can while constantly stimulating Muslim anti-American resentment worldwide. Iraq: Come for the oil, stay for the jihad!

Permanent war is advantageous because it makes the president a "war president"—which makes him seem military-tastic even if he spent Vietnam in Alabama. It makes the "we're at war!" defense available to use against anyone who questions the president on anything. And specifically in the Bush/Cheney era, the use-of-force resolution passed by Congress after 9/11 has been invoked to justify everything from the tribunals at Guantanamo, to the NSA spying on Americans without a court order, to the president's right to make visiting heads of state kiss his bottom while he wears a Burger King crown and hums "God Save the Queen." (Okay, maybe not that last one yet, but there's still time.)

Permanent war means permanent expansion of the president's power. The unitary executive—the growth of the power of the presidency so that it eclipses that of Congress, the Courts, even the rule of law itself—is

> "People like Truman and responsible politicians genuinely feared that we were going to get the Depression all over again. There were thirteen million of us who served in the military in World War II. Thirteen million is a lot of people to find jobs for if they just really don't exist—except if you're constantly armed and on the march. So the decision was made to militarize the economy and to militarize the United States."
>
> —Gore Vidal on *Politically Direct*

the other flaming poop sack that the Bush/Cheney administration is hurling at future presidencies and us poor citizen schmucks. Creating multiple precedents for White House lawbreaking and power grabbing sets up the next president for a heck of a challenge.

The next president will have to expose where the George W. Bush presidential power grab undermined the power of the other branches of government, and our Constitutional democracy. And then undo the damage! Can you imagine the kind of political cojones it will take for a president to voluntarily rein in the powers of his or her own office, for the good of the country, for the protection of the Constitution?

I want the next president of the United States to have those cojones. I want that president to be a progressive standard-bearer. To holler about progressive values openly, articulately, and loudly—to do the right thing by the country and to be able to explain why. And I want a promise that the next president will never, ever, ever appear in public in bike shorts, tights, or a flight-suit codpiece. But other than that, I'm cool with whatever.

Ramon caught up with Vice President Dick Cheney when he was on the road shilling for Bush's doomed Social Security plan.

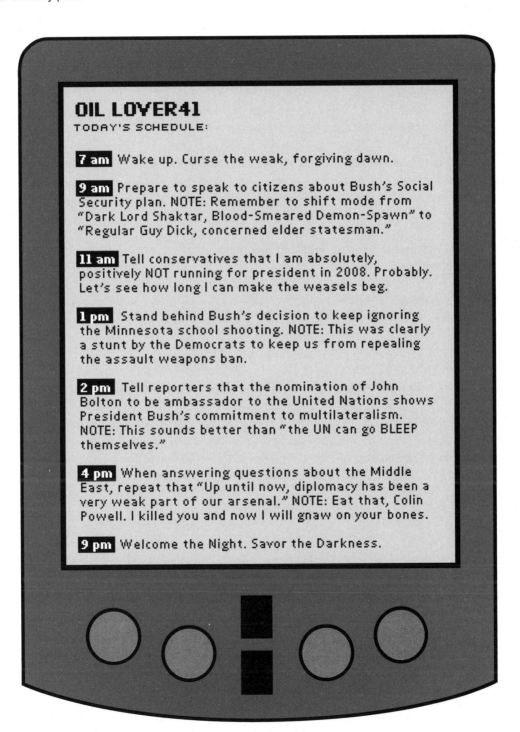

OIL LOVER41
TODAY'S SCHEDULE:

7 am Wake up. Curse the weak, forgiving dawn.

9 am Prepare to speak to citizens about Bush's Social Security plan. NOTE: Remember to shift mode from "Dark Lord Shaktar, Blood-Smeared Demon-Spawn" to "Regular Guy Dick, concerned elder statesman."

11 am Tell conservatives that I am absolutely, positively NOT running for president in 2008. Probably. Let's see how long I can make the weasels beg.

1 pm Stand behind Bush's decision to keep ignoring the Minnesota school shooting. NOTE: This was clearly a stunt by the Democrats to keep us from repealing the assault weapons ban.

2 pm Tell reporters that the nomination of John Bolton to be ambassador to the United Nations shows President Bush's commitment to multilateralism. NOTE: This sounds better than "the UN can go BLEEP themselves."

4 pm When answering questions about the Middle East, repeat that "Up until now, diplomacy has been a very weak part of our arsenal." NOTE: Eat that, Colin Powell. I killed you and now I will gnaw on your bones.

9 pm Welcome the Night. Savor the Darkness.

? Frequently Asked Questions
THE BURNING QUESTIONS THAT YOU NEVER HAD THE GUTS TO ASK!

Is it true that Air America is an idyllic, utopian workplace where the wholesome food in the vending machine is always free and clothing is optional?

So you've been up to see the place! Yes, all of those things are true, although generally we like to wear clothes (made of hemp, organic cotton and recycled tires, of course). And we compost all of our garbage, even used toilet paper.

If it's true that all Jews are liberals, and all Jews are good with money, why is it that Air America never seems to have enough money?

Your premise is somewhat flawed. It's true that all Jews are good with money (Pat Robertson said so), but not everyone who works at Air America is a Jew. If everyone were, we'd have no money problems, obviously.

How does Air America get the word when the homosexual community wants to update its agenda?

Air America maintains the latest in Skype Internet phone technology that keeps us connected via hotline at all times to the homosexual leadership in Hollywood, New York, and Washington. Whenever a lesbian or gay man needs to let us know about a child who needs to be "converted" or a new lifestyle program on Bravo, someone in Gay Agenda Headquarters simply picks up the phone and it automatically rings at Air America's Talking Points nerve center. From there the word is instantly flashed across computer screens in every Air America office.

When it comes to the War on Christianity, is Air America the command and control center or are you all going to cut and run from this one, too?

Oh, no, we're in it to stay. Wherever there is a small-town elementary school Christmas pageant, we'll be there, with our attorneys from the ACLU. If a Wiccan is persecuted on Halloween, we're there to defend her magical rights to cast spells, as long as it's not on city property. And don't ask us what we'll do to your local Hallmark store if we find Christmas cards hidden among the "Happy Holidays" cards!

What could possibly be so wrong with making English the official language of the United States?

The first amendment guarantees Americans the freedom of expression . . . and thus, constitutionally, we cannot mandate the language in which that expression is made. In addition, if passed, this bill would have disastrous repercussions: Politicians would need to learn a new language . . . and Bart Simpson would no longer be permitted to say "*Ay, caramba!*"

What does Air America have against smaller government?

Nothing. We understand that some people believe the economy would be a lot healthier if there were no government to get in the way. We get that. In fact, we once followed Grover Norquist's advice and tried to drown government in a bathtub, but it was like that scene in *Fatal Attraction*. Government just kept coming back. Whenever we got rid of one branch of government another one replaced it. At first we thought we'd turn over a lot of extra government work to churches, but then the ministers turned out to be not so good at fixing roads or feeding troops. That's where Halliburton came in, but then it turned out we needed a new federal agency just to manage all the secret no-bid contracts. Right now, we're working on a plan to transplant all federal government offices to a single-room office, above a 7-Eleven, at some Washington, DC, area strip mall. We'll let you know how that goes.

Is it true that Air America has a secret campus where staff members use war games to explore hypothetical scenarios like a nuclear attack by North Korea or the collapse of the US economy?

No. There was at one point in the past an Air America strategic facility. Certain members of the staff may have conducted war games there. If they did, these were entirely recreational and not sanctioned by Air America. Any such activities would have ceased, anyway, after a series of nuclear end-game simulations wherein Al Franken became a charismatic world leader seven times in a row and decided to run for the US Senate.

In Conclusion

If you still haven't found what you're looking for, we invite you to tune into Air America Radio live in a city near you.

ALASKA
Anchorage KUDO-AM 1080

ARIZONA
Phoenix KPHX-A 1480

ARKANSAS
Little Rock KDXE-AM 1380

CALIFORNIA
Eureka KGOE-A 1480
Fresno KFPT-A 790
Los Angeles KTLK-A 1150
Monterey KOMY-A 1340
Palm Springs KPTR-A 1340
Riverside KCAA-A 1050
Sacramento KCTC-A 1320
Sacramento KSAC-A 1240
Salinas KOMY-A 1340
San Bernardino KCAA-A 1050
San Diego KLSD-A 1360
San Francisco KQKE-A 960
San Luis Obispo KYNS-A 1340
Santa Barbara KIST-A 1340
Santa Cruz KRXA-A 540
Victor Valley KSZL-A 1230

COLORADO
Boulder KKZN-A 760
Denver KKZN-A 760

CONNECTICUT
New Haven WAVZ-A 1300

DISTRICT OF COLUMBIA
Washington WWRC-A 1260

FLORIDA
Boca Raton WJNO-A 1290
Bradenton WSRQ-A 1450
Ft Lauderdale WINZ-A 940
Hollywood WINZ-A 940
Miami WINZ-A 940
Sarasota WSRQ-A 1450
The Keys WKIZ-A 1500
West Palm Beach WJNO-A 1290

GEORGIA
Atlanta WMLB-A 1690

HAWAII
Honolulu KUMU-A 1500
Kauai KQNG-A 570
Maui KAOI-A 1110

IOWA
Cedar Rapids KXIC-A 800
Davenport WKBF-A 1270

ILLINOIS
Canton WBYS-A 1560
Carbondale WINI-A 1420
Chicago WCPT-A 850
Marion WINI-A 1420
Moline WKBF-A 1270
Rock Is WKBF-AMy1270

KENTUCKY
Ashland WRVC-AM 930

LOUISIANA
Baton Rouge WPYR-AM 1380
Lafayette KEUN-AM 1490
New Orleans WSMB-AM 1350

MASSACHUSETTS
Boston WKOX-AM 1200
Boston WXKS-AM 1430
Springfield WHMP-AM 1400
Springfield WHNP-AM 1600
Springfield WHMQ-AM 1240

MAINE
Portland WLVP-AM 870

MICHIGAN
Ann Arbor WLBY-AM 1290
Detroit WDTW-AM 1310
Grand Rapids WTKG-AM 1230
Petoskey WWKK-AM 750
Traverse City WWKK-AM 750

MINNESOTA
Brainerd WWWI-AM 1270
Duluth KQDS-AM 1490
Ely WELY-AM 1450
Hibbing WELY-AM 1450
Minneapolis KTNF-AM 950
St. Paul KTNF-AM 950
Superior KQDS-AM 1490

MISSOURI
St. Louis KRFT-AM 1190

NORTH CAROLINA
Asheville WPEK-AM 880
Durham WCHL-AM 1360
Raleigh WCHL-AM 1360

NEW MEXICO
Albuquerque KABQ-AM 1350
Santa Fe KTRC-AM 1400
Taos KVOT-AM 1340

NEVADA
Reno KJFK-AM 1230

NEW YORK
Binghamton WYOS-AM 1360
Buffalo WHLD-AM 1270
Ithaca WNYY-AM 1470
New York WLIB-AM 1190
Plattsburgh WVAA-AM 1390
Poughkeepsie WKZE-AM 1020
Rochester WROC-AM 950

OHIO
Akron WARF-AM 1350
Cincinnati WSAI-AM 1360
Columbus WTPG-AM 1230

OREGON
Albany KTHH-AM 990
Coos Bay KBBR-AM 1340
Eugene KOPT-AM 1600
Portland KPOJ-AM 620
Springfield KOPT-AM 1600

PENNSYLVANIA
Pittsburgh WPTT-AM 1360
State College WBLF-AM 970

SOUTH CAROLINA
Columbia WOIC-AM 1230

SOUTH DAKOTA
Rapid City KYTI-FM 93.7 (ch.3)

TENNESSEE
Memphis WWTQ-AM 680

TEXAS
Austin KOKE-AM 1600
Corpus Christi KCCT-AM 1150
Dallas-Ft. Worth KXEB-AM 910
El Paso KHRO-AM 1650
San Antonio KTXX-FM 103.1

VIRGINIA
Charlottesville WVAX-AM 1450

VERMONT
Barre WDEV-AM 550
Bennington WBTN-AM 1370
Brattleboro WKVT-AM 1490
Burlington WVAA-AM 1390
Montpelier WDEV-AM 550
St Johnsbury WDEV-AM 550

WASHINGTON
Seattle KPTK-AM 1090
Spokane KPTQ-AM 1280
Tacoma KPTK-AM 1090

WISCONSIN
Madison WXXM-FM 92.1

WEST VIRGINIA
Huntington WRVC-AM 930

Notes on the Contributors

DAVID BENDER hosts *Politically Direct,* the newest addition to Air America's expanding lineup of progressive talk. The news and interview program broadcasts live every Sunday directly from Washington, DC. Bender, whose four-decade career as a political activist began at the age of twelve when he took a "leave of absence" from seventh grade to become a volunteer in the presidential campaign of Senator Robert F. Kennedy, is the author or coauthor of four books, including *Stand and Be Counted*, a chronicle of artist activism in the music industry.

ANGIE COIRO—the award-winning host of Mother Jones Radio—and Air America have a common goal: using the airwaves to make a difference. In the '80s, Coiro hosted an arts feature and a women's networking show on Honolulu talk radio and later spent ten years reporting San Francisco news and traffic. Her show is a fun, fast, and substantive hour of reporting and commentary inspired by stories from *Mother Jones* magazine.

REV. DR. C. WELTON GADDY, host of *State of Belief,* leads the national nonpartisan grassroots and educational organizations, the Interfaith Alliance and the Interfaith Alliance Foundation, and serves as Pastor for Preaching and Worship at Northminster (Baptist) Church in Monroe, Louisiana. Founded in 1994, the Interfaith Alliance challenges those who manipulate religion for partisan political gain or to promote intolerance. In addition to being the author of more than twenty books, Gaddy provides regular commentary to the national media on issues relating to religion and politics.

CHUCK D, cohost of *On the Real* and cofounder of the legendary rap group Public Enemy, served as national spokesperson for Rock the Vote, the National Urban League, and the National Alliance of African American Athletes and appeared in public service announcements for HBO's campaign for national peace and the Partnership for a Drug-Free America. He is also a regular guest on numerous television shows including *Nightline* and *Politically Incorrect* and on CNN. He is currently working on a second book and has formed a rock band.

STEVE EARLE, host of *The Revolution Starts Now,* is a singer and songwriter who was born in Virginia, was raised in Texas, and has resided in Nashville for more than twenty-five years. His 2002 critically acclaimed album, JERUSALEM, garnered him his eighth Grammy nomination. The year 2001 marked the release of *Doghouse Roses,* his first collection of short stories, and in the fall of 2002, the Broadaxe Theatre debuted his first play, entitled *Karla,* about Karla Faye Tucker, the first woman executed in Texas since the Civil War.

LAURA FLANDERS, host of *RadioNation with Laura Flanders,* is the author of *Bushwomen: Tales of a Cynical Species* and *The W Effect: Sexual Politics in the Age of Bush.* Flanders writes regularly for Tompaine.com, *The Nation, Ms. Magazine,* and Znet. Her op-ed pieces have appeared in the *San Francisco Chronicle.* Flanders' TV appearances include *The O'Reilly Factor, Hannity and Colmes,* and C-SPAN's *Washington Journal,* as well as *Good Morning America* and the Canadian news discussion program, *CounterSpin,* on CBC.

AL FRANKEN is an Emmy Award–winning television writer and producer, a *New York Times* best-selling author, a Grammy-winning comedian, and the host of *The Al Franken Show,* the flagship program of Air America Radio. The show launched in March 2004 and delivers three hours a day of fearlessly irreverent commentary, comedy, and interviews. Franken grew up in Minnesota. He has been married to his wife, Franni, for twenty-nine years. They have recently moved back to Minneapolis from New York City and have two children.

GIA'NA GAREL, cohost of *On the Real,* is a writer, producer, and filmmaker who began her film career in 1989 when she produced short films under her company Meridian Pics. In 2004, she coproduced with director Darryl Lassiter the Stellar Award–winning Vickie Winans' video, "Shook." Garel has successfully made a niche in the entertainment industry by spreading her talents into all genres for more than nineteen years.

JACKIE GUERRA, a stand-up comic, actress, author, motivational speaker, and political activist, is the host of *Workin' It,* a new weekly one-hour radio show focusing on working life in America. Growing up, Guerra was inspired by the civil rights, the women's rights, and the farmworkers' rights movements and dreamed of being part of something that could make a difference in the lives of others. The daughter of Mexican immigrants, she learned early on the importance of hard work and of following one's dreams.

ROBERT F. KENNEDY JR., cohost of *Ring of Fire,* is widely recognized as the country's most prominent environmental attorney, working tirelessly to safeguard the environment and public health. He is the founder and director of Pace University's Environmental Litigation Clinic in White Plains, New York; president of the Waterkeeper Alliance, an international coalition of ninety-nine grassroots groups; and senior attorney at the Natural Resources Defense Council. The peripatetic Kennedy also crisscrosses North America several times a year, stirring audiences of college students, community groups, and elected officials.

RACHEL MADDOW hosts the national morning-drive news program *The Rachel Maddow Show.* Launched in April 2005, *The Rachel Maddow Show* airs weekdays on the Air America Radio network in New York, Los Angeles, Miami, and many other markets, as well as nationally online and on XM Satellite Radio. Rachel has a doctorate in politics from Oxford University and a degree in public policy from Stanford. She was the first openly gay American to win a Rhodes Scholarship.

MIKE MALLOY is a traditional Democrat working to return the Democratic Party to its historic liberal roots. Mike Malloy came to talk radio by accident. Writing for CNN in 1987, he heard there was an opening for a talk-show host on the weekends from a friend at an Atlanta radio station; he gave it a try and found a home. Now Mike's nationally syndicated program *The Mike Malloy Show* can be heard weeknights on both Air America Radio and XM Satellite Radio.

MIKE PAPANTONIO is one of the most prominent trial attorneys in the country. He is renowned as the lead counsel in virtually every major product-liability case against the pharmaceutical, industrial products, insurance, and stock-broking industries. In addition to

cohosting *Ring of Fire,* he also sits on the board of directors of Air America Radio. Pap has been described as "part revival preacher, part stand-up comic"—living proof that it's possible to be both laid-back and fired up at the same time.

MARK RILEY, the host of *The Mark Riley Show,* is a veteran talk-show host and has established a reputation for his charismatic approach to controversy. Before joining Air America, Riley worked his way up through a spectrum of roles at WLIB 1190 AM in New York—writer, editor, managing editor, executive editor, program director, and, of course, on-air host. In addition to his live radio program, Riley is a popular TV political analyst, with regular appearances on New York 1 News, CNN, and Fox News Channel.

RANDI RHODES, a Brooklyn native turned South Florida legend turned progressive talk radio pioneer, has been tearing up the airwaves for two decades and counting. A former secretary, waitress, trucker, and US Air Force aircraft mechanic, Randi began her radio odyssey in Seminole, Texas, which led her to Alabama, Milwaukee, Dallas, New York City, and Miami. In March of 2004, Randi moved back to New York to host the afternoon-drive program, *The Randi Rhodes Show,* on Air America. She is listed in *Talkers Magazine*'s Heavy Hundred and is probably watching C-SPAN right now.

BETSY ROSENBERG is an award-winning broadcast journalist who has worked for the three major networks over the course of her twenty-four years in radio. While the show she hosts, *EcoTalk,* began with tips on how to reduce, reuse, and recycle solid waste, it has evolved into a program that chronicles the entire spectrum of "green" living. Betsy lives with her husband and daughter in Mill Valley, California, where she "walks the EcoTalk" by recycling, composting, driving a hybrid car, and being solar-powered.

SAM SEDER, host of *The Majority Report,* is a writer, director, and actor and lives in New York City. He recently published a book with coauthor Stephen Sherrill, titled *F.U.B.A.R.: America's Right-Wing Nightmare.* Raised in Worcester, Massachusetts, Seder's interest in politics first manifested itself when he was in a position serving the Worcester Charter Commission. Later, Seder interned for the Energy Commission in the Connecticut State Assembly, where his decision to earn a living as a comedian was edified.

Credits

ILLUSTRATIONS AND GRAPHICS

PAGES 10, 34, 66, 76, 100, 130, 152, 190, 212, 232, 238, 244 ©2006 by Dustin Amery Hostetler
PAGES 48, 60, 70, 110, 120, 196 Don Asmussen
All other graphic collages by Plinko

PHOTOGRAPHS

PAGE 51 Jim Watson/AFP/Getty Images
PAGE 99 Paul Wolfowitz: Maxim Marmur/AFP/Getty Images; Douglas J. Feith: Scott Davis/DoD via CNP;
        Richard Perle: Miguel Villagran/Action Press/ZUMA Press
PAGE 115 Yuri Gripas/ REUTERS
PAGE 127 Mannie Garcia/REUTERS
PAGE 161 AP Images
PAGE 170 FEMA/IllinoisPhoto.com
PAGE 172 (left middle, bottom; right middle) FEMA/IllinoisPhoto.com
PAGE 177 Scott J. Ferrell
PAGE 227 Farzana Wahidy/AFP/Getty Images

Published by Rodale Inc.

33 East Minor Street, Emmaus, PA 18098   www.rodale.com

MELCHER MEDIA

Produced by Melcher Media Inc.

124 West 13th Street, New York, NY 10011   www.melcher.com

DESIGN BY PLINKO

Air America would like to thank first and foremost our dedicated listeners. Without your support, we would not have a voice. Thanks also to the dedicated believers at Rodale for taking this project on: Leigh Haber, Liz Perl, Jim Berra, Beth Lamb, Leslie Schneider, and Katrina Weidknecht. And thanks to Jonathon Lazear for his expertise and vision from the very beginning.

The indefatigable and superhero teams at Melcher Media and Rodale made this book come to life. Special thanks to Charlie Melcher and his staff at Melcher Media: Bonnie Eldon, associate publisher; Duncan Bock, editor in chief; Carl Robbins, project editor; Shelley Lewis, consulting editor; and Betty Wong, editor. Gratitude for hard work is also due to Jonathan Ambar, Nancy N. Bailey, Keith Biery, David Brown, Pat Brown, Andy Carpenter, Sara Cox, Barry Crimmins, Amelia Hennighausen, Andrea Hirsh, Jonathan Koller, Chris Krogermeier, Lauren Nathan, Lia Ronnen, Holly Rothman, Darlene Schneck, Anthony Serge, Lindsey Stanberry, Shoshana Thaler, Mark Wasserman, and Megan Worman.

Many individuals here at Air America helped this book along the way, and we much appreciate the efforts of Will Craven, Brendan DeMelle, Ron Dodd, Scott Elberg, Lisa Gilbert, Russ Gilbert, Carl Ginsburg, Danny Goldberg, Ben Harrington, Matthew Ianni, Tamara Karcev, Julia Kardon, Billy Kimball, Marty Lynch, John Manzo, Annissa Mason, Jolyn Matsumuro, Scott Millican, Logan Nakyanzi, Chris Nsiah, Andi Parhamovich, Dan Pashman, Thaler Pekar, Naz Rafsanjani, Ray Ramano, Katrina Rill, Bill Schaap, Jon Sinton, Julian Suchman, Jim Wiggett, and Trent Wolbe. Special recognition goes to Jaime Horn, our director of publicity.

Some of the most talented comedy writers in the business have contributed to Air America Radio's unique identity since its inception. We thank them all.